ITALIAN LITERARY ICONS

PRINCETON ESSAYS IN LITERATURE

For a list of titles in this series,
see pages 197-99.

Gian-Paolo Biasin

Italian Literary Icons

PRINCETON UNIVERSITY PRESS

PRINCETON, NEW JERSEY

Copyright © 1985 by Princeton University Press
Published by Princeton University Press, 41 William Street,
Princeton, New Jersey 08540
In the United Kingdom: Princeton University
Press, Guildford, Surrey

All Rights Reserved

Library of Congress Cataloging in Publication Data will
be found on the last printed page of this book

ISBN 0-691-06632-9

Publication of this book has been aided by a grant from
the Paul Mellon Fund of Princeton University Press

This book has been composed in Linotron Palatino

Clothbound editions of Princeton University Press books
are printed on acid-free paper, and binding materials are
chosen for strength and durability

Printed in the United States of America by Princeton
University Press, Princeton, New Jersey

Contents

Illustrations

Acknowledgments

THIS BOOK is a revised version of *Icone italiane*, which was published in Rome by Bulzoni in 1983. All translations of material cited within it, unless otherwise noted, are mine. A few parts have already appeared in English, in preliminary or in any case different versions, as follows: from Chapter Two, "Tears Over Ginevra" in *NEMLA Italian Studies*, vol. 1 (1977), pp. 69–76; from Chapter Five, "Disease as Language" in Enid Rhodes Peschel, ed., *Medicine and Literature* (New York: Neale Watson Academic Publications, 1980), pp. 171–77, and in *Italian Quarterly*, vol. 21, no. 79 (Winter 1980), pp. 77–82; and from Chapter Six, "4/3πr³: Scientific vs. Literary Space" in *Versus. Quaderni di studi semiotici*, vols. 19–20 (January–August 1978), pp. 173–88. I wish to thank the respective editors for having published my work and for permission to reprint it here.

I would also like to thank the University Research Institute of the University of Texas at Austin for a research grant that allowed me time to work on this book. Thanks as well to the readers of the Princeton University Press and Alida Becker, the manuscript editor, whose comments and suggestions led to the improvement of my original text, and above all thanks to the numerous friends, including my students, whose stimulation has enriched me throughout the years.

ITALIAN LITERARY ICONS

Introduction. Taffy's Beavers

IN ONE of his *Just So Stories*, Rudyard Kipling takes us back to the Neolithic Age to show "How the First Letter Was Written." In this tale, a little girl named Taffy sends a stranger home to fetch a new spear for her father, who has broken his while fishing. The stranger, a member of the Tewara tribe, does not know the language of the little girl's people, and the message he carries—a drawing roughly scratched on a piece of bark from a birch tree—is misunderstood. At first, Taffy's mother takes it to mean that the stranger has killed her husband and frightened her daughter, and as a result the Tewara is threatened by the angry tribe. Finally, however, Taffy herself returns and everything is cleared up.

> "I wanted the Stranger-man to fetch Daddy's spear, so I drawded it," said Taffy. "There wasn't lots of spears. There was only one spear. I drawded it three times to make sure. I couldn't help it looking as if it stuck into Daddy's head—there wasn't room on the birch-bark; and those things that Mummy called bad people are my beavers. I drawded them to show him the way through the swamp; and I drawded Mummy at the mouth of the Cave looking pleased because he is a nice Stranger-man, and I think you are just the stupidest people in the world."[1]

---

[1] Rudyard Kipling, "How the First Letter Was Written," *Just So Stories for Little Children* (Garden City, N.Y.: Doubleday, 1926), pp. 123–39, quotation on p. 137. The following quotation is on p. 138.

3

At this explanation, the whole tribe bursts out laughing and the head chief proclaims, with a typically Neolithic (and Victorian) optimism:

"O Small-person-without-any-manners-who-ought-to-be-spanked, you've hit upon a great invention! . . . At present it is only pictures, and, as we have seen to-day, pictures are not always properly understood. But a time will come, o Babe of Tegumai, when we shall make letters— all twenty-six of 'em—and when we shall be able to read as well as to write, and then we shall always say exactly what we mean without any mistakes. Let the Neolithic ladies wash the mud out of the stranger's hair."

This delightful story embraces all the elements that make up the study of semiotics: signification (Taffy wants to express a precise request) and communication (transmitting the information to her mother through signs); the sender and the addressee (Taffy, her mother, and the tribe); the message and the channel (the scratched birch bark and the stranger who carries it); code-making (Taffy invents ideographic writing) and its decoding and interpretation (both of which go much beyond her intentions); the replica (the picture "drawded" by Taffy), and its denotation and connotation (which diverge in the drawing, since the same figure represents "beavers" to Taffy and "bad people" to her mother); the referent and iconism (the broken spear and the new one, the beaver swamp, the cave, the parents, the stranger—in other words, the objective, geographic, and human reality that Taffy must "represent" adequately); aesthetics (Taffy's message is iconic and ambiguous); rhetoric (the broken spear is repeated three times; the whole drawing is emphatic); and culture as a system of signs ("the first letter" is the beginning of culture based on writing, the means of communication par excellence). Of course, the list could go on and on.

Kipling's story is a paradigm of semiosis in its beginning and development, one that ties semiotics to literature with a self-reflexive or metanarrative movement in the concluding words of the head chief. This is a fundamental aspect of semiotics as a critical method and also of literature, both as the field of action and as the means through which the former is manifested.[2] Thus Kipling's story makes an ideal introductory text because it allows me to take for granted as graciously as possible a fact by now obvious in contemporary culture: the emergence of semiotics among the sciences of man.

It would take too long and perhaps be out of place to retrace here the various stages of this emergence: from Giambattista Vico's early insights to the linguistic and anthropological structuralism of Ferdinand de Saussure and Claude Lévi-Strauss; from the linguistics of the Prague School (particularly Roman Jakobson) to "Opoyaz" and Russian formalism (notably N. S. Trubeckoj and Michail Bakhtin); from Charles Sanders Peirce to Charles Morris to Umberto Eco; from Vladimir Propp's morphology of the folktale to the narratology of Algirdas Greimas, Tzvetan Todorov, Roland Barthes, Claude Bremond, and Cesare Segre; from Jacques Derrida's grammatology to Julia Kristeva's intertextuality; from formalism to the Tartu School. . . . In any case, others have already dealt with this fascinating chapter in the history of ideas, either systematically (Terence Hawkes and Gian Paolo Caprettini)[3] or in terms of theory (Carlo Sini, Jonathan Culler, and Marc Eli Blanchard).[4]

For this reason, I shall limit myself to pointing out only the works that are central to my research and the problems around which it is organized. In my view, this sort of discussion is a definite duty for the critic who wants to be clear (and not only on a methodological level) and is an equally necessary

[2] See Wlad Godzich, "The Construction of Meaning," *New Literary History*, vol. 9, no. 2 (Winter 1978), pp. 389–97.

[3] See Terence Hawkes, *Structuralism and Semiotics* (Berkeley: University of California Press, 1977) and Gian Paolo Caprettini, *Letteratura e semiologia in Italia* (Turin: Rosenberg e Sellier, 1979).

[4] These are remarkable works in their respective fields: Carlo Sini, *Semiotica e filosofia. Segno e linguaggio in Peirce, Nietzsche, Heidegger e Foucault* (Bologna: Il Mulino, 1978); Jonathan Culler, *Structuralist Poetics: Structuralism, Linguistics and the Study of Literature* (London: Routledge and Kegan Paul, 1975) and *The Pursuit of Signs: Semiotics, Literature, Deconstruction* (Ithaca: Cornell University Press, 1981); and Marc Eli Blanchard, *Description: Sign, Self, Desire: Critical Theory in the Wake of Semiotics* (The Hague: Mouton, 1980).

reflection a posteriori on the critical itinerary followed in writing this book.

The first work I wish to mention is Umberto Eco's *A Theory of Semiotics*, stressing in particular one of its conclusions:[5]

> The labor of sign production releases social forces and itself represents a social force. It can produce both ideologies and criticism of ideologies. Thus semiotics (in its double guise as a theory of codes and a theory of sign production) is also a form of *social criticism*, and therefore one among the many forms of *social practice*. (p. 298)

This conclusion, which is so important for the literary critic, is typical of Eco, and distinguishes him from the French writers of *Tel Quel*, whose collective work *Théorie d'ensemble* is aimed at deconstructing the metaphysical foundations of Western thought. (One thinks especially of Jacques Derrida, while Julia Kristeva and Philippe Sollers can be subsumed within the semiotic perspective with a remarkably "subversive" thrust.) On the other hand, this conclusion connects Eco not only (or not so much) with Gramscian criticism but also with the semiotics of culture developed by the Tartu School, in particular that of Yuri Lotman and Boris Uspensky.[6]

A Theory of Semiotics develops Eco's preceding work in the following directions and seems important for the following reasons: first, semiotics is conceived and articulated as "a critique of culture"—in other words, the treatise provides the theoretical foundations for a semiotic practice of which Eco himself is a valuable representative;[7] secondly, and perhaps

---

[5] Umberto Eco, *A Theory of Semiotics* (Bloomington: Indiana University Press, 1975); all quotations will refer to this edition. See also the Italian edition, which varies in some instances from the English one: *Trattato di semiotica generale* (Milan: Bompiani, 1975). It is perhaps useful to point out that Eco's theory of codes could be linked with Roland Barthes' own interest in and use of codes both in culture (food or fashion) and in literary texts (e.g., *S/Z*, Paris: Seuil, 1970). However, in addition to fusing Saussurean and Peircean concepts, Eco's code is more systematic and less idiosyncratic than Barthes'.

[6] See Yuri Lotman and Boris Uspensky, *Tipologia della cultura*, Italian tr. (Milan: Bompiani, 1975) and *Ricerche semiotiche. Nuove tendenze delle scienze umane nell'URSS*, Italian tr. (Turin: Einaudi, 1973).

[7] I am referring in particular to Umberto Eco, *Il superuomo di massa. Studi sul romanzo popolare* (Milan: Cooperativa Scrittori, 1976).

in reply to certain critical suggestions put forth by Segre, Eco proposes the sign function and the inference as notions that seem indispensable for literary criticism in that they open up the text to a wealth of nuances that might escape an analysis not sufficiently equipped with interpretive tools;[8] and thirdly, practical semiotics (above all the typology of modes of sign production) dialectically completes pure semiotics and allows the literary critic to analyze certain semiotic phenomena (especially aesthetic ones) from a genetic viewpoint, which in my opinion will become ever more valuable in the future.

Eco's *Theory*, even in this brief and necessarily incomplete précis, is shown to be an important catalyzer for a whole series of ideas and problems. These are discussed in other critical texts that, for their part, are equally fundamental as far as my research is concerned.

I refer first of all to Cesare Segre's *Structures and Time*, which is perhaps the most significant text in Italian literary semiotics.[9] This volume is linked with a long and authoritative tradition of textual and philological criticism (so much so that Segre's latest work is actually entitled *Semiotica filologica*),[10] while at the same time it is open to the contributions of Russian formalism and French narratology, as can be seen in its profitable and keen exchange with Victor Shklovsky and Boris Tomashevsky, as well as with Todorov and Greimas.[11] Segre has a rigorous respect for the texts he examines and an equally rigorous respect for their historicity. These features are characteristic of Italian literary semiotics in general and are its specific distinguishing trait.

[8] See Cesare Segre, *I segni e la critica. Fra strutturalismo e semiologia* (Turin: Einaudi, 1969), p. 52. See also Eco's further development of these proposals in *The Role of the Reader: Explorations in the Semiotics of Texts* (Bloomington: Indiana University Press, 1979) and Maria Corti, *An Introduction to Literary Semiotics*, tr. by Margherita Bogat and Allen Mandelbaum (Bloomington: Indiana University Press, 1978).

[9] Cesare Segre, *Structures and Time: Narration, Poetry, Models*, tr. by John Meddemmen (Chicago: University of Chicago Press, 1979).

[10] Cesare Segre, *Semiotica filologica. Testo e modelli culturali* (Turin: Einaudi, 1979); see also his *Semiotica, storia e cultura* (Padua: Liviana, 1977).

[11] Cf. Tzvetan Todorov, ed., *Théorie de la littérature. Textes des formalistes russes* (Paris: Seuil, 1966).

Like Segre, I too am interested in the contributions of French structural formalists such as Gérard Genette and Philippe Hamon; and among the Russian formalists, I prefer Tomashevsky, whose "thematics" seems to me more systematic and stimulating than Shklovsky's, particularly because he establishes a fruitful and dynamic interrelationship between story and plot, and enriches it with correlative notions such as those concerning bound and free motifs.[12] I am also greatly indebted to Yuri Lotman, whose *The Structure of the Artistic Text* is not only a valid contribution in itself,[13] but is above all a link between formalism *strictu sensu* (or conceived in too restricted a sense) and that other formalism of a more sociological type, proposed by Bakhtin, that is emerging today as a "dialogic" conception of literature and culture, and in which the central notion is an interaction, not a gap, between *langue* and *parole*, between utterance and competence.[14] An utterance is determined by its historical and social context. Hence it is made up (in semiotic terms) of a multiplicity of codes, which are of

[12] Boris Tomashevsky, "Thematics," in Lee Lemon and Marion Reis, eds., *Russian Formalist Criticism: Four Essays* (Lincoln: University of Nebraska Press, 1965), pp. 61–95. A more complete version is available in Tomashevsky's *Teoria della letteratura*, Italian tr. (Milan: Feltrinelli, 1979).

[13] Yuri Lotman, *The Structure of the Artistic Text*, tr. by Roland Vroon (Ann Arbor: University of Michigan Press, 1977). Another useful contribution is Boris Uspensky, *The Poetics of Composition: Structure of the Artistic Text and the Typology of Compositional Form*, tr. by V. Zavarin and S. Wittig (Berkeley: University of California Press, 1974).

[14] See Pavel Medvedev and Michail Bakhtin, *The Formal Method in Literary Scholarship: A Critical Introduction to Sociological Poetics*, tr. by Albert J. Wehrle (Baltimore: Johns Hopkins University Press, 1978), and Michail Bakhtin, *The Dialogical Imagination*, tr. by Caryl Emerson and Michael Holquist (Austin: University of Texas Press, 1981). It should be noted that Lotman explicitly refers to "Bakhtin's seminal thought on the structure of dialogical texts" in relation to his own proposal to consider culture as "a dialogical structure" possessing at least two languages: *Testo e contesto. Semiotica dell'arte e della cultura* (Bari: Laterza, 1980), p. 42. Vittorio Strada stresses the historical-hermeneutic element in Bakhtin's thought (with precise references to Martin Heidegger, Karl Jaspers, Hans Gadamer, and Martin Buber) in "Dialogo con Bachtin," *Intersezioni*, vol. 1, no. 1 (April 1980), pp. 115–24. Cf. also *Strumenti critici*, vols. 42–43 (October 1980), special issue ed. by D'Arco Silvio Avalle, "La cultura nella tradizione russa del xix e xx secolo," and Tzvetan Todorov, *Michail Bakhtine. Le principe dialogique* (Paris: Seuil, 1981).

course the basis of culture. Furthermore, in Bakhtin's conception the relationship between sender and receiver is seen
as essential: a message is completed only by a reception on
the part of an audience—or, as Elio Vittorini might have said,
we are always dealing with "a manuscript *found* in a bottle."
Bakhtin paved the way for a semiotics of culture (represented today especially by Lotman) that is perhaps the most
tentative, but also the most challenging and promising branch
of semiotic studies. This can be traced to its stress on the
interrelations of codes (a "dialogic structure") and its emphasis on the spatial and dynamic characteristics of imagination and hence of verbal signs as well.[15]

If my research has been inspired by the major theoretical
works mentioned so far, it is also deeply rooted in that practice
of historicist intertextuality and methodological alertness of
which Ezio Raimondi is perhaps the most effective representative in Italy.[16] In fact, I believe that through the model
provided by Raimondi it is possible to understand my own
present research as the logical development of my earlier in-
quiries into thematic, structural, and symbolic fields, precisely
because semiotics helps to understand how themes, structures, and symbols function in a broad cultural context, that
is to say, how they become vehicles of communication.

But before this introductory overview turns into a kind of
autobibliography, I will shift my attention to the notions and
problems that are dealt with at a theoretical level in the works
mentioned so far, which are assumed here as cornerstones of
my own critical discourse. In doing so, my intention is not
to offer a theoretical system of my own, but rather to single

[15] I refer particularly to "Sul meccanismo semiotico della cultura" in Lotman
and Uspensky's *Tipologia della cultura*, pp. 39–68; idem, "Il metalinguaggio
delle descrizioni tipologiche," ibid., pp. 143–81, and Lotman's *Testo e contesto*.
On the philosophic and critical problems of the imaginary, see the deconstructive approach of Jean-François Lyotard, *Discourse, figure* (Paris: Klincksieck, 1971).

[16] Ezio Raimondi, *Tecniche della critica letteraria*, *Metafora e storia*, and *Scienza
e letteratura* (Turin: Einaudi, 1967, 1970, and 1978), and "Dal formalismo alla
pragmatica della letteratura," *Lingua e stile*, vol. 14, nos. 2–3 (September 1979),
pp. 381–93. These are the works that have a major, methodological interest
for me, but there are others that I shall quote in specific contexts as well.

out, discuss, and apply certain crucial theoretical tenets that
are scattered in the writings of many other critics, and to bring
these tenets to bear on an interpretative operation of my own
that is focused on the Italian (and European) culture of the
last two centuries.

Cultural Semiotics

If we start with the observation that culture is a network
of sign functions, that it is made up of a multiplicity of codes
and their interrelationships, that it is in sum a system of social
communications, then the notion of culture as text will be
clearly revealed. It is a complex text, of which those other
complex texts called literature are a part, and a central part
indeed. Both culture and literature, furthermore, are modeling systems for understanding the world. Hence the cultural
relevance of literary criticism, which today more than ever
must explain its own object in a context that conditions it
synchronically as well as diachronically. Such a contextuali-
zation of *langue* and *parole*, of competence and performance,
of artistic text and cultural text is essential for semiotic criticism. This means, of course, that the relationships of homology or differentiation that may or may not exist among
the many cultural codes (the literary, the pictorial, the ideological, the scientific, and so on) must be hypothesized, posited, and verified. The difficulty of such a task is increased
by a phenomenon described by Lotman:

> The development of self-enclosed and multifaceted for-
> mations is essential to the mechanism of culture and fa-
> cilitates an increase in the information circulating inside
> a given culture, thereby facilitating as well the capacity
> of this culture to orient itself in the world. However, the
> development of such formations is loaded with dangers
> in that it can cause a certain "schizophrenia of culture"
> and its crumbling down into manifold cultural entities
> that are antagonistic to one another. In other words, the
> multiplicity of languages might become a "Tower of Ba-
> bel" of cultural semiosis.[17]

[17] Lotman, *Testo e contesto*, p. 39.

To avoid such a proliferation of languages, every culture must describe itself and "elaborate its own particular model" through a metalanguage and what Lotman calls a "regulating meta-mechanism." I believe that the creation of such a metalanguage necessarily involves interdisciplinarity, which today's criticism seems more and more to embrace. This book is itself intended as a contribution to this interdisciplinarity, this metalanguage.

Literary Semiotics

There are numerous theoretical-methodological problems of semiotics that are specifically interesting in terms of the literary phenomenon. One of them in particular seems to me to be fundamental. This is the problem of referentiality, which involves the concepts of sign function and infinite semiosis on the one hand (by proposing a semiotic solution to the philosophic problems of "knowledge," "the real," "the essence"), and on the other hand can be translated into the corresponding literary problems of realism, ideology, and self-reflexivity.

Eco's treatise has already inspired notable contributions on this subject; it seems significant, for example, that both Teresa De Lauretis and Thomas E. Lewis have connected semiotics with Marxism.[18] Lewis uses Louis Althusser for the Marxian part of his analysis, and his conclusions are worth quoting at length:

> The marxist distinction between the real object and the object of knowledge parallels at the level of epistemological premise the semiotic discrimination between the interpretant and the referent defined as "thing" within a theory of codes. Furthermore, the marxist profile of the mode of production of knowledge as a transformative

---

[18] Teresa De Lauretis, "Semiosis Unlimited," *PTL: A Journal for Descriptive Poetics and Theory of Literature*, vol. 2 (1977), pp. 367–83, and "Semiotics in Italy" in R. W. Bailey, L. Matejka, and P. Steiner, eds., *The Sign: Semiotics Around the World* (Ann Arbor: Michigan Slavic Publications, 1978), pp. 248–57; and Thomas E. Lewis, "Notes Toward a Theory of the Referent," *PMLA*, vol. 94, no. 3 (May 1979), pp. 459–75.

labor carried out on raw materials that are already cultural units, and as productive of knowledge effects that then become new cultural units available for further transformations, maintains a deep affinity with the epistemological and methodological bases of the theory of sign production as a whole. Thus, we find within Marxism, as well as within semiotics, compelling theoretical reasons for redefining the literary referent as "cultural unit": it is the surest way, from both perspectives, to ground textual signification in history, while avoiding the necessary idealist ramifications of a staunch adherence to a metaphysics of the referent.[19]

These conclusions seem to me particularly important because they emphasize the strategy of semiotics: by redefining meaning as a cultural unit, the philosophical problem is put in parentheses and the ground is cleared for the operational functioning of the discipline. Such a philosophical *epoché* is in my opinion the theoretical basis on which certain parallels between semiotics and deconstruction are made possible for the literary critic, while still respecting their differences. It is within this *epoché* that the major effort of deconstruction takes place, while it is at the operational or pragmatic level that semiotics displays its usefulness and effectiveness. Incidentally, this *epoché* also explains why I feel free, later in the book, to quote such a deconstructionist as Paul De Man without subsuming him into the semiotic field—exactly as I shall quote other critics like Francesco Arcangeli, René Girard, and Peter Brooks, without necessarily sharing all their premises or implications. In other words, quoting these critics is also a not too cryptic indication of the limits (as well as the possibilities) of semiotics in literary criticism.[20]

In any case, both semiotics and deconstruction struggle

[19] Lewis, p. 469.

[20] For a philosophical discussion of Lyotard, Derrida, and De Man, see Rodolphe Gasché, "Deconstruction as Criticism," *Glyph*, vol. 6 (1979), pp. 177–215. Cf. also Peter Steiner, "In Defense of Semiotics: The Dual Asymmetry of Cultural Signs," *New Literary History*, vol. 12, no. 3 (Spring 1981), pp. 415–36.

against "a metaphysics of the referent"; in this common struggle, deconstruction goes further than semiotics because it rejects history and self-reflexivity. In contrast, by rejecting "any ontological claim for referentiality,"[21] semiotics also explains the contextual, historicized self-reflexivity of the literary text. This is possible because when a given referent is constituted by a semiotic sign in the text itself, there is a case of metalanguage, of a text speaking about itself.[22]

Practical Semiotics

My interest is in the philological and historicist empiricism of a precise, faithful textual analysis and the theoretical constructions that are based on or derive from it. It is this practice, this empiricism that I have sought in my book, following the example of Taffy in Kipling's story, who did not ask questions about the future implications of sending a message "drawded" on a piece of birch bark, but simply sent it along with the Tewara stranger. This does not mean, however, that I have deliberately neglected theory; it only means that my semiotic itinerary goes from practice to theory, remembering that theory must always be verified by practice.

Hence, I propose that the reader approach the following chapters by keeping in mind the three levels on which they are articulated: the first is that of literary history (practical semiotics of given texts); the second is that of methodology (literary semiotics); and the third is that which deals with homologies between signifying systems (cultural semiotics). Any one of these levels may be given a certain preeminence in a particular chapter, but all three will always be present. Of course, I have chosen specific texts, problems, and homologies according to that mysterious relationship that always occurs between the text and the critic. Nevertheless,

[21] Lewis, p. 473.
[22] See Michel Riffaterre, *Semiotics of Poetry* (Bloomington: Indiana University Press, 1978) and Paolo Valesio, *The Practice of Literary Semiotics: A Theoretical Proposal* (Urbino: Centro Internazionale di Semiotica e Linguistica, Working Papers and prepublications, vol. 71, no. D, February 1978), especially pp. 20–21.

this does not preclude the scientific quality of the critical act. After all, even in "exact" sciences, intuition plays a fundamental role.

The three levels I have just mentioned are obvious in this introductory chapter, but it might be worth listing them briefly for those that follow:

Chapter One: (1) Romanticism: Ugo Foscolo's *Ultime lettere di Jacopo Ortis* and "Alla sera"; (2) poetic space, iconic elements of style, point of view, perspective, and conceptualization; (3) the intersystemic relationship between painting (Jacques-Louis David, J.W.M. Turner) and poetry.

Chapter Two: (1) "minor" Romanticism: Massimo D'Azeglio's *Ettore Fieramosca*; (2) the notion of genre; the selection of theme, story and plot, and motivation; (3) the historical novel, the novel as a genre, and melodrama with references to Alessandro Manzoni and Giuseppe Verdi.

Chapter Three: (1) *verismo* and its aftermath: Giovanni Verga, Luigi Pirandello, Giuseppe Tomasi di Lampedusa, Leonardo Sciascia, and Vincenzo Consolo; (2) referentiality, representation, code-making, sign production, diegesis, and ideology; (3) the relationship between literature and nature (landscape).

Chapter Four: (1) symbolism: G. A. Borgese's *Rubè*; (2) ideologemes, separate worlds, and hypersign; (3) the relationship between literature and society (the rise of fascism).

Chapter Five: (1) contemporary explorations: Carmelo Samonà's *Fratelli*; (2) semiosis, discourse, contact, and meaning; (3) the relationship between literature and medicine.

Chapter Six: (1) post-modernism: Italo Calvino's *Le cosmicomiche* and *Ti con zero*; (2) space, model, self-reflexivity; (3) the relationship between literature and science.

I hope this outline does not give too distorted an idea of my intentions or, a posteriori, of my results, and that the three levels, here separated for clarity's sake, will actually appear united in the chapters themselves. It should be immediately obvious that I have chosen first-rate works as the basis of my inquiry, works that have a high aesthetic value and rightly belong in the history of Italian literature, even when judged according to the strictest standards of the traditional canon. The exception, of course, is *Ettore Fieramosca*, a "minor" text in that canon, but still an extremely interesting, challenging, and necessary one. It has been included because it seems to me an almost paradigmatic specimen of the culture I am studying, a specimen that presents its mechanisms and values in elementary patterns, which in turn help us to understand the more elaborate ones to be found in the "high" literary works of the same period. In other words, the choice of *Fieramosca* was deliberately made as a necessary integration "from below" of traditional literary history, in order to make it a real part of culture, which is always both "high" and "low." The resulting "lowering" of tone seemed an appropriate price to pay.

Another remark should be made here, namely that each one of the intersystemic relationships explored in my six chapters could conceivably be, by itself, the subject of a book. Rather than pursue this course, I have preferred to try different and multiple approaches, partly to give an overview of Italian culture, partly to have my chosen methodology tested from several viewpoints, and partly to reaffirm the centrality of literature to my enterprise. However, I have pursued one relationship, the homology between literature and the visual arts, beyond the first chapter, where it belongs, because it is peculiarly important in our civilization and as such is worth exploring at length. I have done this by means of illustrations that are directly related to the texts under examination, with appropriate references and brief comments that should bring further unity to the cultural "picture" I am "drawing."

Throughout my book, I have tried to explain how the chosen texts work and why they work in their constitutive elements—from the space of writing to symbolic images. And perhaps space can be considered the unifying category for the whole project: space not as theme but as structure, as form, even when it is not the specific object of my analysis, or when it is linked with the coordinate of time in the diachrony of history.

Certainly space intended in this sense has inspired the title of my book. I have used the term "icon" not so much in a

strictly technical, semiotic sense à la Peirce,[23] as in the sense
of the spatial implications that are contained in it. These implications might be defined as metaphoric, at least in the sense
in which Jakobson spoke of the "iconic aspects" of the literary
text when he referred, for example, to syntax.[24] This is one
of those formal elements I have often emphasized in my own
analysis. It should also be remembered that, at the level of
interpretation, symbol and icon often coexist in the same image or figure.

As for the semantic marker "Italian," it is obviously (though
only partially) self-explanatory, in that it refers to the fact that
I am examining texts written in the Italian language since the
end of the eighteenth century. But it also refers to the conclusions of each of the six analyses that make up this book,
that is, to the "cultural unit" that against the European background is defined as pertaining to Italy and not, let us say,
to France or Germany.[25] Even a "geographic expression," with
its minimal common denominator of spatiality, gives rise to
culture. On the other hand, I hope that the historical period
I have chosen, from Foscolo to Calvino, clearly shows the
development and change of this cultural unit—from the birth
of the nation to the advent of a national role of cooperation
and exchange (both economic and intellectual, involving both
power and desire) in a context that is no longer merely European but international.

Before closing, I should like to go back for a moment to
that "semiotic" short story by Kipling. A lot of water has
flowed through Taffy's swamps since the Neolithic Age, but
the optimism of the chief of her tribe ("A time will come . . .
when we shall be able to read as well as to write, and then
we shall always say exactly what we mean without any mis-

---

[23] For instance: "Anything whatever, be it quality, existent individual, or
law, is an icon of anything, in so far as it is like that thing and used as a
sign of it." Charles Sanders Peirce, *Collected Papers* (Cambridge, Mass.: Harvard University Press, 1965), vol. 3, par. 247.

[24] Roman Jakobson, *Essais de linguistique générale* (Paris: Minuit, 1964).

[25] Cf. Giuseppe Galasso, *L'Italia come problema storiografico* (Turin: UTET,
1980), on the historical and cultural implications of the adjective "italiano"
as opposed to "italico" or "italiota."

takes") is not contradicted by the enormous and subtle complexity of the global semantic universe in which we move today. And it is semiotic theory and practice that help us to understand and communicate within this universe, to be "civilized," enabling us to avoid making mistakes such as taking Taffy's harmless beavers for bad people.

One. In the Primordial Origin of Evening

IN A MEMORABLE essay entitled "Romantic Space," the late Francesco Arcangeli wrote: "In my opinion one *ought* to risk a definition of Romanticism, and I believe that, as for any other art movement, the only criterion must necessarily be to try to define what Romanticism has given that is *newer* in comparision to preceding epochs and movements."[1]

Arcangeli proposes an interpretation of Romanticism that is no longer centered upon the commonly accepted Latin and French line of Géricault and Delacroix. Instead, he turns to a Nordic and British line featuring Constable and Turner because it expresses a new spatiality of the pictorial image, which reflects a new relationship between conscience and universe. It is an image that

> appears as *something unseizable and ambiguously definable within a space no longer delimited* by perspective [*i.e.*, from the given, traditional perspective]. This might seem nebulous at first, but actually I believe it is not, and it is clear

---

[1] Francesco Arcangeli, "Lo spazio romantico," originally in *Paragone*, no. 271, September 1972, pp. 3–25, now in his *Dal romanticismo all'informale. Dallo "spazio romantico" al primo Novecento* (Turin: Einaudi, 1977), pp. 3–22, quotation on p. 7. All quotations will refer to this edition. It should be noted that Arcangeli continues the investigations of Roberto Longhi's great school of criticism, with original and remarkable results. Longhi had explored the spatiality of the pictorial image (in, for example, his emphasis on *luminismo* and *chiaroscuro*), but had not dealt with Romanticism; see his *Da Cimabue a Morandi*, ed. by Gianfranco Contini (Milan: Mondadori, 1973).

that in that visual effect, in that particular spatiality, there are implied the *Sehnsucht*, the fluctuating of world appearances for the Romantic eye, man's breaking away from every preceding certitude. . . . No one had so radically destroyed Renaissance space and any idea of a concluded form as Turner did. (p. 9)

This destruction of Renaissance space is obtained in oil paintings and watercolors that suggest "the primordial origin or the end of things," a tension that is very different from the "linear simplifications" of John Flaxman, William Blake, and (in part) Jean Auguste Ingres. In fact, these simplifications always "lead one to retrace the beginning of classical art, that is, the beginning of an institutionalized and substantially well-known civilization, rather than the primordial origin of a life that is presumed to be anterior to civilization, as happens in the true Romantics." Arcangeli insists: "if one does not keep in mind the distinction between beginning (*arché*) and origin (*primordio*), which is in my opinion fundamental, one ends by confusing an archeology, however modern it may be, with an equally modern invention of life" (p. 10). As Arcangeli points out, the difference is truly fundamental, especially when considering the consequences of such an approach:

Romantic space, close [and] remote, placed at an undefined distance, is not the space of an intellectual conscience, or it is so only implicitly; it is a space that can risk inquiry into, and intuition by images of, the immensity of a universe that is no longer centered in man because, at the same time, it presupposes an inner exploration that knows no boundaries. (pp. 10–11)

From the start, Arcangeli deals with this inner exploration (an exploration also examined by Giuliano Briganti, who rightly speaks of a "psychological revolution"),[2] and defines it as "the discovery of a limitlessness unknown by traditional psychology." He then draws an extremely significant conclusion: namely that in the dialogue between inner limitlessness and

[2] Giuliano Briganti, *I pittori dell'immaginario. Arte e rivoluzione psicologica* (Milan: Electa, 1977).

the immensity of the universe, what cannot find a place is "the human body as an ideal body or a protagonist, . . . the measure of the universe in its imagined, but no longer verifiable, proportions." In a peremptory tone reminiscent of Pirandello's Mattia Pascal (and of Northrop Frye), Arcangeli continues:

> Copernicus opened up a whole dimension that destroys such an ideal condition. Man as the measure of things is an ancient illusion, which inertia and pride can still drag along, but which has substantially crumbled after that astronomical, but terribly human, revolution. After Copernicus it can be said that the conscience-universe relationship is our measure of things. (p. 11)

In nineteenth-century England, "the minimal quantity of man vis-à-vis the universe (at least on a physical level), his minimal scale vis-à-vis the cosmic dimension, are systematically taken for the first time as themes of painting" (p. 12). Arcangeli registers the initial glimmerings of such a conception in certain Danubian painters of the sixteenth century, such as Albrecht Altdorfer, and in Pieter Brueghel, but especially in Michelangelo da Caravaggio and Rembrandt van Rijn, both of whom are the true precursors of Turner, because in them "the terms of conscience and universe do not work any longer along a 'self-centered' balance, but as appearances suspended on the brink of the unknowable" (p. 17). Thus it becomes "legitimate" to speak about Turner's "informal" painting (p. 18)—and here "informal" would also seem to define twentieth-century painting by, say, Jackson Pollock, much better than the equivalent American term "abstract expressionism."

According to Arcangeli, the preeminence and novelty of British painting in the nineteenth century can be explained as well in relation to a whole milieu, a whole cultural climate, that finds poetic expression in the work of William Wordsworth. Two poems in particular are cited: "To the Cuckoo," in which the cuckoo is no longer a bird but "an invisible thing,/ a voice, a mystery" ("an ambiguous, undefined, spatially unrelated image, like an aerolite traveling in space," p. 13), and

"The Solitary Reaper," in which the song of the girl from the Hebrides can express both "old, unhappy, far-off things,/ and battles long ago," and "some more humble lay,/ familiar matter of to-day." In Arcangeli's view,

Romantic art's meaning as a meaning for life is clarified here, in the polarity between a "here and now" in which the whole poetics of "moderate" Romanticism is declared (from Wordsworth to Constable to Manzoni) and the unreachable "beyond" of what is spatially or temporally remote, what causes Coleridge's, Shelley's, and Turner's *Sehnsucht*. It is the same polarity between present, daily anguish and the echoing of past, fallen ages to be found in Leopardi's "La sera del dì di festa" (p. 14).[3]

Hence the tremendous power of innovation and discovery to be found in the "extreme" Romantic painting: "What did Turner do, with his 'vortex-like' space, but throw the appearances of the world at an infinite distance" (p. 21) and "remeasure man vis-à-vis the immensity enveloping him?" (p. 12). The most conclusive and persuasive example given by Arcangeli is *Snowstorm: Hannibal and his Army crossing the Alps*, painted by Turner in 1812, in which "the huge, cosmic storm seems to overcome the tension of the hero's will." In analyzing this painting, "one can never sufficiently stress the shocking reversal of the historical theme," especially if one compares it with *Napoleon crossing the Great St. Bernard Pass*, painted by Jacques-Louis David in 1800, in which "the protagonist overcomes a humiliated nature," and Napoleon, the "great Latin and still humanistic hero," is a "living embodiment of neo-classic, not Romantic civilization and, let us say, 'will' " (p. 21).

I shall not enter here into the details of the polite polemic formulated by Arcangeli against the will-oriented notion of Romantic art held by Giulio Carlo Argan and the modernistic line of Pierre Francastel because this polemic, however nec-

[3] "Moderate" Romanticism is analyzed by Karl Kroeber in *Romantic Landscape Vision: Constable and Wordsworth* (Madison: University of Wisconsin Press, 1975).

essary it may be, is of no immediate interest to the literary critic, and above all because it seems to me that the "reading of the forms" of pictorial works—a reading made by Arcangeli in order to arrive at "the history of meanings" (p. 20)—is better suited to my interests than an idealist approach based on general, philosophical concepts from which particular interpretations are then derived.

In any case, in Arcangeli's essay there are some features that should be noted:

(1) The introduction of the criterion of *novelty*, which in the field of literary criticism can be made to correspond to the concept of *innovation* (never merely aesthetic, but also historical, in terms of the first audience's "horizon of expectation")[4] and the concept of *modernity*, which is intended as a "radical renewal."[5] The introduction of such a criterion is a salutary reaction against a tendency, present even in literary criticism, to consider a definition of Romanticism as impossible or useless (the work of Mario Praz is as good an example of this as any).[6]

(2) A remarkable proposal in the field of historiography concerning the definition of Romanticism as a new relationship between conscience and universe. In painting, this is revealed through a nonanthropocentric perspective, which can also be applied to literature. Among the most important corollaries of this definition are: (a) a clear-cut distinction between Romanticism (the poetics of "the natural sublime," reflecting a concern with the primordial origin of life) and Neoclassicism (the "poetics of the statue," reflecting a concern with the beginning of civilization), which nevertheless respects the coexistence of both continuity (*tramando*) and the dialectical relationship; (b) the positing of a line from Cara-

---

[4] Hans Robert Jauss, *Perché la storia della letteratura?*, Italian tr. (Naples: Guida, 1977), pp. 83–86.

[5] Paul De Man, *Blindness and Insight: Essays in the Rhetoric of Contemporary Criticism* (New York: Oxford University Press, 1971), p. 150.

[6] Mario Praz, *The Romantic Agony*, tr. by Angus Davidson (London: Oxford University Press, 1970). For a well-documented overview of the subject, see Olga Ragusa, "Italy/Romantico-Romanticismo," in Hans Eichner, ed., *"Romantic" and Its Cognates: The European History of a Word* (Toronto: University of Toronto Press, 1973), pp. 293–340.

vaggio to Rembrandt to Turner to abstract expressionism that is very revealing, at least for me, when considering the nature of modern art.

(3) An extremely coherent methodological approach, which can be viewed a posteriori as a true, *ante litteram* semiotic insight, of the type represented in France by Jean-Louis Schefer and Louis Marin and recently outlined in Italy by Cesare Segre.[7]

Starting from Arcangeli's historiographic proposal, I believe that the new relationship between conscience and universe can and actually should be taken as paradigmatic for a definition of literary Romanticism. Something similar has already occurred in American criticism, for beyond the often harsh polemics that divide them, critics like Arthur Lovejoy, René Welleck, Morse Peckham, Earl Wasserman, M. H. Abrams, and Northrop Frye have all formulated interpretations of Romanticism in which a central role is played by the new conception, no longer mechanistic but organicistic, of the universe.[8] This conception on the one hand differentiates Romanticism from the Enlightenment, while on the other it constitutes the link between Neoclassicism and Romanticism. In fact, organicism derives from and is tied to the various eighteenth-century poetics of the sublime (Anthony Shaftesbury, Edmund Burke, A. G. Baumgarten, harking back to

[7] Jean-Louis Schefer, *Scénographie d'un tableau* (Paris: Seuil, 1968); Louis Marin, *Etudes sémiologiques. Ecritures, Peintures* (Paris: Klincksieck, 1971); and Cesare Segre, "La descrizione al futuro: Leonardo da Vinci," in his *Semiotica filologica* (Turin: Einaudi, 1979), pp. 131–60.

[8] I am referring in particular to: Arthur Lovejoy, *The Great Chain of Being* (Baltimore: Johns Hopkins University Press, 1936); René Welleck, *Concepts in Criticism* (New Haven: Yale University Press, 1963); Morse Peckham, *The Triumph of Romanticism* (Columbia, S.C.: University of South Carolina Press, 1970); Earl Wasserman, *The Subtler Langauge* (Baltimore: Johns Hopkins University Press, 1959); M. H. Abrams, *Natural Supernaturalism* (New York: Norton, 1971); and Northrop Frye, ed., *Romanticism Reconsidered* (New York: Oxford University Press, 1963). For the latest developments, see at least David Thornburn and Geoffrey Hartman, eds., *Romanticism: Vistas, Instances, Continuities* (Ithaca: Cornell University Press, 1973), and Hans Eichner, "The Rise of Modern Science and the Genesis of Romanticism," *PMLA*, vol. 97, no. 1 (January 1982), pp. 8–30.

Longinus) and of the primitive (Jean Jacques Rousseau, but above all Vico).[9]

In Giovanni Macchia's words, which singularly echo Arcangeli's, "it is a fact that in Italy the great Romantic poetry was written by the 'classicists.' This classicism had nothing to do with the classicism of the eighteenth century. It was itself a part of *a current of vital exaltation that seemed to bring man back to the sources of life*. The modern discovery of classicism was made by the Romantics."[10] For the moment, let us accept the organicistic conception (which is homologous to Arcangeli's historiographic proposal) as a valid hypothesis as far as Italian literature is concerned, a hypothesis we will later verify through some basic texts by Ugo Foscolo. As Glauco Cambon and Gustavo Costa have demonstrated, Foscolo was deeply influenced by the eighteenth-century poetics of the sublime and the primitive (Longinus, Vico). Macchia even unified these poetics when he wrote: "those who, like Foscolo, in defending Greek mythology defended a supernatural degree of imagination, which Christendom had not been able to destroy, asserted a form of *primitive sublime*."[11] I hasten to add that this primitive sublime should be intended, as far as Foscolo is concerned, not so much or not only as the revival of a concern with beginnings, but as a return to the consideration of a primordial origin.

Meanwhile, it is necessary to comment upon Arcangeli's methodological approach. I have said that Arcangeli has had a semiotic insight *ante litteram*; in fact, he pursues a *reading* of the *forms* of some works from which a *history* of *meanings* is derived. Of course, Arcangeli is not at all concerned with problems of semiotic theory, as Emile Benveniste or Boris

[9] Chapters 2 and 3 in Briganti's book have useful examinations of eighteenth-century poetics, as does James Engell's *The Creative Imagination: Enlightenment to Romanticism* (Cambridge, Mass.: Harvard University Press, 1981).

[10] Giovanni Macchia, "Origini europee del Romanticismo," in Emilio Cecchi and Natalino Sapegno, eds., *Storia della letteratura italiana* (Milan: Garzanti, 1969), vol. 7, *L'Ottocento*, p. 429, italics added.

[11] Ibid., p. 488, italics added. See also Gustavo Costa, "Foscolo e la poetica del sublime," and Glauco Cambon, "Vico e Foscolo" in *Forum Italicum*, vol. 12, no. 4 (Winter 1978, Special Issue: A Homage to Ugo Foscolo), pp. 472–97 and 498–511.

Uspensky are. Rather, his concern is a practical one, and in his perspective-oriented analysis, he considers a painting as an "epistemological space."[12]

Let us then read a semiotic critic like Cesare Segre, keeping Arcangeli in mind: "The movement of sight not only inserts temporality into spatial co-presence, but establishes the meaning of the work by instituting its overall significance."[13] Furthermore, by ordering the content of the work into a "chain that can be enunciated verbally," the analyses of perspective and iconology "snatch the painting from its simultaneity and give it a discursive duration" (p. 135). In other words (and here Segre completes Benveniste), a verbal narration transposes an iconic representation through "processes of figurative syntax achieved in the representation itself" (p. 136), but "only the globality of discourse assigns their qualifications to the elements. In any case, even the word 'discourse' is used metaphorically. It is more exact to speak of perspective, because it is perspective that institutes and supports the syntax of the image" (p. 137). In fact (and here, while Segre is commenting upon Uspensky, in my view he is also confirming Arcangeli's insight), perspective is "a relational system homologous to a given conception of the world," because "it is vision that precedes and causes concepts, not vice versa" (pp. 137 and 142).

Indeed, Arcangeli's itinerary of perspective to verbalization to conceptuality seems to be at the core of the contemporary debate on the semiotic nature of painting.[14] Let us briefly go

[12] Cf. Emile Benveniste's "Sémiologie de la langue," in *Problèmes de linguistique générale*, and Boris Uspensky's analysis of ancient Russian icons in his *Poetics of Composition*, tr. by V. Zavarin and S. Wittig (Berkeley: University of California Press, 1974). Also cf. Dora Vallier, "Malévitch et le modèle linguistique en peinture," *Critique*, vol. 334 (March 1975), pp. 284–96. It is necessary to emphasize that although he knows Erwin Panofsky quite well indeed, Arcangeli refuses to accept his "symbolic meanings," preferring instead a search for "real meanings dealing with natural and modern truth" (p. 20).

[13] Segre, "La descrizione al futuro," p. 134. The following quotations from this essay will be identified with page numbers in parentheses.

[14] In this connection cf. Segre, p. 139: "At the core of the problem there is the definition of communicative content. Between information and com-

over this itinerary, revealing what remained implicit in the art critic's discourse.

It is perspective that allows the reading of David's *Napoleon crossing the Great St. Bernard Pass* as a celebration of the hero. In this painting, Napoleon is physically handsome, and possessed of all the attributes of leadership. He is both realistic and idealized as he stands out on his horse in the foreground. The boulders of the Alps literally are his pedestal (according to the iconological code of Renaissance *condottieri*, not only in painting, as for example in the works of Paolo Uccello, but also and above all in the sculpture of such artists as Andrea del Verrocchio; indeed, here the neoclassic poetics of the statue find a brilliant confirmation). It is a pedestal because the majestic horse's hind hoofs stand on the rock; it is also a pedestal because on that very rock is freshly carved the name of the hero, "Bonaparte," a name much more clearly visible than those of his historical predecessors. One, "Karolus Magnus," is badly eroded, while the other, "Hannibal," is almost completely illegible. The hero's cloak and imperious index finger stand out on top—above the snow-capped peaks, which are lower in the background—and spur on the soldiers and artillerymen who are laboring up the slope in the middle distance. The date of the painting (1800) and the title, with its precise onomastic and geographic data, confirm the refer-

---

munication there is the gamut that encompasses all the forms of art: verbal arts hold the informative attitudes of language and its substitutes (gestures, signals, and so on); music is exclusively communicative; and painting stands in the middle, because of the amount of reality to which it refers, not by means of signs but of images, at times even by elaborating messages with a temporal (narrative) character. While 'informal' art has brought painting toward the level of music—the coupling of shapes and colors being analogous to the coupling of chords and notes—from the Middle Ages to the Renaissance and the Baroque, the figurative arts have stressed the informative elements, at least as a support." In this context, a number of essays on different forms of art are of particular interest, especially those in the *New Literary History* issue dedicated to "Literary and Art History," vol. 3, no. 3 (Spring 1972), with contributions by Svetlana and Paul Alpers (pp. 437–58), Jean Laude (pp. 471–86) and Oleg Grabar (pp. 559–68), among others. A more traditional approach is found in Mario Praz, *Mnemosyne: The Parallel Between Literature and the Visual Arts* (Princeton: Princeton University Press, 1970).

Fig. 1. Jacques-Louis David (1748–1825), *Napoleon crossing the Great St. Bernard Pass*, 1800, Musée Nationale, Malmaison.

entiality of the work and confer further authority upon its laudatory representation of the hero.

Now let us look at the "shocking reversal of the historical theme" brought about by Turner in *Snowstorm: Hannibal and his Army crossing the Alps*. Already the title is a key for the reading. It is the syntactical element bringing the pictorial aspects together, and as such is indispensable for an understanding of them in their referentiality.[15] The title shifts the

[15] This painting was shown for the first time at London's Royal Academy with the title *Snowstorm: Hannibal and his Army crossing the Alps* and was listed in the catalogue together with a poem by the artist, "Fallacies of Hope," which deals with ancient Carthage and the frailty and dangers of glory. In this connection, consider the following entry from the catalogue of a recent Turner exhibit: "Hannibal crossing the Alps in 218 B.C. was a common source

Fig. 2. James William Mallord Turner (1775–1851),
Snowstorm: Hannibal and his Army crossing the Alps,
1812, Tate Gallery, London.

attention from history to nature ("Snowstorm") and relegates
the historical character ("Hannibal") to the subtitle. Furthermore, this character is not shown in his triumphant individ-
uality but is united with, if not confused amidst, an anonymous mass ("and his Army"). If we remember the date of
the work (1812) and the historical events that are associated
with it (the Russian campaign), it seems clear that Turner is

of Romantic and post-Romantic inspiration. Mrs. Radcliffe's *The Mysteries of
Udolpho*, 1794, describes the scene shown by Turner, who was also inspired
by the lost oil painting by J. R. Cozens, which passed through the sale-rooms
in 1802. . . . On his visit to Paris in 1802 Turner had visited David's studio
and seen his picture of *Napoleon on the St. Bernard Pass* in which Napoleon
was shown as the modern Hannibal." *Turner 1775–1851* (London: Tate Gallery
Publication Department, 1975), p. 57. This catalogue also reports an anecdote
that accounts for the inspiration for the painting. Looking out at a snowstorm
from within the shelter of Walter Fawkes' house, Farnley Hall, in Yorkshire,
in 1810, Turner remarked to his host, "There, Hawkey; in two years you will
see this again, and call it Hannibal crossing the Alps" (p. 58). See also Graham
Reynolds, *Turner* (London: Thames and Hudson, 1969), pp. 86–88, and Hugh
Honour, *Romanticism* (New York: Harper and Row, 1970), p. 34.

directing his polemical discourse against David, literally hooking on to the pictorial *text* of 1800 (the "Hannibal" that is so faintly etched on Napoleon's rock-pedestal) in order to achieve a *diminutio antiaulica* of the leader and to warn him about the alternating fortunes of human destinies. In fact, Arcangeli says that "Turner already thinks like Tolstoi" (p. 21). The figurative syntax of Turner's painting corresponds exactly to the directions of its title. The space of the work is almost entirely dominated not by a human figure, as in David, but by the huge, white vortex of the snowstorm that blurs the dark lines of the mountain peaks with its enveloping movement and stands out at the center with a menacing emptiness.[16] In the foreground, whose scale is strongly reduced, the contrasting forms of the huge boulders serve to emphasize the swirling snow, making the human figures even more minute and helpless than they appear in themselves and in their postures. Some, terrified, raise their arms to the sky; others lie exhausted on the ground, lost and humiliated in the midst of a mighty nature that overwhelms them. Thus the relationship between man and nature becomes also an ideological one, and is exactly the opposite of that painted by David.

It should be noted that these two examples given by Arcangeli are focal points for the meeting and development of two, true *topoi* of the Romantic period: the climax and decline of Napoleon as a cultural model (the historical sublime), and

[16] When considering the importance and novelty of the vortex, it should be remembered that Turner wanted the picture hung at a man's height, not high above a door, as planned by the curators of the Royal Academy: "Turner's insistence that the picture should be hung low reveals his understanding of the novel effect of his vortex-like composition, which draws the spectator into its swirling depths," *Turner 1775–1851*, p. 58. Furthermore, this image is one in which external and internal limitlessness can be said to meet. It is present in numerous works by Turner, and can perhaps be subjected to the type of psychoanalytic interpretation put forth by Gilles Deleuze and Félix Guattari in *Capitalisme et Schizophrénie: L'Anti-Oedipe* (Paris: Minuit, 1972), p. 157. In their description of the vortex, Deleuze and Guattari use the terms "breakthrough" and (not) "breakdown," which are the same as those employed by R. D. Laing in *The Politics of Experience* (New York: Pantheon, 1967) to define madness as the fundamental and transcendental experience of the loss of the Self, the loss of personal identity.

the belief that the mountains are a privileged place for poetical contemplation, either melancholic or glorious (the natural sublime).[17] The ascending and descending parable of nature (with its metaphoric component connected with the semantic field "mountain") and the parable of the Napoleonic myth can be taken together as a useful point of reference for an analysis of corresponding developments in literature and, particularly in Foscolo, of the new relationship between conscience and universe as shown by Arcangeli.

It is quite well known that Napoleon was the subject as well as the object of an intricate web of cultural models in which literature and life exchanged their respective roles. Instead of delving deeply into this already familiar ground, let us simply recall that the trichotomy of fame, misfortune, and beauty, so prominent in *Ultime lettere di Jacopo Ortis*, had "its immediate roots" in *Ossian*, which was greatly admired by poets like Vittori Alfieri, Giacomo Leopardi, and Ugo Foscolo, as well as by Napoleon himself.[18] Equally well known is the historical disillusionment toward Napoleon felt by Foscolo, of which *Ortis* is a primary example. (One thinks of the beginning of the novel, or of the famous letter dated March 17, 1798.)

Let us, then, consider those pages from *Ortis* in which mountains appear as privileged places and, at an intersystemic level, function as literary correlatives of the pictorial "texts" that have been examined so far. For instance, the letter dated May 13 begins with a desire ("If I were a painter!") that is immediately denied ("but supreme nature, immense, in-

---

[17] On the first *topos*, see Eileen Ann Miller, *Napoleon in Italian Literature, 1796–1821* (Rome: Edizioni di Storia e letteratura, 1977); Roberto Cardini, "Tracollo napoleonico e fine dell'età neoclassica," *La Rassegna della letteratura italiana*, vol. 80, no. 1 (1976), pp. 32–69, especially pp. 62–69; and Biancamaria Frabotta, "Ugo Foscolo e la crisi del giacobinismo: le due inconciliabili libertà," *La Rassegna della letteratura italiana*, vol. 81, no. 3 (1977), pp. 306–330. On the second *topos*, see Majorie Nicolson, *Mountain Gloom and Mountain Glory: The Development of the Aesthetics of the Infinite* (Ithaca: Cornell University Press, 1959).

[18] Marcello Pagnini, "Il sonetto [A Zacinto]. Saggio teorico e critico sulla polivalenza funzionale dell'opera poetica," *Strumenti critici*, vol. 23 (February 1974), pp. 41–64, quotation on p. 58.

imitable—I've never seen her [painted]"). The letter continues with a description of a mountain in which anguish and serenity alternate ("barren ravines," "dark and frightening depth," "the mouth of a whirlpool" on the one hand; and on the other, "the horizon, where everything grows smaller and blends together," "and I, as though in the middle of the ocean, I can find only the sky") and is finally concluded with an invocation-meditation that takes place in a Gray-like country cemetery at the foot of a mountain:

> Rest in peace, you relics of a past life! Dust has returned to dust; nothing diminishes, nothing grows; everything is transformed and reproduced—oh human destiny! The man who fears his destiny less knows less unhappiness than others.[19]

Foscolo's Romantic organicism seems concentrated in this passage, while in the letter dated May 25 the relationship between soul and landscape (conscience and universe) is described again: "I have climbed the highest mountain; the winds were raging. . . . There in the terrifying majesty of nature my soul, stunned and dazed as it was, forgot its troubles and for a short while returned to peace with itself." This is the same situation that has its most successful poetical expression in the sonnet "Alla sera." Then Jacopo moves on toward the places associated with Napoleon ("rocky roads, craggy mountains, all the cold of the season," in the letter of February 15, 1797, from La Pietra). And although he is going toward exile, not conquest, he too is about to cross the Alps:

> Finally . . . I am enjoying some peace! What kind of peace? Exhaustion, the torpor of the grave. I've wandered through these mountains. There isn't a tree, a hut, a single blade of grass. Nothing but tree-stumps. Rugged and leaden-colored boulders, here and there several crosses which

---

[19] All prose quotations are from Ugo Foscolo's *Ultime lettere di Jacopo Ortis*, tr. by Douglas Radcliff-Umstead (Chapel Hill: University of North Carolina Press, 1970). The poems are from Ugo Foscolo, *Poesie*, ed. by Guido Bezzola (Milan: Rizzoli, 1976) and *The Penguin Book of Italian Verse*, intro. and ed. by George R. Kay, with plain prose translations of each poem (Harmondsworth: Penguin, 1972), pp. 245, 248, 235–36, 237, and 255.

mark the spot where travelers have been murdered. Down below I can see the Roja, a stream which becomes a raging torrent when the ice melts up in the Alps; it cuts these immense mountains in two. . . . I stopped at the bridge, and looked out as far as my sight could reach. Crossing over two mounds of very high rocks and cavernous cliffs you can just barely make out other snowy Alpine mountains which grow vague and confused in the distant clouds [literally: which are immersed in the sky and everything is white and blurred]. The northwind comes down from the wide-open Alps and sweeps through those openings to strike the Mediterranean. Nature sits here solitary and threatening while it chases away all living things. (Letter from Ventimiglia, February 19 and 20, 1799.)

It seems to me that this text by Foscolo can be read in much the same way as Turner's *Snowstorm* because of its human (no longer humanistic) perspective from below (the viewer is belittled) to above (the peaks triumph), climaxing in the phrase "snowy Alpine mountains which are immersed in the sky and everything is white and blurred," which could be a literal description of Turner's vortex. Furthermore, this vision is the secret spring that pushes Jacopo to formulate the ensuing (patriotic) historical-political and moral considerations; they too provide a new dimension for the human figure and contribute an integral part of the character's *prise de conscience* in the face of the spatio-temporal universe—so much so, in fact, that because of them he will not cross the Alps but instead turns back. Clearly, the model of Napoleon triumphing over humiliated nature no longer works for the young poet.

Like Jacopo, Foscolo was modern (and Romantic) because he posited the relationship between conscience and universe in new terms, because he felt nature and the world in an organicistic manner. And if we move from *Ortis* to the great poem *Dei Sepolcri*, further textual confirmations of Foscolo's perspective abound. Here, for example, are lines 19 through 22 (which illustrate this point despite a sure echo from Antoine Lavoisier's mechanicism):

E una forza operosa le affatica
Di moto in moto; e l'uomo e le sue tombe
E l'estreme sembianze e le reliquie
Della terra e del ciel traveste il tempo.

And a busy force wears them [all things] from one movement to the next; and time disguises man and his tombs
and last appearances and the relics of earth and sky.

Or lines 95 and 96:

I miserandi avanzi che Natura
Con veci eterne a sensi altri destina.

Those [pitiful] remains, which Nature with constant vary-
ing destines for other purposes.

In these and similar verses by Foscolo, man is "placed in a
relationship." He is no longer at center stage, no longer dom-
ineering and triumphant like Napoleon on the Great St. Bernard Pass.

But in order to illustrate Foscolo's novelty in a comprehen-
sive manner, it is necessary to analyze the sonnet "Alla sera."
This poem is a stupendous meditation on the new relationship
between conscience and universe which Foscolo was the first
to offer in nineteenth-century Italy (it was published there in
1803). As such, it is a radical renewal from within of the
traditional form of the sonnet (the "poetic space"), one that
is perfectly consistent with the thematic innovation. Here is
the text:

1   Forse perché della fatal quïete
2   Tu sei l'immago a me sì cara vieni
3   O sera! E quando ti corteggian liete
4   Le nubi estive e i zeffiri sereni,

5   E quando dal nevoso aere inquïete
6   Tenebre e lunghe all'universo meni
7   Sempre scendi invocata, e le secrete
8   Vie del mio cor soavemente tieni.

9   Vagar mi fai co' miei pensier su l'orme
10 Che vanno al nulla eterno; e intanto fugge
11 Questo reo tempo, e van con lui le torme

12   Delle cure onde meco egli si strugge;
13 E mentre io guardo la tua pace, dorme
14 Quello spirto guerrier ch'entro mi rugge.

Perhaps because you are the image of that fatal quiet your coming is so dear to me, o evening! When the summer clouds and calm breezes woo you, and again when from the snowy air you bring long and troubled shades to the world, you always come down as one prayed for, and gently follow out the secret ways of my heart.

You make me linger in thought, upon the paths that go towards eternal nothingness; and, meanwhile, this evil time flies, and with it go the swarms of cares in which it wastes itself and me; and as I look upon your peace, that warrior spirit which roars in me is sleeping.

I do not intend to present a formal analysis of this sonnet, complete with isotopies and codes. Instead I shall limit myself to pointing out and emphasizing those elements (of both form and content) that justify the homology with Turner's Romantic space.

Foscolo's poetic discourse in "Alla sera" constantly pushes against the limits of metrics, and it can be said to overflow the dykes of the hendecasyllables, of the quatrains and tercets, as if it equated poetic space with the limitlessness of the poet's inner contemplation, the limitlessness of his physical and mental vision. In this connection, one remembers that according to Lotman "the structure of the space of a text becomes a model of the structure of the space of the universe, and the internal syntagmatics of the elements within a text becomes the language of spatial modeling."[20] These remarks are of fundamental importance to an understanding of Foscolo's novelty, especially considering the fact that the syn-

---

[20] Yuri Lotman, *The Structure of the Artistic Text*, tr. by Ronald Vroon (Ann Arbor: University of Michigan Press, 1977), p. 217.

tagmatics of the elements inside the text corresponds to what Jakobson has called "the iconic aspects" of language. For it is by acting on these iconic aspects that Foscolo has made the structure of poetic space into the model of the structure of the space of the universe. This is enormously enlarged vis-à-vis traditional (external) perspective and (inner) psychology, which are by now obsolete.

Foscolo uses three technical means to activate the iconic elements in order to reach such a result:

(1) At the phonological level, there is the dieresis *in rhyme*, which causes a prolongation of the line (*quïete . . . inquïete*).

(2) At the rhythmic level, there is the *enjambment*, which occurs *seven* times, one of which is between the two tercets (*vieni/ O sera . . . liete/ Le nubi . . . inquïete/ Tenebre . . . le secrete/ Vie . . . fugge/ Questo reo tempo . . . le torme/ Delle cure . . . dorme/ Quello spirto*).

(3) At the syntactic level, there is not only the very effective position of the adjectives, which has already been noted by Luigi Russo (*inquïete Tenebre e lunghe*), but above all the polysyndeton: there are two long sentences linking quatrain to quatrain and tercet to tercet, each sustained paratactically by three conjunctions (*e*), which predominate over the temporal and causal connections: *e quando, e quando, e intanto, e mentre*. The amplification, the enlargement, the vortex effect is also increased by two other *e*'s that are used morphologically to tie adjectives and nouns instead of clauses (*Le nubi estive e i zeffiri sereni . . . inquïete Tenebre e lunghe*). The sum total of these "iconic"—that is, visually "spatial"—conjunctions is eight.[21]

[21] Cf. Luigi Russo, *I classici italiani* (Florence: Sansoni, 1946), vol. 3, p. 105: "The beauty of the sonnet consists principally in the lyrical syntax of its sentences, of that width of melodic movement that enlarges the images." See also Glauco Cambon, *Ugo Foscolo: Poet of Exile* (Princeton: Princeton University Press, 1980), p. 139: "Syntax conspires with sound to insinuate the psychic implications of the cosmic event, by flooding over the successive sluices of each major prosodic unit in rhythmic waves upon waves which counteract the strict definiteness of stanza and verse through enjambment and strategic pause." See also Marco Cerruti, *Neoclassici e giacobini* (Milan: Silva, 1969), pp. 230 and 249, in which "the polysyndetic basis of the sonnet" and the "intensive use of the conjunction *e*" are briefly noted as elements

The formal as well as thematic novelty of the enlargement of the poetic text in "Alla sera" has not been sufficiently emphasized by critics, with two notable exceptions. Glauco Cambon states that "it is as if the sharp outlines of things were dissolving in the twilight [notice how close the images used by the literary critic are to those of the art critic, Arcangeli], and as if the measured length of each eleven-syllable line were melting into pulses of measureless duration." Similarly, Antonino Musumeci, in examining Foscolo's so-called "major" sonnets, points out the "decisive break with the institutionalized structure of the sonnet with its traditional code."[22]

But there is another formal aspect of "Alla sera" that has a crucial importance: the apostrophe. In this connection, Jonathan Culler's remarks on the vocative form in poetry and its founding function should be applied to Foscolo in their entirety:

> The vocative of apostrophe is a device which the poetic voice uses to establish with an object a relationship which helps to constitute him. The object is treated as subject, an *I* which implies a certain type of *you* in its turn. One who successfully invokes nature is one to whom nature might, in its turn, speak. He makes himself poet, visionary. Thus, invocation is a figure of vocation. . . . The vocative . . . is precisely the attempt to bring about the condition to which it alludes: the condition of visionary poet who can engage in dialogue with the universe. If, as we tend to assume, post-enlightenment poetry seeks to overcome the alienation of subject from object, then

---

of a "compositional dynamics" capable of revealing Foscolo's perplexities and irrationality vis-à-vis the "failure" of history. Finally, see Antonino Musumeci, "Foscolo: Poesia come violazione," *Forum Italicum*, vol. 12, no. 4 (Winter 1978), pp. 512–27, in which he points out "the jumping movement" of the sonnet, caused by the alternate use of caesurae and enjambments, and emphasizes "the phonic element of the vowel *e* as a relaxing and fascinating sound," which in fact "appears 79 times" in the brief poem (p. 518).

[22] Cambon, p. 139, and Musumeci, p. 515. See also the most recent biography of the poet by Enzo Mandruzzato, *Foscolo* (Milan: Rizzoli, 1977), p. 125: "In a magnificent sonnet, *Alla sera*, the secret of the light containers [the signifiers] confirms Foscolo's truly new and truly Nordic Romanticism."

apostrophe takes the crucial step of constituting the object as another subject with whom the poetic subject might hope to strike up a harmonious relationship.[23]

The formation of the relationship between the poetic conscience and the universe could not be described in better terms. If it is Foscolo who invokes evening, it is evening that constitutes "Foscolo." Furthermore, Culler's words clearly illustrate Foscolo's strong desire to be a "visionary" poet, one who enters into a dialogue with the universe, instituting a "harmonious relationship" with his interlocutor, nature. However, this is not a question of attempting to anthropomorphize nature. On the contrary, the vocative reveals the pretense of the poet at the same time that it constitutes him as a poet: the human *I* is fragile, no longer self-centered and self-sufficient. Nature is the necessary referent that the poet, more than others, is able to represent and make speak. In a sense, it can be said that the poet depends on the universe and on his discourse, which are indissolubly linked by the vocative.

With all this in mind, let us consider the thematic novelty of "Alla sera" in Arcangeli's terms:

(1) The polarity between conscience and universe. The poet is lost in and consoled by his contemplation of the temporal infinite (*il nulla eterno*), which is summoned up by the view and by the consideration, repeated in an atemporal present, of the spatial infinite. This is just hinted at but is still decisive (*nubi, zeffiri, tenebre, universo, guardo la tua pace*). Thus evening, a temporal and real moment, becomes a true *image*. It becomes *immago*, a symbol, an emblem of spatiality. It should be noted that such contemplation leads one toward an acknowledgment of the limitlessness of the inner life, a concept unknown to traditional psychology. This is expressed through such im-

<hr>

[23] Jonathan Culler, "Apostrophe," *Diacritics*, vol. 7, no. 4 (Winter 1977), pp. 59–69, quotation on p. 63; now in his *The Pursuit of Signs* (Ithaca: Cornell University Press, 1981), pp. 135–54. Pagnini speaks of a "conative elocution" that is a direct consequence of apostrophe (p. 48); Musumeci emphasizes the "affective quality" of such an elocution (p. 516); and Cambon underlines Foscolo's combination of apostrophe with prolepsis (pp. 21–22).

ages as *l'orme/ Che vanno al nulla eterno*, which is as ambiguous and indefinite as any.

(2) The polarity between an anguished "here and now" (*questo reo tempo, le torme delle cure*) and an unreachable "beyond" that is spatially and temporally remote (*il nulla eterno*). But even beyond its consideration in Arcangeli's terms, the novelty of "Alla sera" is important because, at the intertextual level, it precedes by sixteen years the other climax of Italian Romanticism, Giacomo Leopardi's "L'infinito," which in this perspective appears as the necessary development of the insights contained in Foscolo's sonnet.[24] Let us begin with the text of Leopardi's poem:[25]

1   Sempre caro mi fu quest'ermo colle,
2   E questa siepe, che da tanta parte
3   Dell'ultimo orizzonte il guardo esclude.
4   Ma sedendo e mirando, interminati
5   Spazi di là da quella, e sovrumani
6   Silenzi, e profondissima quiete
7   Io nel pensier mi fingo; ove per poco
8   Il cor non si spaura. E come il vento
9   Odo stormir tra queste piante, io quello
10   Infinito silenzio a questa voce
11   Vo comparando: e mi sovvien l'eterno,
12   E le morte stagioni, e la presente
13   E viva, e il suon di lei. Così tra questa
14   Immensità s'annega il pensier mio:
15   E il naufragar m'è dolce in questo mare.

[24] Therefore I agree with Bruno Biral, who in *La posizione storica di Giacomo Leopardi* (Turin: Einaudi, 1974) rejects the traditional links that critics have made between "L'infinito" and a well-known passage from Alfieri's *Vita* as being both misleading and unjustified (pp. 188–91 and 206–207). However, as Ezio Raimondi reminds us, "without the shock provoked by Alfieri's tragedies it would be difficult to imagine the lyrical monologue of the new Italian poetry [of the nineteenth century], its dramatization of a destiny engaged in a dialogue with its own history." *Il concerto interrotto* (Pisa: Pacini, 1979), p. 12.

[25] Giacomo Leopardi, *Tutte le opere*, ed. by F. Flora (Milan: Mondadori, 1937–49), vol. 1, *Poesie e prose*. The translation is by George R. Kay in *The Penguin Book of Italian Verse*, p. 272.

It was always dear to me, this solitary hill, and this hedge which shuts off the gaze from so large a part of the uttermost horizon. But sitting and looking out, in thought I fashion for myself endless spaces beyond, more-than-human silences, and deepest quiet; where the heart is all but terrified. And as I hear the wind rustling among these plants, I go on and compare this voice to that infinite silence: and I recall the eternal, and the dead seasons, and the present, living one and her sound. So in this immensity my thoughts drown: and shipwreck is sweet to me in this sea.

If I am not mistaken, only Mario Fubini has noted that "as far as the subject is concerned 'L'infinito' can be compared with the sonnet 'Alla sera.'" By focusing his analysis on the rhythmic element, he concluded that Leopardi penetrates "more deeply [than Foscolo] into the realm of innermost thoughts: Leopardi lives and makes us live from within what Foscolo embraces synthetically in one line (*vagar mi fai co' miei pensier su l'orme*). The discovery of a new rhythm corresponds to the discovery of a new world."[26] This last remark coincides with that of Arcangeli, already quoted, according to which the new intuition of the immensity of space "presupposes an inner exploration that knows no boundaries." It should only be dated back and referred to Foscolo *in primis*.

At this point, it would be useful to analyze the thematic level of "L'infinito" vis-à-vis the concept of Romantic space. In this context, its novelty can be seen in two areas:

(1) The polarity between conscience and universe. As in Foscolo's sonnet, so in Leopardi's poem a poet is lost in and consoled by the contemplation of the temporal infinite (*mi sovvien l'eterno*), which is caused more by imagination than by the actual sight of spatial infinity (*questa siepe, che da tanta parte Dell'ultimo orizzonte il guardo esclude*: therefore *interminati Spazi . . . Io nel pensier mi fingo*), not to mention the auditory

---

[26] Mario Fubini, *Metrica e poesia* (Milan: Feltrinelli, 1962), pp. 63–70. Fubini has noted that the numerous *e*'s of "L'infinito" "contribute to the widening of the verses," but he does not refer them back to Foscolo's precedent. Fine remarks on this subject are also made in Costanzo di Girolamo, "Gli endecasillabi de *L'infinito*," *Yearbook of Italian Studies*, vol. 2, 1972, pp. 102–110.

stimulus, which is absent in Foscolo, of the wind (*silenzio . . . voce*). This contemplation leads to an awareness of the limitlessness of the inner life, with ambiguous and indefinite images that are linked to the unknowable, as are those in Foscolo (*interminati spazi, sovrumani silenzi, le morte stagioni, immensità*).[27]

(2) The polarity between a barely perceived "here and now" (*il vento* of *queste piante*, the *presente E viva* season) and an unreachable "beyond" that is spatially and temporally remote. (The textual statement should be emphasized: *interminati spazi* DI LÀ DA *quella*; and also *quello Infinito silenzio, l'eterno, E le morte stagioni, questa immensità, questo mare*.)

I believe the thematic homology between "Alla sera" and "L'infinito" has already been indisputably established. But if further proof is required, it can be found at the lexical level in the presence of no fewer than seven identical key-words in each of the two poems. Key-words are literary signs whose importance cannot be underestimated because "we can consider them as a second discourse, a hypodiscourse. They are connected among themselves from point to point in the context; they create a sort of asyntactic discourse in which isolated conceptual elements, rather than consequential connections and developments, are emphasized."[28] These are the seven key-words:

> *quiete* (Foscolo, line 1; Leopardi, line 6)
> *cara/o* (F 2, L 1)
> *sempre* (F 7, L 1)

[27] Leopardi's ideas on the vague and the indefinite are well known. Recurring throughout his *Zibaldone*, they constitute a true poetics that has been duly noted by literary critics, but is still cast in a new light by Arcangeli's notion of Romantic space. Among the recent contributions on this subject, see Nicolas Perella, *Night and the Sublime in Giacomo Leopardi* (Berkeley: University of California Press, 1970) and Luigi Blasucci, "Leopardi e i segnali dell'*Infinito*," *Strumenti critici*, vols. 36–37 (October 1978), pp. 146–70, on "the various processes to 'activate' the semantic elements."

[28] Segre, *Semiotica filologica*, p. 42. One should remember that even in the narrative field, key-words, whether "abundantly distributed" or "only strategically placed" in a given text, are very important signals for the "reconstruction of the topic" by the "Model Reader." Umberto Eco, *The Role of the Reader* (Bloomington: Indiana University Press, 1979).

cor (F 8, L 8)
pensier (F 9, pl.; L 7 and 14, sing.)
eterno (F 10, adj.; L 11, noun)
guardo (F 13, verb; L 3, noun)

To these key-words we might add two others: *soavemente* (F 8) and *dolce* (L 15), which belong to the same semantic family. But in any case, these seven key-words are eloquent in themselves in that each one of them, and all of them together, constitute the fundamental thematic motifs (the hypodiscourse) of both Foscolo and Leopardi. I should add that *sempre* and *quiete* are accented, respectively, at the beginning and at the end of the line in both poems (not to mention Leopardi's initial *raccourci*-intensification, *Sempre caro*) and that in Leopardi *cor* is accented at the beginning of the line and *eterno* at the end. The complementary relationship between *cor* and *pensier* (between feeling and reason), placed as it is at the very center of the hypodiscourse, is indispensable to the correct understanding of both the poetics and the ideology governing the two poems.

Finally, the thematic homology has a precise, formal correspondence in the structure of the poetic discourse. In "L'infinito," Leopardi abandons the by now too restrictive rules of the sonnet in order to be able to radicalize Foscolo's "lyrical syntax" to the utmost. It should be remembered that in order to equate poetic space with epistemological space Foscolo had already expanded the metric measure of the hendecasyllable enormously and did not abide by the traditional limits between quatrain and quatrain, tercet and tercet. To achieve such a result, not only does Leopardi renounce the poetic form of the "sonnet" *tout court*—by eliminating quatrains and tercets, and furthermore by adding that fifteenth line, which is extremely significant as the seal of the poetic innovation (the "idyll")—but he also uses and even intensifies the same means that are employed by Foscolo, with the obvious exception of the dieresis in rhyme, of which, however, there remains a revealing echo in *quiete*. These means are the enjambment (*tanta parte/ Dell'ultimo orizzonte . . . interminati/ Spazi . . . sovrumani/ Silenzi . . . quello/ Infinito silenzio . . . la presente/*

E viva . . . questa/Immensità) and the polysyndeton (there are eight *e*'s in "Alla sera," as there are eleven in "L'infinito," of which four perform a paratactic and seven a morphological function, reinforced also by the adversative *ma*). However, there is no apostrophe, which made possible the dialogue between the individual conscience and the nature-universe constellation in Foscolo. Leopardi, who does use the apostrophe in his *Canti* with splendid results, here is able to do without it, perhaps because, or precisely because, he is carrying on the poetic discourse Foscolo had begun.

The poetic space that is enlarged to reproduce the new relationship between conscience and universe at the formal level is, therefore, the literary equivalent of what Arcangeli defined as "the new spatiality of the image" in English Romantic painting. In fact, his words can be applied directly to the two poems that have just been examined:

> The two apparent dimensions of so many images by Turner open up to reveal the vertigo of a place that is "really" unlimited. The infinite but solid space assigned by the Middle Ages to personal divinity has disappeared; the earthly certitude of Italian perspective is abandoned; and the image becomes isolated or is diffused into a cosmos of an unlimited, unmeasurable depth. Perhaps conscience may think it is at the level of the new cosmic space, but at this level there is no longer, in Turner as well as in any other true Romantic artist, a body-protagonist or any other humanistic proportion. If it is present, the body is continually obliterated or internally minimized vis-à-vis the immensity surrounding it (p. 12).

The ultimate meaning of the peace of evening in which Foscolo's *spirto guerrier* finally sleeps, as well as the meaning of Leopardi's *naufragar dolce*, could not be stated in better terms than Arcangeli's. Sleep and shipwreck are the two figures of the inner vortex that is caused by the contemplation of nature's immensity, in comparison with which the poetic voice is minimized. This is the reason why "Alla sera" and "L'infinito" are truly emblematic of an entire epoch of Italian literary history.

If in Foscolo's "Alla sera" the relationship between conscience and universe is expressed according to a wholly new conception, it must also be emphasized that such a novel approach is not isolated, but is instead manifested in a variety of existential attitudes and texts that contribute to make Foscolo the first great Italian Romantic. A systematic examination of these attitudes and texts would require an entire volume, but perhaps it would be worth while to point out a few directions a critical inquiry might take in order to integrate the preceding proposals. In outlining these directions, I shall use the categories of new social roles that were "invented" by the Romantics and were described by Morse Peckham as "designed to symbolize the difference between role and self,"[29] and hence were also called anti-roles: the Byronic hero, the visionary poet, the dandy, and the historian, all of which are true cultural codes.

Foscolo was a Romantic—that is, modern, new—because he was a Jacobin, a traveler, an exile. The anti-role of the Byronic hero fits him as well as it does his best-known character, Jacopo Ortis, and his poetic persona: *"Un dì, s'io non andrò sempre fuggendo/ Di gente in gente. . . ."* ("One day, if I am not to keep fleeing from people to people . . . ," "In morte del fratello Giovanni," lines 1–2); or *"quando lontano/ Non prescrivano i fati anche il sepolcro"* ("if the fates do not decree that even my tomb should be a distant one," *Le Grazie*, part 3, lines 256–57); or *"e me che i tempi ed il desio d'onore/ Fan per diversa gente ir fuggitivo"* ("and me whom the times and the wish for honor cause to seek refuge among different peoples," *Dei Sepolcri*, lines 226–27). It is worth adding that a formal literary innovation—at least for Italy—corresponded to this new attitude: *Ultime lettere di Jacopo Ortis*, an epistolary novel and as such traditionally and mainly intended to communicate or even to persuade at the intersubjective level (one thinks

[29] Peckham, p. 38. Two other Romantic roles described by Peckham, the virtuoso and the Bohemian, do not seem to be applicable to Foscolo, at least in part because of chronological reasons. The need to examine Foscolo's modernity is also stated in Walter Binni, "Foscolo oggi: proposta di una interpretazione storico-critica," *La Rassegna della letteratura italiana*, vol. 82 (September–December 1978), pp. 333–51, especially pp. 333–36 and 340–43.

of *Les Liaisons dangereuses*), is instead bent on the expression of the whole interiority of the self.[30] Furthermore, the "ironic" distance that is gained by inserting a character who is the editor of the letters between the author and the writing protagonist (Foscolo-Lorenzo-Ortis) is minimal here, but will become typical of the twentieth-century novel (e.g., Italo Svevo-Dr. S.-Zeno).

Foscolo was also modern because he was a visionary poet, a bard. Seen in its entirety, the development of his work shows a progressive deepening of the creative and salutary value of the poetic word, from the very first insight in the ode "Alla amica risanata" (lines 91–94), through the conscious adoption of the role of the bard in *Dei Sepolcri*, together with the parallel celebration of Homer, the *sacro vate* (*"Me ad evocar gli eroi chiamin le Muse/ Del mortale pensiero animatrici,"* "let the Muses, the inspirers of mortal thought, summon me to invoke heroes," lines 228–29), and finally to the triumphant, visionary quality of *Le Grazie*, in which the poetic word is a guarantee of both compassion and modesty, two eminently civic virtues.[31]

Foscolo was also modern because he was a "dandy" (even Montale spoke of Foscolo's "humanistic dandyism").[32] Undoubtedly he was so because he was an ironic bourgeois who lived in a time that was still primarily aristocratic (one thinks of the nobility of such families as the Manzonis and the Leopardis). Yet in the end Foscolo's game became too serious to

[30] On this novel, the remarks of Fubini are still valid: "Lettura dell' 'Ortis,' " in *Ortis e Didimo. Ricerche e interpretazioni foscoliane* (Milan: Feltrinelli, 1963), pp. 11–85. There is also a remarkable essay by Giorgio Bàrberi-Squarotti, "L'itinerario tragico di Jacopo Ortis," *Forum Italicum*, vol. 12, no. 4 (Winter 1978), pp. 554–95.

[31] In this connection, see Karl Kroeber, *The Artifice of Reality: Poetic Style in Wordsworth, Foscolo, Keats, and Leopardi* (Madison: University of Wisconsin Press, 1964). A Derridian interpretation can be found in Eugenio Donato, "The Mnemonics of History: Notes for a Contextual Reading of Foscolo's *Dei Sepolcri*," *Yale Italian Studies*, vol. 1, no. 1 (Winter 1977), pp. 1–23.

[32] Eugenio Montale, *Fuori di casa* (Milan, Naples: Ricciardi, 1969), p. 49. The influence of Foscolo on Montale, the "echoes of rhymes," is studied by Gilberto Lonardi in "I padri metafisici: appunti sullo spazio del privato in Montale," *Strumenti critici*, vol. 30 (June 1976), pp. 281–303.

be carried on. In fact, it became sorrowful and tragic, as was also the case with Oscar Wilde in that same England where Foscolo died. What remains, in literary terms, of Foscolo's attitude is in Didimo Chierico, the figure who is the counterpart of those of Jacopo Ortis and above all of the "visionary" poet, the bard.[33] It should also be noted that the Sternean irony in Didimo is focused on the words themselves (as will be seen later on in the works of Carlo Dossi and Carlo Emilio Gadda). In this regard, it is enough to read a passage in which Foscolo pretends he is quoting from Didimo, and more precisely from "one of his many scribbling pads" entitled *Itinerario lungo la Repubblica Letteraria*. This passage describes "an implacable war between the letters of the alphabet and the arabic numerals, which finally won through clever tricks, keeping hostage the *a*, the *b*, and the *x* that had gone as ambassadors and were then tyrannically burdened with inexpressible and anguishing labors."[34]

Finally, Foscolo was modern because he was a historian—and the enormous importance of historicism in the nineteenth century is well known. First it was a reaction against the tabula rasa of the French Enlightenment, then it was a deliberate search for and documentation of origins, and finally it became a scientific and philosophic attitude. Foscolo was a historian in that he was a philologist, a critic and historiographer of Italian literature. In this role, he propounded insights and remarks, truly new and full of promise, that are only today beginning to be studied and appreciated. One thinks, for example, of his discussions of the periods of Italian literary history, of his interest in the linguistic sign and the notion of text, of his meditations on art intended not as mimesis but as creation (a concept that is itself a typically Romantic one).[35]

But there is also a second, and conclusive, meaning of the term "modernity," one that we have approached little by

[33] Cf. Armand Tripet, " 'Spirto guerrier' e parola civilizzatrice nell'esperienza del Foscolo," *Forum Italicum*, vol. 12, no. 4 (Winter 1978), pp. 462–71.

[34] In Ugo Foscolo, *Edizione Nazionale*, vol. 5, *Prose varie d'arte*, ed. by Mario Fubini (Florence: Le Monnier, 1951), p. 182.

[35] Foscolo's writings on criticism and literary history are in vols. 7–12 of *Edizione Nazionale*.

little: modernity no longer as novelty but as contemporariness. The reasons why Foscolo was modern in his own era also explain why Foscolo is still modern now. The relationship he saw between conscience and universe, with its new dimension of the human figure, conforms to the perception of man held by today's science and philosophy (one thinks of the notions of relativity, structure, and ecology). And his celebration of the poetic word is also in tune with today's formalistic criticism, and with other modes of criticism as well. Thus his insights are well worth our consideration.[36]

If novelty and contemporaneity coincide after almost two centuries, this means that Paul De Man is correct when he writes that "modernity turns out to be one of the concepts by means of which the distinctive nature of literature can be revealed in all its intricacy." The writer "cannot renounce the claim to being modern but also cannot resign himself to his dependence on predecessors—who, for that matter, were caught in the same situation."[37] This is the reason why, "considered as a principle of life, modernity becomes a principle of origination and turns at once into a generative power that is in itself historical." Modernity and history are tied to the same destiny, and if their link seems (and is) paradoxical, the paradox is inherent to the literary phenomenon and is its nature, its specificity.[38]

Clearly, De Man is dealing with a fundamental problem, one that is treated as well by T. S. Eliot (tradition and the individual talent), Harold Bloom (the anxiety of influence), and of course Arcangeli, who is by now well-known to the readers of this chapter (the dialectical relationship and the

[36] Furthermore, it is possible to acknowledge that Foscolo has "some typical traits of the progressive, modern intellectual," as Gennaro Barbarisi stated in an article entitled (presumably by editorial intervention) "Che fascino: è tanto dissensuale!," *L'Espresso*, 12 February 1978, p. 72.

[37] De Man, pp. 161–62.

[38] Ibid., pp. 150–51. See also on p. 162: "The continuous appeal of modernity, the desire to break out of literature toward the reality of the moment, prevails and, in its turn, folding back upon itself, engenders the repetition and the continuation of literature. Thus modernity, which is fundamentally a falling away from literature and a rejection of history, also acts as the principle that gives literature duration and historical existence."

relationship of continuity or *tramando*).[39] Therefore, let us also apply De Man's remarks to painting (or to music) and speak not only of the specificity of literature but of art as a whole (every single art being in turn specified by its own expressive means, such as words, colors, or notes). One can then say, with De Man, that true art is always "modern" because modernity is a principle of life, a generative power that renews itself in every historical epoch, as is demonstrated at the beginning of the nineteenth century by Turner's painting and Foscolo's poetry.

[39] T. S. Eliot, *The Sacred Wood* (London: Methuen, 1960), and Harold Bloom, *The Anxiety of Influence: A Theory of Poetry* (New York: Oxford University Press, 1973). Bloom continues and expands W. Jackson Bate's *The Burden of the Past and the English Poet* (New York: Norton, 1970). There are numerous other contributions on the subject. Prominent among these are Robert Langbaum, *The Poetry of Experience* (London: Chatto and Windus, 1957), especially the introduction on "Romanticism as a Modern Tradition," and his subsequent *The Modern Spirit: Essays on the Continuity of Nineteenth- and Twentieth-Century Literature* (New York: Oxford University Press, 1970); and Frank Kermode, *Romantic Image* (New York: Macmillan, 1957), *Continuities* (New York: Random House, 1968), and *The Classic: Literary Images of Permanence and Change* (New York: Viking, 1975).

THE READER CAN DRAW HIS OWN CONCLU-
SION. OUR STORY IS ENDED.
Massimo D'Azèglio

LITERATURE'S A STRANGE TRADE; ANYONE
TAKES IT UP FROM ONE DAY TO THE NEXT!
LOOK AT MASSIMO: HE FEELS AN ITCH TO
WRITE A NOVEL AND HE REALLY DOESN'T
DO HALF BADLY.
Alessandro Manzoni

HENCE, IF THE BLACK CORSAIR WEEPS, WOE
TO THE INFAMOUS READER WHO LAUGHS
AT HIM. BUT WOE TO THE STOLID WHO LIM-
ITS HIMSELF TO WEEPING. IT IS ALSO NEC-
ESSARY TO DISASSEMBLE THE MECHANISM.
Umberto Eco

Two. Fieramosca's Challenge

From History to a Story

IN THE YEAR 1829, the Marquis Massimo D'Azeglio produced
a large oil painting entitled *La sfida di Barletta*. It was done in
a grand manner that combined British landscape description
(à la Constable) and French-Italian historical representation
(à la Francesco Hayez); a manner we could term as belonging
not with Turner but with "moderate" Romanticism. D'Azeglio was not a professional painter. He was, rather, a not
unworthy amateur whose pictures are listed by the poet Guido
Gozzano among "le buone cose di pessimo gusto," or "good
things in the worst taste."

While he was painting, D'Azeglio had an inspiration: he
would relate the same historical episode with his pen that he
had with his brush.[1] This was the origin of *Ettore Fieramosca*,

---

[1] According to Sandra Pinto, the year should be 1831, as it is written on
the back of the picture. See Sandra Pinto, ed., *Romanticismo storico. Catalogo
della mostra* (Florence: Centro D Edizioni, 1974), p. 351.

Fig. 3. Massimo D'Azeglio (1798–1866), *The Challenge of Barletta*, 1829, Collection of Count Gaetano Porro Schiaffinati, Milan.

ovvero La disfida di Barletta, one of the most successful and popular historical novels of nineteenth-century Italy. In his memoirs, D'Azeglio describes how he came to write such a work:

> I too searched, first of all, for a good subject. I found it in Italian history of the year 1503, in the Challenge of Barletta. . . . The subject permitted a lovely sky, rich vegetation, . . . arms, rich dresses, [a different people]. Moreover, it had the great merit, the condition *sine qua non* of all I have done that is any good, of serving the Italian cause. . . . One day, I remember it as though it were yesterday, I was putting the finishing touches to that group of battling horses in the middle, when the idea came to me that, considering the importance of the

event and the opportunity it gave to stir up [literally: to put a bit of fire into] the Italians, it would really achieve its purpose better if narrated, rather than painted. "All right, let's tell it," I said. "But how? A poem? Oh no! Prose, it must be prose if one is to speak so as to be understood by the man in the street and not on Mount Helicon!" I flung myself into my new task and to the enthusiasm of painting there was added the enthusiasm of writing. Where could I undertake the historical research into the period, the topographical and artistic research about the locality; or better still, could I go there, see the place, make it mine, so that I could describe it? I hardly had the patience to read the relative pages of Guicciardini, but immediately started to describe the scene in the Piazza of Barletta at sunset, without the shadow of an idea what was going to come out of it. What did I know of those places?[2]

This well-known passage is nicely autobiographic, vividly conveying the vivacious and youthful image of the author. It is also the statement of an extraordinary awareness, in the choice between literature and painting, of what Walter Benjamin would later call "the work of art in the age of its mechanical reproduction." Above all, however, it is a critical document of unequalled cultural value, a reflection by an author on his own intentions and on his tastes as well as those that prevailed in his time. Hence, it makes references to certain codes that must be pointed out.

Such an operation will be all the more fruitful in that we are dealing with the text of a "minor" author who meditates on the literary genre called the "historical novel," a genre to which he had contributed. This is because minor authors "are actually the connecting tissue of literary institutions, the protagonists of their stability" and because, among the literary institutions mediating between collective consciousness and

---

[2] Massimo D'Azeglio, *Things I Remember (I miei ricordi)*, tr. by E. R. Vincent (London: Oxford University Press, 1966), pp. 297–98; and *Ettore Fieramosca: or The Challenge of Barletta* (Boston: Phillips, Sampson, 1859). All subsequent references to D'Azeglio will be from these editions.

artistic works, genres are undoubtedly of the greatest importance "because of their 'reality' and because even minor writers make use of them," so that they "are more linked to the sociocultural context and its stratifications than are single works," even major ones.[3]

D'Azeglio's novel is emblematically "minor" because it allows us to verify: (1) an aspect of the collective consciousness that was Romanticism, as examined by Northrop Frye; (2) some of Georg Lukàcs's theses on the historical novel as a literary institution; and (3) the importance of the selection of themes in the formal analysis of a given work, whether it be minor or major, a subject that has been discussed especially by Boris Tomashevsky.

Of course I do not mean to imply that these three critics have actually analyzed D'Azeglio's work, which is not the case at all. Given the present state of modern Italian studies, it is remarkable enough that Lukàcs devotes even a few paragraphs to Manzoni, recognizing him, hastily as well as peremptorily, as "the superior of Scott."[4] Nevertheless, D'Azeglio's work should be important to a contemporary critic who is interested in literary history and theory, and above all in their cultural implications.

In analyzing the various ramifications of the "Romantic myth" in English literature, Northrop Frye discussed the impact and importance of the sublime in some literary forms and pointed out that the sublime "emphasized a sense of mystery and vagueness, not of order or purpose, coming through uncultivated nature, and addressing the individual or solitary man rather than the community."[5] As an example, Frye cited

the Gothic novels of the 1790s, with their shivery occult imagery, their emphasis on the sensibilities engendered

[3] Maria Corti, *An Introduction to Literary Semiotics*, tr. by Margherita Bogat and Allen Mandelbaum (Bloomington: Indiana University Press, 1978), pp. 132 and 118.

[4] Georg Lukàcs, *The Historical Novel*, tr. by Hannah and Stanley Mitchell (London: Merlin Press, 1962), p. 70.

[5] Northrop Frye, *A Study of English Romanticism* (New York: Random House, 1968), p. 28.

by solitude and sublime landscape, their paternalistic
nostalgic conservatism, and their exploiting of the picturesque (the alienated seen as happy) and the exotic (the
unfamiliar seen as pleasurable).[6]

Clearly D'Azeglio is not Ann Radcliffe, and his novel is only
minimally "Gothic," yet for him it is quite natural to appeal
to the picturesque and the exotic, which are part of the tastes
and attitudes of his time: "The subject permitted a lovely sky,
rich vegetation, . . . arms, rich dresses, [a different people]."
We shall see later on whether the textual results fulfill D'A-
zeglio's intentions, but for now these intentions are eloquent
in themselves, for they testify to the persistence in "minor"
Italian Romanticism of those tastes and attitudes that are found,
decades earlier, in English Romanticism. (After all, as Arcangeli remarked, in Italy Foscolo, Leopardi, and Manzoni had
not been "the rule, nor had they made a civilization.")
Similarly, another point raised by Frye deserves consideration:

> It may seem very strange to describe Romanticism as anti-
> historical, when we think of how central historical novels
> and narrative poems are to it. Yet when we look more
> carefully at the historical fictions in Romanticism, we see
> that earlier ages of history are being recreated in a spe-
> cifically Romantic form, as symbols of certain aspects of
> the poet's own age.[7]

Frye is referring here to Walter Scott and William Morris, in
whose works "what is being rejected, one feels, is the social
reality of the earlier ages." However, his remarks cannot be
accepted unconditionally, as in fact they cannot be accepted
in relation to Foscolo's philological historicism. Neither would
they be acceptable to Lukàcs as far as Scott is concerned. But
because of the delay of Italian Romanticism vis-à-vis the English, what Frye has to say can well describe the continuing a-
historicity of the Italian historical novel (with the obvious
exception of Manzoni, the forerunner of the later bourgeois
realism). In particular, Frye's statement can be applied to

[6] Ibid., p. 29.
[7] Ibid., p. 36.

D'Azeglio, from whose very explicit confession they actually receive a candid confirmation: "I hardly had the patience to read the relative pages of Guicciardini. . . . What did I know of those places?"

Given the above, it should not be surprising to discover that *Fieramosca* is full of "poetical licenses" in which D'Azeglio disregards history with fine nonchalance: the letter by Pope Alexander VI is said by the author to come "from his own bag," the character of Graiano D'Asti is transformed from a Frenchman into a Piedmontese, the ending of Fieramosca becomes legendary (instead of banal). All these appear in addition to the "impassioned anachronisms" of the novel, which form a link "between a late and prestigious revival of Ariosto's ancient knights, and the new Romantic-Risorgimento recreation of chivalric epic."[8]

Another aspect of D'Azeglio's novel can now be better analyzed if we pass from Frye to Lukàcs, from a theory on the culture of Romanticism to a critical view of the historical novel. Perhaps in this sense *Fieramosca*,

> without its author even realizing it, in the end was the Italian novel closest of all to the spirit of the Scottish narrator, because of its positive climate and its nonchalant historical reconstruction which, however, went straight to the point. After all, as a young man Scott had enjoyed the great texts of the Italian Renaissance, which he read in the original, and above all admired Ariosto's chivalric world.[9]

Therefore it is *Fieramosca*, even more than D'Azeglio's second novel *Niccolò de' Lapi*, that lends itself to a Lukàcsian critical analysis. This can be carried out on at least three points: "the intensive character" of the "picture of history," patriotism (consisting of "bringing the past to life as the prehistory of

---

[8] Renato Bertacchini, *Il romanzo italiano dell'Ottocento* (Rome: Studium, 1964), pp. 27 and 28, n. 1: "Not even Airone, one of Ettore's battle horses, is exempted from his service of *Italianità*."

[9] Sergio Romagnoli, "Narratori e prosatori del Romanticismo," in Emilio Cecchi and Natalino Sapegno, eds., *Storia della letteratura italiana* (Milan: Garzanti, 1969), vol. 8, *Dall'Ottocento al Novecento*, pp. 5–192, quotation on p. 61.

the present"), and the "vigorous popular character" of the historical novel.[10]

On the first two points, the passage from D'Azeglio's memoirs is explicit: "I too searched, first of all, for a good subject. I found it in Italian history of the year 1503, in the Challenge of Barletta." This is one of those "outwardly insignificant events," one of those "smaller (from without) relationships" that according to Lukàcs "are better suited than the great monumental dramas of world history" to illustrate "the social and human motives which led men to think, feel and act just as they did."[11] On the other hand, the Challenge of Barletta had for D'Azeglio "the great merit . . . of serving the Italian cause," and he considered it an important historical event, so important as to justify the opportunity to recall it in order "to put a bit of fire into the Italians." But—and here is the great difference between D'Azeglio and Scott and Manzoni— in *Fieramosca* D'Azeglio did not succeed in achieving that "historical faithfulness" (hence that truly great historical art) that consists "in giving poetic life to those historical, social, and human forces which, in the course of a long evolution, have made our present-day life what it is and as we experience it."[12] It should be noted, on the other hand, that D'Azeglio is one of the most representative figures of the Italian historical novel, partaking of that "liberal Romanticism, which in outlook and form has very much in common with the original basis of Romanticism, with the ideological struggle against the French Revolution, but which, nevertheless, upon these contradictory and uncertain foundations stands for the ideology of moderate progress."[13]

[10] Lukàcs, pp. 43, 53, and 49. However, other aspects Lukàcs points out in Scott are not applicable to D'Azeglio: for instance, the epic quality and the presence of "middle" heroes.

[11] Ibid., p. 42.

[12] Ibid., pp. 59 and 53.

[13] Ibid., p. 63. See also Alberto Asor Rosa, *Scrittori e popolo* (Rome: Samonà e Savelli, 1965), p. 55: "During the Risorgimento and until about the end of the nineteenth century, there remains a clear-cut distinction between two contrasting views of populism: on the one hand, the radical and democratic one . . . ; on the other, the catholic and moderate one, which considers the *popolo* as the child to be educated."

I should say that Lukàcs's definition is quite a valid interpretation, one that has inspired recent research on the Italian historical novel, in particular Vincenzo Cuoco's *Platone in Italia*, "an ideological *summa* of Risorgimento moderation" and "the archetype of the historical novel conceived with civic and patriotic intentions, at the very origins of that trend in which Balbo, Santarosa, then Guerrazzi, D'Azeglio, Ruffini, and Nievo belong."[14]

I will only add that in this trend one cannot find the idyllic and reactionary idealization of the past (particularly of the Middle Ages) that for Lukàcs characterizes, for example, François René de Chateaubriand. On the contrary, following the great Manzonian model there is a predominant "sorrowful interpretation of Italian history"[15] (so that *I promessi sposi* has been effectively called "a novel without idyll").[16]

We now come to the third point to be analyzed, the "vigorous popular character" of the historical novel. And on this as well D'Azeglio is equally explicit: "Prose, it must be prose if one is to speak so as to be understood by the man in the street and not on Mount Helicon!" But this assertion immediately reveals the limitation of the popular character of *Fieramosca*: D'Azeglio is not concerned with a representation of the "great transformations of history as transformations of popular life" à la Scott,[17] but with the intelligibility of the language and the genre he has chosen.[18]

[14] Piero De Tommaso, "Sul romanzo storico," in *Nievo e altri studi sul romanzo storico* (Padua: Liviana, 1975), pp. 1–26.

[15] Romagnoli, p. 9.

[16] Ezio Raimondi, *Il romanzo senza idillio. Saggio sui "Promessi Sposi"* (Turin: Einaudi, 1974).

[17] Lukàcs, pp. 48–49.

[18] See D'Azeglio, *Things I Remember*, p. 315: "To sum up, it was a howling success. Did I deserve it or not? Here a curious question arises about the fate of books, which is often the least understandable and the most anomalous of proceedings. On the whole, in speaking, for example, of *Guerrin meschino*, *Paris e Vienna*, *Cal[l]oandro fedele*, the *Reali di Francia*, *Bertoldo*, one says: Trash! Certainly trash; but, from time immemorable, they have persisted, first in manuscript, then printed, reprinted, and they keep on being printed. So they must have appealed to men's hearts and minds; they must have some merit." See also Bertacchini, p. 17.

There are no doubts that the novel had "a howling success," according to its author, who also indicates that it was read by everyone from prima donnas and tenors to schoolgirls, seminarians, and military cadets. These examples, however, seem to point up the fact that the historical novel was "a prized object for intellectual consumption by the Italian bourgeoisie,"[19] rather than an object for mass consumption by the people, *il popolo*. At that time, according to Bruno Migliorini's estimate, four fifths of the population was illiterate,[20] although there are no precise statistics.[21]

In any case, it might be useful now to recall that the illustrated editions of both *I promessi sposi* and *Ettore Fieramosca* had a "great success" in the second half of the nineteenth century, and that their success "helps to explain the concomitant decadence of historical genre painting" in Italy.[22] We also know that in 1872 *Fieramosca* was published by Paolo Carrara in Milan in "a popular edition sold in installments at 15 cents each,"[23] and that even today it is available in a truly popular series such as the Biblioteca Universale Rizzoli.

Leaving aside for the moment the complex relationship between the historical novel and the popular novel (and without forgetting "high" literature and opera), it should be noted that the problem of the popularity of a novel is strictly connected to the problem of the reader. In formalistic criticism, particularly that of Tomashevsky, the problem of the reader has a remarkable importance in the "selection of themes" and

[19] Romagnoli, p. 34. Evidence of the popular success of *Fieramosca* is given by Luigi Settembrini and Francesco De Sanctis, in Romagnoli, pp. 45–46. D'Azeglio himself says that he earned five thousand francs from the first edition.

[20] Bruno Migliorini, *Storia della lingua italiana* (Florence: Sansoni, 1971), p. 553.

[21] In this connection, Folco Portinari has also noted that "the *popolo* was intended as a national soul, a sort of *Weltanschauung*," but that it was "an entity difficult to define." Thus "the *popolo* was socially limited to a petit bourgeois and agrarian milieu, to which the new cultural fruits were donated as a benign concession by the cultural aristocracy." *Le parabole del reale* (Turin: Einaudi, 1976), p. 81.

[22] Pinto, p. 55.

[23] Romagnoli, p. 62, n. 1.

hence in "plot construction."[24] At this level and from this point of view, D'Azeglio's autobiographic statement is an explicit document that shows the way an author has arrived at the selection of his theme, or, as D'Azeglio puts it, the way he finds "a good subject." D'Azeglio searched for and found it in "Italian history," exactly as Manzoni wrote the "story or report" of the facts of "History." But since D'Azeglio's statement is a document, it remains a pre-text. Thus it is necessary to move on to the text of *Fieramosca* itself and to verify within it the conditions and consequences of the preliminary selection of the theme: first as it pertains to the interest and attention of the reader, and then to the story and the plot.

A Well-constructed Plot

According to Tomashevsky, a writer "always considers the reader, at least abstractly," and must arouse his interest through "real" themes. These may be either "general human" ones—"(problems of love and death) which are the fixed bases of the entire course of human history"—or "historical" ones—"from a given period," which "can be received with perhaps greater interest than the presentation of what is more obviously contemporary." "General interest in a theme, then, is determined by the historical conditions prevailing when the work appears; the literary tradition and the problems it poses are among the most important of these historical conditions."[25] But for Tomashevsky "the selection of an interesting theme is not enough. Interest must also be maintained, attention stimulated. The theme does both. The emotion at-

---

[24] Boris Tomashevsky, *Teoria della letteratura*, Italian tr. (Milan, Feltrinelli, 1979), pp. 62 and 92. Of course, it is entirely conceivable that an analysis of D'Azeglio's novel could be based on formalistic categories of French narratology. However, since *Fieramosca* is a relatively elementary text, it seems that a basic approach, such as Tomashevsky's, is the most appropriate here. More sophisticated contributions will be used in the next chapter, particularly in connection with the diachronic functioning of a literary code through its successive readers.

[25] *Ibid.*, pp. 64–65.

tached to the theme [its "emotional coloration"] plays a major role in maintaining interest."[26]

Fieramosca seems a perfect illustration of Tomashevsky's theory. For D'Azeglio wanted to and knew how to arouse the reader's interest by means of a "real" theme, one that unites the nationalism of the time (presented and camouflaged[27] through both the historicity of the fact that is narrated and through the literary tradition, which encompasses the chivalric motif, echoes from the "Gothic" novel, and the Manzonian model) with more general human interests (such as love and honor, which are expressed in the structure of the plot, in the choice of the characters, and in the author's ironic or moralizing interventions).

As for the reality and contemporaneity of the nationalistic theme, it can be seen that D'Azeglio superimposes it upon the chivalric one, at the cost of giving up historical truth or even verisimilitude, or of deliberately distorting them in passing from Renaissance to Risorgimento. A single but eloquent example will suffice. After the victory in the Challenge of Barletta, which reaches a climax with the killing of the "traitor" Graiano D'Asti by Brancaleone, Ettore turns to the latter and tells him with "a sigh from his inmost heart":

> "This weapon of thine," and he pointed to the battle-axe held in his friend's grasp, still dripping with blood, "has this day accomplished a great justice. But can we enjoy this victory? is not this earth imbued with Italian blood? Ah! might he not, strong and valiant as he was on the battle field, have shed it to his and our glory against the common enemy. Then Graiano's tomb would have been honored and glorious! his memory a monument of pride! But now there he lies in infamy, and the malediction on the traitor against his country weighs heavy upon him." (p. 344)

[26] Ibid., p. 65.

[27] Cf. D'Azeglio, *Things I Remember*, p. 317: "The problem to be settled was just this. Admitting the fact of an Austrian censorship, one wanted to publish a book written with the object of inciting the Italians to attack the foreigner. Was this a trifling difficulty?"

As for the "general human" interests, they are centered above all in the love between Ettore and Ginevra di Monreale, which is opposed on the one hand by the imposed marriage between her and Graiano, and on the other by the dark schemes of Duke Valentino. These vicissitudes are the private part of the story, the indispensable complement of the public one of the challenge, the novelistic and a-historical element intertwined with history.

However, in *Fieramosca* the interest and attention of the reader also seem to be an integral part of the narrative structure. They are recognized as such by the author, who intervenes with ironic and distancing remarks that soften his moralism. From the very beginning of the novel, there is no doubt that D'Azeglio is an omniscient author. He not only knows the thoughts and feelings of his characters, but feels free to interject his own comments on the various actions and narrative situations. These remarks are intended to convey certain moral messages, which are expressed through maxims such as, "How seldom it is that a man can foretell the truth!" (p. 58), or through long tirades, such as the one against the corrupt Pope Alexander VI.[28] The interventions of the omniscient author also concern the characters and the events of the story he is telling, as in: "The morning of that day in which fate had reserved the most dreadful blows for Ginevra" (p. 203) or "We will now resume the thread of events, narrating what happened to Brancaleone on the evening before" (p. 301). Above all, D'Azeglio does not hesitate to involve the reader, at first with hints at the temporal and spatial distance separating him from the story (Piedmont/North vs. Barletta/ South; nineteenth vs. sixteenth century),[29] and then, in a more substantial and repeated manner, by arousing the reader's complicity, his active participation in the narrated events and the sentiments they evoke. This is accomplished by putting the reader on the same plane as the author himself or as any

[28] D'Azeglio, *Fieramosca*, pp. 262–63.
[29] There are numerous other passages involving the reader throughout the novel, which it seems unnecessary to quote.

given character. Consider, for example, the following particularly meaningful passage:

> Those among my readers who have happened to converse with a woman of noble spirit about generous deeds to be done in behalf of one's country, must remember how their heart quickened in its pulsations, and will know how impassionate must have been Ettore's words,—how fervid with love of country and aspirations of glory, and how the presence of Ginevra must have increased the fire of his soul. (p. 121)

But the most successful interventions are those that produce irony from the play that is established between author, reader, and text. For instance, let us read the following passage, in which the author "suddenly stops and all but *sotto voce* intervenes":[30]

> And here we seem to hear the reader exclaiming:—When will there be an end to all these agonizing accounts of assassins, traitors, dungeons, deaths, devils, and worse? But, to please our reader, while we have been so fortunate as to guess his thoughts, he has not been equally fortunate in giving us credit for the resolution which we had already made of putting an end to these stories and send to the—[devil] Martin and Pietraccio. We must in a confidential way declare that they were growing loathsome even to us,—and we were just about inviting our readers to transfer themselves to the very centre of the Barletta castle, which will present a far different appearance from that when we last met there in company with Don Miguel. (p. 167)

These and similar interventions of the author into the story he is telling,[31] and the related invitation to the reader to participate actively in the literary game, provide part of the vivacity and modernity of D'Azeglio's novel. As such they are undoubtedly of interest to the reader-critic of today.

---

[30] Romagnoli, p. 63.
[31] Again, it seems burdensome to quote all the authorial interventions that occur throughout the text.

Proceeding on with his formalistic analysis, Tomashevsky deals with "plot construction" in the literary work and makes the by now classic distinction between "story" and "plot."[32] He then formulates a systematic nomenclature that includes the situation, the conflict of interests, the intrigue, the peripety, the tension, the ending, and especially the splitting up of a theme into different motifs. These motifs can be either bound (those that "cannot be omitted") or free (those that "may be omitted without disturbing the whole causal-chronological course of events"); the former are relevant to the story, the latter to the plot.[33] Motifs can also be dynamic (those that "change the situation") or static ("those that do not").[34]

When it comes to the "formation of a plot from the material of the story," Tomashevsky distinguishes between immediate exposition and delayed exposition, with the related "time shift in the elaboration of the story material," between the omniscient and the limited narration, and between the time and place in a given narration. He also analyzes the motivation of the motifs that appear in a particular work of art, which can be compositional, realistic, and artistic. Another important element is, of course, the character ("the living embodiment of a given collection of motifs"), and particularly the hero or protagonist.[35]

It is not my intention here to examine Tomashevsky's categories from the viewpoint of literary theory.[36] Rather, they are interesting to me as "models for the reading of narrative texts,"[37] and are therefore filtered also through the critical considerations of Cesare Segre, beginning with those on the

[32] "Both include the same events," but in the story "causal-temporal relationships exist between the thematic elements," while in the plot "the events are *arranged* and connected according to the orderly sequence in which they were presented in the work." Tomashevsky, pp. 66–67.

[33] Ibid., pp. 67–68.

[34] Ibid., p. 70.

[35] Ibid., pp. 74–78 and 78–88, *passim*.

[36] For example, in comparing these categories with Shklovsky's, Cesare Segre defined them as "fundamental even in their defects." *Structures and Time*, tr. by John Meddemmen (Chicago: University of Chicago Press, 1979), p. 16.

[37] Ibid., p. 56.

segmentation" of the text, that is, on the problem of the

"segmentation" of the text, that is, on the problem of the "summary" or critical "paraphrase."[38]

An example of a summary of *Fieramosca* is the following, by Ronald Marshall: "The plot of the novel is a dual one—of Ettore's devotion to Ginevra, and of his championship of Italian renown in arms. . . . The two climaxes are made to coincide exactly in time—Ettore's personal tragedy with his public triumph."[39] Another example—and a very interesting one because it testifies to the lasting popularity of D'Azeglio, despite being itself a half-mocking, parodic distortion—is the following by Gianni Celati:

> Ettore Fieramosca was a grand warrior at the challenge of Barletta. This guy could not bear hearing his Italian fatherland insulted by a Frenchman named De La Motte. He became enraged, throwing all the other knights off their horses, and this made the challenge of Barletta a celebrated historical event throughout the nation. Afterward, however, he got a lump in his throat, produced by a certain Ginevra, who was not willing to give him her love and her kisses. This made him half demented, that is, so unhappy that Ettore was always telling himself: oh, how unhappy I am. Then what does he do? He goes and throws himself down a cliff with his horse and kills himself.[40]

To avoid testing the patience of my reader, I will not analyze D'Azeglio's text systematically. Instead I will provide an illustration of the procedure in Tables 1 and 2, which divide the text into narrative units (or situations) that can be considered to fall somewhere between the extremely laconic summary by Marshall and the equally extreme particularity of the indivisible or basic motifs.[41]

The tables are intended to give an overall view of some aspects of the novel and to relate them briefly to Toma-

---

[38] Ibid., pp. 17 and 37–40.
[39] Ronald Marshall, *Massimo D'Azeglio, An Artist in Politics* (New York: Oxford University Press, 1966), p. 61.
[40] Gianni Celati, *La banda dei sospiri* (Turin: Einaudi, 1976), p. 187.
[41] "Each sentence, in fact, has its own motif." Tomashevsky, p. 67.

Table 1. *The Beginning*

1. Challenge	Initial situation: 1503, Barletta, Spanish mercenary soldiers. (Static motif, delayed exposition, abstract narration, time, place)		French prisoners arrive: their stories about Ginevra, the Duke, Ettore. (Dynamic motif, concrete narration)
2. Villain		Investigation: two mysterious characters appear at the Inn of the Sun and are recognized by Boscherino. (Intrigue, tension, dynamic motif, →)	[Lusts and schemes of the Duke about Ginevra]
3. Hero			[Ettore and the seemingly dead Ginevra] (Simulated motivation)
4. Victim			[Still love story between Ginevra and Ettore] (Conflict, ⇄)

LEGEND: ( ) critical commentary; ⇄ time shift; relationships between narrative levels; [ ] story within the story.

Table 2. *A Narrative Climax*

1.	Fanfulla wears Ettore's cloak and tricks Donna Elvira. A mysterious cry.		
2.			Villainy: the Duke finds Ginevra, who has fainted, and rapes her.
3.	Ettore and Pietraccio set out for St. Ursula's Convent in a boat.	Their struggle with the Duke's *bravi*: Pietraccio is taken prisoner; Ettore is wounded and saved by Zorais at the convent.	
4.		Ginevra goes to Barletta by boat, passing, but not recognizing Ettore in the night. She sees Fanfulla with Elvira and believes him to be Ettore; she cries and faints.	Ginevra is raped by the Duke.

shevsky's categories, without any pretense at systematic coverage. They clearly show "the structuring of a finely tense and complicated plot according to the canons of the genre."[42] I should also note that I have taken from Propp the descriptive terms "investigation" and "villainy,"[43] while the division into four narrative planes reflects the complexity of the story/plot dialectics in *Fieramosca*, in which the author, according to Manzoni's amused and surprised observation, "really doesn't do half badly." At the same time, this division shows the permanence as well as the variation of certain cultural themes and narrative models. For example, under the level of the historical challenge of the title, the archetypal and Proppian triangle of villain-hero-victim could also be formulated, according to the "recipe" by Louis Reybaud made famous by Mario Praz, as "bloody and brutal tyrant, sensitive and virtuous page, unhappy and persecuted damsel."[44]

But a consideration of story and plot does not exhaust D'Azeglio's extraordinary narrative effectiveness. He has also paid particular attention to the motivations of his novel: the compositional (Fieramosca's cloak, Ghita's medallion, the depiction of the various characters—including secondary ones like Venom the innkeeper and the lively Fanfulla—and the many landscape descriptions, which reflect the eye and hand of a moderate Romantic painter); the realistic (in the choice and use of historical facts and characters, aside from their documentary truthfulness); and the artistic (in a smaller measure than the first two, with the "defamiliarization" process achieved especially in the exotic character of Zorais[45] and in some ad-

[42] Romagnoli, p. 58.

[43] Vladimir Propp, *Morphology of the Folktale*, tr. by Laurence Scott (Austin: University of Texas Press, 1979), *passim*.

[44] Mario Praz, *The Romantic Agony*, tr. by Angus Davidson (London: Oxford University Press, 1970), ch. 3. The same "recipe" is also quoted and used by Angela Bianchini, *Il romanzo d'appendice* (Turin: ERI, 1969). In this connection, cf. Alexander Veselovsky and the Marquis de Sade, *La fanciulla perseguitata*, ed. by D'Arco Silvio Avalle (Milan: Bompiani, 1977).

[45] There is a typical observation of Zorais concerning the Kingdom of the Two Sicilies, which according to the prevailing opinion of the times should have been considered a fief of the Roman See: "It is curious! and who gave it to the Roman See?" (p. 124).

dresses to the reader that bring about a spatial and temporal distance that has already been discussed).

As far as the hero is concerned, D'Azeglio also seems to provide a perfect illustration of Tomashevsky's categories. The characterization of Ettore Fieramosca, the protagonist, is made either directly by the narrator, through dialogue among other characters, or by means of stories and confessions told by the hero himself. Fieramosca's characterization is then completed by his actions and behavior, which are always extremely noble, and by the descriptions of his features and clothes, which are always extremely beautiful. But above all, "the emotional relationship to the character (sympathy or revulsion) is worked out morally"[46] on a human and patriotic basis, which is intended by the author to arouse piety and pride in the reader.

It should be noted that the analysis conducted so far has not lost sight of the fact that Tomashevsky's categories have been "filtered" by Segre. It is perhaps proper to recall here that Segre, by integrating Tomashevsky's theory with a combination of Shklovsky's, Propp's, and his own, proposes a description of the narrative text that is divided into four elements: discourse, plot, *fabula* or story, and narrative model.[47] So far, our examination of *Fieramosca* has dealt only incidentally with the first element (the verbal aspect of the text: prose, popular language, the genre of the "historical novel") and has focused on the two central elements of plot and story, concluding with a few brief considerations of the narrative model (the functions, the motivations). In other words, the whole examination has been conducted almost exclusively on the textual side, with minimal references to the cultural one.

It is perhaps worth noting that Segre himself has taken up again his own old four-level model and (with the minimal variation of "intrigue" instead of "plot") has expanded it to the cultural realm, within the framework of the "semiotic itinerary" that develops between the author (or sender) and the reader (or addressee), and vice versa. This framework

---

[46] Tomashevsky, p. 89.
[47] Segre, p. 10.

includes language, exposition techniques, autobiographical materials, and the key concepts and logic of the action as cultural levels integrating the textual ones.[48] It sums up a broad scheme of narratological research, clearly showing how the various levels of an inventive (and critical) project

> are integral parts of the perspective of signification; and how, beneath the surface of the text, numerous signifying systems develop, which cooperate in the sense-making of the work (from a centripetal viewpoint) and are at the same time connected with the polysystem "culture" (from a centrifugal viewpoint).[49]

And so we must now turn our attention to the cultural context of *Fieramosca*. Our analysis, which is the analysis of a literary text, albeit a "minor" one in the Italian canon, will be conducted by concentrating on the last three elements of Segre's scheme, then concluding with a brief look at the first.

Consolation and Astonishment

Fieramosca is undoubtedly the most successful and pleasant representative of the "historical novel" genre in nineteenth-century Italian fiction. Perhaps one of the reasons is that "since there is a chemistry of emotions, and one of the elements that by ancient tradition originate emotions is a well-constructed plot, if a plot is well-constructed it provokes the emotions it was intended to cause."[50]

But whether *Fieramosca* is also a great novel is an entirely different question, one that I believe should be approached and solved in critical terms according to the two different models of Aristotelian catharsis that are examined by Umberto

---

[48] Cesare Segre, *Semiotica filologica* (Turin: Einaudi, 1979), p. 12.

[49] Ibid., pp. 12–13.

[50] Umberto Eco, "Le lacrime del Corsaro Nero," in *Il superuomo di massa* (Milan: Cooperativa Scrittori, 1976), p. 13. Cf. D'Azeglio, *Things I Remember*, p. 316: "The best of studies is, therefore, to discover what moves and persuades men most. This discovery can be made by observing the most ordinary people. I have often heard peasants telling some tale of woe, some poor mother speaking of the idleness of a son, or perhaps his goodness toward her, and I have felt deeply moved."

Eco—the problematic and the consoling. In Eco's view, the problematic model gives rise to artistic literature, while the consoling one produces the popular novel. The latter is "popular not because it is understandable by the people, but because, as Aristotle knew when he related the problems of *Poetics* with those of *Rhetorics*, ultimately the builder of plots must know what his audience expects." Consequently, the author must fulfill certain expectations.

> There is a constant feature that distinguishes the popular from the problematic novel: in the former there will always be a fight of Good against Evil, a fight that will be resolved in any case, whether the ending is filled with happiness or sorrow, in favor of Good—this Good being defined in terms of current morality, values, and ideology. In contrast, the problematic novel proposes ambiguous endings because both Rastignac's happiness and Emma Bovary's desperation exactly and ferociously put into question the accepted notions of "Good" (and "Evil"). In a word, the popular novel tends toward peace, while the problematic novel sets the reader to war with himself.[51]

Clearly, *Fieramosca* belongs in the dichotomy proposed by Eco, who actually quotes it as an example of a nonambiguous ending: "But also a large section of the popular novel—much of the Risorgimento-type historical novel—wanted the death of the beloved and the pitiful end of the hero as a pathetic seal to a solution according to the public reasons of the heart, which considered crying as a marketable purifying moment."[52] I should also add that Denis de Rougemont would have additional reasons to explain the "impossibility" of the love affair between the knight-page (Tristan, Ettore) and the married lady (Isotta, Ginevra) in our Western culture. So we are back within the "terms of current morality, values, and ideology," that is, within the key concepts of the novel, the

[51] Eco, pp. 17 and 19.
[52] Ibid., p. 19.

logic of its action, and the anthropological materials it incorporates.

There is another critical area that is useful in distinguishing the qualitative differences that separate the historical from the serious novel. In it, the author, the narrator, and the reader are involved in a literary game, a game that is found in both the historical novel and the serious novel.

In this area, D'Azeglio's *Fieramosca* and Manzoni's *Fermo e Lucia* can be considered, if not on the same level, then at least on a contiguous plane, because of the explicit and imposing presence of their authors.[53] If one analyzes Manzoni's work from *Fermo e Lucia* to the later *I promessi sposi*, one can "measure the magnitude of Manzoni's narrative experiment and the vigor of his choices, even where they have the appearance of a renunciation."[54] It will also be possible, by analogy, to measure the difference between D'Azeglio's historical novel and Manzoni's novel, between romance and *romanzo*:

> The fact is that from a Manzonian viewpoint the true narrator is the one of *I promessi sposi*, who is by now free from the indignation, the eye-catching prancing of the commentator of *Fermo e Lucia*, not because of a process of weakening in his ideology, but because of a coherent development of the function of the character. More than a precious or picturesque background, history must lend the character a social consistency, a support of ideas and biases that are fundamental to his role and the modifications of his personality within the flux of events. In this place the character lowers his level of consciousness to that of the surrounding historical society, is self-limited and de-heroicized. . . . At the same time the narrating *I*, in his dialogue with the manuscript, occupies a more elevated plane from which a changing light of irony em-

[53] In this connection, there are some pertinent remarks by Eco, p. 84: "The historical novel is so conscious of possessing functions that go beyond the narrative machinery that at any point it generates its own metanarrative reflection, it interrogates itself about its own ends, it discusses with its readers, as in the case of Manzoni's, the greatest of all."

[54] Raimondi, p. 69.

anates, and is subsequently destined to illuminate even the storyteller, because there is no privileged time that can put in parenthesis the destiny of man, the ambiguous truth of us men in general.[55]

These words by Raimondi seem fundamental to the present discussion, not only because the "indignation" and the "eye-catching prancing" of the commentator of *Fermo e Lucia* can be directly applied to the narrator of *Fieramosca*, but also because Raimondi leads us back, on a different level, to critical exigencies and conclusions that have been examined by Lukàcs (the "social consistency" of the character) and by Eco ("the ambiguous truth" of man).

Above all, this citation from Raimondi outlines the development of the novelistic character in relation to the story, concomitant with the parallel revaluation of the character vis-à-vis the functions in Segre's semiotic analysis, in order to judge the artistic quality of the fictional text.[56] In doing so, Raimondi also outlines the development from the historical novel to the novel, illustrating what Tomashevsky called "the process of canonization of inferior genres."[57] This process, which was also pointed out by Antonio Gramsci,[58] is central

[55] Ibid., pp. 69–70.

[56] Cf. Segre, *Structures and Time*, pp. 34–35.

[57] Since the English translation of "Thematics" in Lee Lemon and Marion Reis, eds., *Russian Formalist Criticism* (Lincoln: University of Nebraska Press, 1965) does not include the last section of the essay, I shall paraphrase the French translation of Tomashevsky's text in Tzvetan Todorov, ed., *Théorie de la littérature* (Paris: Seuil, 1966), p. 305: "The process of 'canonization of inferior genres,' even if it is not a universal law, is so typical that the literary historian, while looking for the sources of any important literary phenomenon, is obliged to turn not to the great, preceding literary facts, but to the minor ones. These less outstanding, inferior phenomena, spread out in strata and literary genres with a relatively minor status, are those that are canonized and introduced into the superior genres by the great writers, and they give rise to new aesthetic effects, absolutely unheard of and profoundly original."

[58] Aldo Rossi, "Parenti poveri?" in Umberto Eco and Cesare Sughi, *Cent'anni dopo. Il ritorno dell'intreccio* (Milan: Almanacco Bompiani, 1972), p. 78. Cf. Antonio Gramsci, *Letteratura e vita nazionale* (Turin: Einaudi, 1952), pp. 101–142. In any case, the Marxian, or at least sociological, roots are evident also in Tomashevsky, as for instance on p. 304: "In the succession of literary

to the critical concern of the present chapter and is its *raison d'être* at the very core of the "cultural context."

It will be noted that in nineteenth-century Italy at least two other great writers beside Manzoni passed from "inferior" to "higher" literature, but with different nuances: Ippolito Nievo went from the historical and *campagnolo* novel to *Le confessioni di un italiano*, and Giovanni Verga went from the historical novel and from the *feuilleton* proper (*Sulle lagune*) to *Mastro-don Gesualdo*.[59] To measure the continuity and vitality of the passage from the historical novel to the novel, I shall simply mention two contemporary (although quite different) examples: Giuseppe Tomasi di Lampedusa's *Il Gattopardo* and Elsa Morante's *La storia*.

But the canonization process can also be considered from another viewpoint. When Raimondi speaks of the "level of consciousness" of the character juxtaposed against the narrating *I*, it seems to me that he is referring to a problem that is developed in many of its implications by Gianni Celati: that is, the problem of consciousness as a discriminating factor between the serious novel (*romanzo*) and the romance, between maintenance of the social order and marginality, between criticism and storytelling—to the detriment of romance, marginality, and storytelling.[60]

If a well-constructed plot is taken as a fundamental expression of storytelling, one understands how Manzoni's transi-

---

genres the superior ones are constantly being substituted for by the inferior ones. We can trace an interesting parallel with social evolution, in which the 'high,' ruling classes are gradually superceded by the 'lower,' democratic strata."

[59] In this connection, see my "Il romanzo 'Sulle lagune' del giovane Verga," *La Rassegna della letteratura italiana*, vol. 74, nos. 2–3 (May–December 1970), pp. 394–416. In recent years, critical contributions on "inferior" literature have multiplied. In addition to *Cent'anni dopo* and the works by Bianchini, Eco, and Portinari that have already been quoted, there are also Massimo Romano, *Mitologia romantica e letteratura popolare* (Ravenna: Longo, 1977); Giuseppe Zaccaria, ed., *Il romanzo d'appendice* (Turin: Paravia, 1977); and Vittorio Brunori, *La grande impostura. Indagine sul romanzo popolare* (Padua: Marsilio, 1979).

[60] Gianni Celati, *Finzioni occidentali. Fabulazione comicità e scrittura* (Turin: Einaudi, 1975), pp. 3–49.

tion from *Fermo e Lucia* to *I promessi sposi* is perfectly inserted in the cycle of transformation that leads from romance to novel, or from the historical and popular novel to the serious, problematic, analytical novel, so that storytelling as such is kept only "as memory and margin," as "a social reservoir of unconscious productivity, from which a return cycle can always begin anew."[61] One also understands how *Fieramosca* is situated precisely on the line dividing romance from novel because of the liveliness of its plot (the success of its storytelling) and its "Risorgimento-type anachronisms" (its flaw of consciousness or, more precisely, of historical consciousness).

On the basis of the preceding considerations, it is possible now to broaden the cultural context by examining the function of the popular historical novel in nineteenth-century Italy. It is well-known that Gramsci, by positing the equation of the popular novel with melodrama, recognized the hegemony of French culture in the field of *feuilletons* and the hegemony of Italian culture in the field of melodrama. In a similar fashion, the music critic Massimo Mila has recently analyzed the opera as a "popular form of artistic communication" ("popular, indeed, for its capacity of diffusion, although it is a mirror of eminently bourgeois customs").[62] Among other things, Mila states that opera "replaces not only theater, of which Italy was substantially deprived, but also the novel, which at that

---

[61] Ibid., p. 43. Fredric Jameson, in "Magical Narratives: Romance As Genre," *New Literary History*, vol. 7, no. 1 (1975), pp. 135–63, indirectly confirms the importance of storytelling when he demonstrates the persistence of the romance and its transformation into the novel. For instance, in *I promessi sposi* he notices the coexistence of the gothic novel in the story of Lucia and the adventure novel in the story of Renzo, with the ensuing enrichment of the narrative texture (pp. 143 and 151). But I doubt that it is useful to speak of "historical romance" for the Manzonian novel, precisely because of the reasons that have been so persuasively offered by Raimondi.

[62] Massimo Mila, "L''opera' come forma popolare della comunicazione artistica," in Vittore Branca and Tibor Kardos, eds., *Il Romanticismo. Atti del VI Congresso dell'AISLLI* (Budapest: Akadémiai Kiadó, 1968), pp. 193–203, quotation on pp. 198–99. There is also an interesting essay by Carlo Varese (1828), "Di Rossini e di Walter Scott messi a confronto come genii d'indole identica e del Romanzo in generale," in Renato Bertacchini, ed., *Documenti e prefazioni del romanzo italiano dell'Ottocento* (Rome: Studium, 1969), pp. 25–32.

time in other countries had the functions of an *école du coeur* which *chez nous* could not be reasonably attributed even to Manzoni's masterpiece, not to mention *L'assedio di Firenze* or *Marco Visconti*," two very popular historical novels, although not quite so popular as *Fieramosca*.[63] Furthermore, Mila maintains that "in its attempt to make the chord of patriotic and national enthusiasm vibrate, early nineteenth-century society and the music in which it expressed itself were not yet mature: such a task had to be undertaken a bit later by Giuseppe Verdi—and then indeed the Romantic idea of the *popolo* and the nation blazed in music with very high flames."[64]

I would like to keep Mila's metaphor by also suggesting that a historical novel like *Fieramosca* undoubtedly "put a bit of fire into the Italians" (as D'Azeglio intended) and sparked the flame of Romantic nationalism that then blazed in Verdi's operas.[65] Two other obvious factors contributed to this flame: "the political reawakening of Italy toward ideals of freedom" in the decade between 1830 and 1840 and the teachings of Giuseppe Mazzini, which are summed up in the motto "God and People!" This motto in particular seemed to channel the Romantic, individual longing for the infinite away from "the amorous communion with another person" toward an absorption "into that collective entity, the people. Italian music, 'high' and aristocratic because of a centuries-old tradition," discovered the people, and with it the nation, in the figure of Verdi, especially the Verdi who composed the "grandiose, choral, and collective opera, almost opera-*oratorio*." His *Na-*

[63] Mila, p. 199.

[64] Mila, p. 197. A literary critic, Luigi Baldacci, goes even beyond Mila's well-balanced remarks: "It could be said that the Italian *feuilleton* in the first half of the nineteenth century is represented and substituted for by Donizetti's theater; . . . Notice that Donizetti's *feuilleton* had nothing to do with the historical novel Italian-style, which was not a form of popular but of learned literature. In fact, the historical novel begun by Manzoni became popular only in Verdi's dramatic theater: only with Verdi can we speak of a mass Manzonism." *Libretti d'opera e altri saggi* (Florence: Vallecchi, 1974), p. 172.

[65] It is to be noted that thirteen operas were derived from the novel *Fieramosca*, but "none of them had a particularly brilliant success." A list of these can be found in Pinto, pp. 270–72.

bucco is dated 1842, and *I Lombardi alla prima crociata* followed it the next year.[66]

In dealing with the function of an *école du coeur*, it seems important to consider briefly the conclusions arrived at by Peter Brooks in his analysis of the French melodrama of the nineteenth century, a theatrical form that not by chance is often based on what Frye calls the mode of romance,[67] and that in turn has undoubtedly influenced opera.[68]

In French melodrama, Brooks points out and emphasizes: (1) "the aesthetics of astonishment," which is based on clear conflicts of pure theatrical signs (action, suspense, *coups de théâtre*, reassurance); (2) "moral manicheism," the clear-cut division between vice and virtue, victim and persecutor, good and evil; and (3) "the rhetoric of excess":

Melodramatic rhetoric, as our accumulating examples sufficiently suggest, tends toward the inflated and the sententious. Its typical figures are hyperbole, antithesis, and oxymoron: those figures, precisely, that evidence a refusal of nuance and the insistence on dealing in pure, integral concepts.[69]

Hence, given its characteristics, this rhetoric represents "a victory over repression" (precisely because everything, even evil, is named, called by its name, has its own sign that is clearly legible and immediately understandable). This rhetoric

[66] Massimo Mila, *Breve storia della musica* (Turin: Einaudi, 1977), pp. 269–70. See also his "Il romanticismo nella musica," *Belfagor*, vol. 34, no. 5 (30 September 1979), pp. 493–503, quotation on p. 497: "Verdi lends his voice to the Italian national redemption, Wagner donates the Germanic musical epic to German unity." Finally, a similar view is also found in Peter Conrad, *Romantic Opera and Literary Form* (Berkeley: University of California Press, 1977), p. 52: "in Verdi history is the incorporation of private emotion in a community."

[67] Peter Brooks, *The Melodramatic Imagination: Balzac, Henry James, Melodrama, and the Mode of Excess* (New Haven: Yale University Press, 1976), p. 30. Cf. Northrop Frye, *Anatomy of Criticism* (Princeton: Princeton University Press, 1957), pp. 158–239, and *The Secular Scripture: A Study of the Structure of Romance* (Cambridge, Mass.: Harvard University Press, 1976).

[68] Brooks, pp. 49, 75ff., and *passim*.

[69] Ibid., p. 40.

also achieves a rediscovery of morality in a universe that had been desacralized by the French Revolution ("it relocates and rearticulates the most basic moral sentiments and celebrates the sign of the right"). Above all, it is "a democratization of morality and its signs" because the villains often are tyrants and the victims, whatever their social class may be, believe in merit and not in privilege.[70]

Keeping Gramsci in mind, I believe that Brooks' conclusions can be applied to the non-hegemonic artistic genre in Italian culture that corresponds to French melodrama, that is, to the popular novel (including the historical novel) and in particular to *Fieramosca*. It is enough to think of the novel's eponymous central character, who can and must be considered a "sign of virtue" (in Brooks' theatrical, "melodramatic" sense) even more than a hero or a protagonist.[71] But consider also the continuing *coups de théâtre*, intrigues, recognitions, conflicts, and peripeties that sustain the narrative tension of the plot (the aesthetics of astonishment). And note as well the clearcut juxtaposition between the good characters (Ettore, Fanfulla, Ginevra, the Italians) and the bad (Duke Valentino, Graiano d'Asti, De La Motte, the Frenchmen), a juxtaposition typical of moral manicheism. Finally, as a result of this manicheism, one should remember the rhetoric of excess in the syntactically hyperbolic and structurally antithetical descriptions of Good and Evil. For example, at one point a character describes the hero, Ettore Fieramosca, in the following terms: "I never saw a handsomer youth, and a more pensive brow" (p. 34). In contrast, his antagonist, the villain, Duke Valentino Borgia is portrayed quite differently: "Indeed, a countenance, which with physical deformity united the expression of crime, could never be exhibited under a more hideous aspect" (p. 267).

Umberto Eco has also recognized "the manichean struggle of Good against Evil" as "the central theme" of the popular novel,[72] while Folco Portinari offers some considerations that seem dictated by the passages just quoted from *Fieramosca* but

[70] Ibid., pp. 41–44.
[71] Ibid., p. 24.
[72] Eco, p. 88.

are actually inspired by G. B. Bazzoni's *Il castello di Trezzo* and refer to an entire literary genre:

> Because of its elementary, pedagogic function, the traditional structure governing the historical novel is epic-manichean. That is, in its ideology, the organization of good and evil, God and Satan are quantitatively balanced and clearly juxtaposed on the qualitative level. That is why the characterization of the negative hero has to be modeled after that of the positive hero, with an opposite sign: dark and nocturnal as much as the other is clear and sunbright.[73]

This is exactly what I wished to demonstrate through the exemplariness of *Fieramosca*. This exemplariness can be viewed as an alternative to a systematic typology of the historical novel in nineteenth-century Italy, a typology that is perhaps similar to the one tried by Mario Lavagetto for "those more modest novels" that are Verdi's opera libretti, in which "the *coup de théâtre* is quite common and at the same time the characters, even the most exotic ones, are endowed with a moral code and a psychological set-up typical of the bourgeoisie."[74] These conclusions are not dissimilar from those of Brooks'. In fact, they confirm the centrality and modernity of melodrama in a desacralized universe in which tragedy is no longer possible.[75]

Before concluding, it is perhaps worth noting that opera also owes its popularity during the past century to that immediacy of reception that a literary text can have in a much lower degree—for instance, by means of those "real" themes, "historical" but above all "general human" ones, that are considered in the preceding analysis of *Fieramosca*. Obviously, these themes are to be found in opera as well, and are rein-

[73] Portinari, p. 5; also, on p. 18 Tommaso Grossi's historical novel *Marco Visconti* is defined a "melonovel."

[74] Mario Lavagetto, "Quei più modesti romanzi," *Nuovi argomenti*, vols. 43-44 (January–April 1975), pp. 205–267, quotation on p. 266. Cf. also Enrico Chierici, "Verdi nei libretti," *Nuovi Argomenti*, vol. 50 (April 1976), pp. 78–115.

[75] Brooks, p. 21. Conrad, p. 42, also has fine remarks on Verdi's treatment of Shakespeare's plays as "frustrated novels."

forced by its expressive means: words *plus* music, or libretto *plus* score.[76] It is therefore also possible in opera to verify the structure of the "aesthetic response" that is present in folklore: a given performance causes both a cognitive response (with its underlying *vision du monde*) and an affective response (with its underlying values), and the four terms are all interrelated.[77] Since at the core of Verdi's opera there are, above all, "affective-emotive situations,"[78] there can be no doubt about the type of reception and response opera evokes, and consequently about the function of its *école du coeur*. However, this does not exclude a parallel function for literature as well.

In fact, returning to the literary genre from which we started, we may follow a line that begins with Cuoco and Foscolo, passes through D'Azeglio and Manzoni, and arrives at Nievo and the young Verga. In doing so, we can consider the less problematic and most popular historical novels of the nineteenth century in Italy, such as those by Giuseppe Garibaldi, a name that on the symbolic level is certainly equal to that of Verdi.[79] In these novels the aesthetics of astonishment, moral manicheism, and the rhetoric of excess are brought to extreme

[76] Cf. the discussion of Luigi Dallapiccola in Baldacci, pp. 203–216 and especially pp. 217–30.

[77] Robert Jerome Smith, "The Structure of Aesthetic Response," in Américo Paredes and Richard Bauman, eds., *Toward New Perspectives in Folklore* (Austin: University of Texas Press, 1972), pp. 68–79.

[78] Franco Fornari,"Chi ha detto che baritono vuol dire padre?" in *Il corriere della sera*, 3 February 1978, p. 3. His proposal is interesting: "Depression and persecution, as basic affective conditions, seem to direct love and hatred in Verdi's opera according to canons that choose a slow or feverish rhythm, a narrow or ample sound on the musical score. These are merely hints, yet they might open the way for an 'affective semiology' of opera."

[79] Giuseppe Garibaldi was the author of four historical novels. The first three are: *Clelia. Il governo dei preti*, 1870, now reprinted in the series *Il Feuilleton*, ed. by Giovanni Arpino (Turin: MEB, 1973); *Cantoni il volontario*, 1870 (Milan: Edizioni Tascabili Italiane, 1970); and *I Mille*, 1874, which has not been reprinted recently, as far as I know. For a critical appraisal of these novels, see C.E.J. Griffiths, "The Novels of Garibaldi," *Italian Studies*, vol. 30 (1975), pp. 86–98, and a brilliant essay by Alberto Arbasino, "La gallina e il generale," in his *Certi romanzi. Nuova edizione seguita da La Belle Epoque per le scuole* (Turin: Einaudi, 1977), pp. 287–98. The fourth novel by Garibaldi, *Manlio*, has only recently been discovered and published (Naples: Guida, 1982).

consequences (logical if not artistic) as functions of the *école du coeur*, of civic education, and of the democratization of morality and its signs. All this is the coherent as well as unexpected result of that goal of "regeneration of the national character" the Marquis Massimo D'Azeglio had in mind when he first thought of writing the historical novel *Ettore Fieramosca, ovvero La disfida di Barletta* while painting a picture on that distant day in the year 1829.

THE AGONY IN STONY PLACES. . . .

T. S. Eliot

IF A SIGN OUGHT TO BE DIRECTLY
COMPARED TO ITS OBJECT, INTENDED IN
AN EXTENSIONAL WAY, NO METAPHOR
WOULD BE POSSIBLE.

Umberto Eco

Three. Sicilian Epiphanies

AMONG the critics who have recently written about Giovanni Verga, two have focused their attention on part one, chapter four, of *Mastro-don Gesualdo* (a chapter that is a true, paradigmatic *summa* of the protagonist's destiny) and on the crucial and determining function that is displayed in it by the landscape.

In examining the "construction" of the novel and noting its perfect division into two parts (corresponding to the ascent and fall of the eponymous character), Guido Guglielmi has organized every aspect of the narrative according to a perspective that could be defined, at least initially, as Proppian:

> The character who passes through tests expresses a strong antagonism, manifested in his relationship with society and with nature. Hence, there is a type of Verghian treatment of the landscape that is not different, from a functional viewpoint, from that in chapter ten of *I Malavoglia.*
> . . . The representation, which becomes epic, evidently contains a dynamic-narrative value; the landscape functions as an obstacle that Gesualdo overcomes, while the other characters fail. . . . However, the meaning of his action cannot be said to be heroic because there is in it something not grandiose but excessive and contemp-

78

tuous, as when at the Giolio oil-press don Gesualdo risks being killed while pushing the millstone on the platform.[1]

From such a perspective, Guglielmi derives his concluding judgment: "Don Gesualdo's indomitable stance is put to a test by the harshness of the landscape; but if energy, decision, and 'heroism' cause awe and admiration, they also cause perplexity. The old man's words illuminate the indefatigability of the 'hero' from another viewpoint, which antithetically reveals his senselessness; therefore the context becomes ironic instead of epic, and the epic, reduced within the limits of daily life, takes on comic overtones."[2] This very perceptive judgment is used in the present chapter as an initial point of departure, one that is indispensable to the analysis that follows.

Taking up Guglielmi's remarks and using them in a formal reading centered on the writer-character relationship, Roberto Bigazzi notes that the two main landscapes in chapter four "certainly depend on Gesualdo's point of view," even if "style is spared the personal coloring of the *discours indirect libre* or any affective trace whatsoever."[3] He then arrives at some conclusions that appear to be fundamental:

> The "things" in which Gesualdo sees only obstacles, thus stopping at the surface, at fatigue and aridity, actually have quite a different resonance. These are "epiphanic" landscapes, where the domain of death is revealed, a death that makes the type of "progress" aimed at by Gesualdo useless, and therefore dangerous. If he is not aware of the gap between his "fever" and the limits imposed by nature, and hence cannot discover this aspect of things by himself, it is the task of the writer to intervene (as he did in "Vagabondaggio") in order to emphasize what the protagonist sees but does not understand; the emphasis is achieved through linguistic-syntactical means, never with an explicit commentary or with scenographic exaggerations, which was the common practice among

[1] Guido Guglielmi, "Sulla costruzione del *Mastro-don Gesualdo*," in *Ironia e negazione* (Turin: Einaudi, 1974), p. 97.
[2] Ibid., p. 98.
[3] Roberto Bigazzi, *Su Verga novelliere* (Pisa: Nistri-Lischi, 1975), p. 198.

contemporary narrators. Hence, the many notes of desolation, the attention given to adjectives, the tendency toward parataxis and nominal style—all of which break up reality into a series of hostile "objects," lifeless, refractory to the unifying possession Gesualdo believes he is able to impose on everything.[4]

Both Guglielmi's and Bigazzi's conclusions are successful and significant examples of the interest of twentieth-century criticism in what Gérard Genette called the "boundaries of narrative": both critics examine "the *diegetic* functions of the description, *i.e.* the role played by the descriptive passages or aspects in the general system of the narrative."[5] Following Genette, it seems clear that Guglielmi and Bigazzi rightly attribute to the Verghian landscape not a "decorative" function ("a pause or an amusement during the narrative") "similar to that of a piece of sculpture in a classical building," but a function "at once explicative and symbolic":

In Balzac and his realist successors, physical portraits and descriptions of clothing and furnishings tend to reveal and at the same time to justify the psychology of the characters, of which they are at once sign, cause, and effect. The description becomes a major element of the exposition as it was not during the classical period. . . . The evolution of narrative forms, by substituting the signifying description for the ornamental description, has tended to reinforce the narrative's domination (at least until the beginning of the twentieth century). Description has doubtless lost in autonomy what it has gained in dramatic importance.[6]

4 Ibid., pp. 198–99.
5 Gérard Genette, "Boundaries of Narrative," *New Literary History*, vol. 8, no. 1 (Autumn 1976), pp. 1–15, quotation on p. 6. Cf. also Giacomo Debenedetti, *Il romanzo del Novecento* (Milan: Garzanti, 1971), p. 292: "Objects, facts, events" are important for their contribution to "the plot or the construction of a given character."
6 Genette, pp. 6–7. In contrast, Blanchard strongly argues for the autonomy of description vis-à-vis narration, although their respective "boundaries" are not so easy to discern. Marc Eli Blanchard, *Description: Sign, Self, Desire: Critical Theory in the Wake of Semiotics* (The Hague: Mouton, 1980), *passim*.

Such a trajectory for realistic description is certainly valid in Italian literary history as well, especially in the period under examination here.

But realistic description has also been defined and classified by Philippe Hamon from a strictly formal viewpoint.[7] Without delving into his systematization, I wish to emphasize his approach to the problem of mimesis, which is implicit in every description: "The realistic attitude rests on a linguistic illusion, that of a language monopolized by its referential function alone, in which signs would be the adequate analogues of things, a transparent grid duplicating the discontinuity of reality."[8] Hamon takes up the question again in a later article in which he examines, among others, the fundamental contributions of Erich Auerbach and Michel Riffaterre, reaching conclusions that are of great semiotic interest.[9] "Actually it is never the 'real' that is attained in a text, but a rationalization, a pre-textualization of the real, an a posteriori reconstruction encoded by and in the text, which does not have an anchorage and is kept within the circularity without the closure of the 'interpretants' (Peirce), of the clichés, of the copies or stereotypes of culture."[10] Therefore, "it is not a matter of replying

[7] Philippe Hamon, "Qu'est-ce qu'une description?," *Poétique*, vol. 12 (1972), pp. 465–85. On pp. 483–84, he lists the functions of description as demarcating, dilatory, decorative, organizing, and focalizing.

[8] Ibid., p. 484.

[9] Philippe Hamon, "Un discours contraint," *Poétique*, vol. 13 (1973), pp. 411–45. For analogous problems in the visual arts, the obvious references are to E. H. Gombrich and Pierre Francastel.

[10] Hamon, "Un discours contraint," p. 420. In this connection cf. Umberto Eco's position: "Semiosis explains itself by itself: this continual circularity is the normal condition of signification and even allows communication processes to use signs in order to mention things and states of the world. If a sign ought to be directly compared to its object, intended in an extensional way, no metaphor would be possible." "Peirce's Notion of Interpretant," *MLN*, vol. 91, no. 6 (December 1976), p. 1471. At this point, semiotics and Derrida's (and Nietzsche's) deconstructive thought are most closely related, as can be seen in the following remarks by Eugenio Donato: "Inasmuch as a text is fundamentally constructed, its naturalness can only be a will to signification aware of itself. The difference from text to text lies primarily in their relative manner of ignoring, hiding, or on the contrary overtly manipulating their *Bedeutung*, their will to signification." " 'Here, Now'/ 'Always Already': Incidental Remarks On Some Recent Characterizations of the Text," *Diacritics*, vol. 6, no. 3 (Fall 1973), pp. 24–29, quotation on p. 28.

to a question of the type, how does literature copy reality?, which is a question without interest by now, but of considering realism as a sort of speech act (Austin, Searle) defined by a specific situation of communication, hence of replying to a question of the type, how does literature make us believe that it copies reality?"[11] The reply lies in the text's readability and coherence, which take the place of reality and correspond to Jakobson's "motivation," Greimas' "isotopy," and Auerbach's "hypotaxis."[12]

In this chapter, I would like to explore the semiotic level of the problem, which precedes Hamon's formalistic analysis. To do so (still keeping in mind the methodological problems implicit in Guglielmi's and Bigazzi's remarks and explicitly formulated by Hamon), I shall concentrate first on Lotman's theory of "artistic space" as "demarcated" space.[13]

According to Lotman, "the special character of visual perception inherent to man is such that visible spatial objects serve as the denotata of verbal signs; as a result verbal models are perceived in a particular way. The iconic principle and a graphic quality are wholly peculiar to verbal models as well,"[14] in particular and *pour cause* in a "realistic" landscape description, such as those by Verga. For Lotman, literary texts can be divided into two groups, "those without and those with plot." The former have "a distinctly classificatory character" (such as "the calendar, the telephone directory, or a plotless lyrical poem") and the latter are built on the former as their negation, so that "the plot is the 'revolutionary element' in relation to the world picture."[15] Hence there is an extremely important consequence for the diegetic function of the landscape description in any given narrative:

A map is a good example of classificatory (plotless) text. . . . But if we draw a line across the map to indicate, say,

[11] Hamon, "Un discours contraint," p. 421.
[12] Ibid., p. 424.
[13] Yuri Lotman, *The Structure of the Artistic Text*, tr. by Ronald Vroon (Ann Arbor: University of Michigan Press, 1977), p. 217.
[14] Ibid.
[15] Ibid., pp. 236 and 238.

the posssible sea or air routes, the text then assumes a plot: an action will have been introduced which surmounts the structure (in this case geographical).[16]

The example of the map allows Lotman to consider the three different levels on which the text with plot is articulated: "the level of plotless semantic structure; the level of typal action within the limits of the given structure; [and] the level of concrete action."[17] Here a crucial semiotic element enters the picture: "the interrelations of the levels change depending on where we draw the basic structural opposition," so that "level two can be perceived both as code and as message, depending on the point of view. Beginning with Propp's *Morphology of the Folktale* it has become evident that a persona represents an intersection of structural functions."[18]

The relationship between the persona of Gesualdo and the Sicilian landscape as it appears in the initial interpretations by the two Italian critics seems to illustrate Lotman's theory in an exemplary way, and is therefore part of a semiotic-literary system that is well worth exploring.

In *A Theory of Semiotics*, Umberto Eco proposes a "theory of sign production" that on the one hand broadens and completes the more traditional theory of codes, and on the other seems to open up interesting perspectives for literary criticism, since it focuses on the passage from the universe of experience to that of signs, and in particular to the verbal universe.[19] The theory of sign production, which is a major part of Eco's treatise, can be considered as a new and original critical and cognitive instrument, one that allows us to view the creation of a literary work from a perspective very different from those of genetic structuralism and the various branches of psychoanalysis.

After a forceful critique of the notion of iconism, Eco proposes a classification of the modes of sign production. This

[16] Ibid., p. 239.
[17] Ibid., p. 240.
[18] Ibid.
[19] Umberto Eco, *A Theory of Semiotics* (Bloomington: Indiana University Press, 1975). This volume has already been discussed in the introduction.

Fig. 4. Giovanni Verga (1840–1922), *Vizzini from the South Side*, 1892, from *Specchio e realtà: 84 foto inedite*, ed. by Wladimiro Settimelli (Rome: Magma, 1976), p. 58.

classification is presented in tabular form, with the physical labor necessary to produce expressions, the type-token ratio, the continuum to be shaped, and the mode and rate of articulation laid out on the vertical axis, and recognition, ostension, replica, and invention laid out on the horizontal axis.[20]

For the literary critic, the left side of the table (recognition and ostension) corresponds to the pre-textual area. In our case, we can refer historically to Mr. Giovanni Verga, who traveled around Sicily equipped with a camera, ready to point out to himself those places (like Vizzini, near Catania) that he would use as an author. Thus the important side of Eco's table for us is the right one (replica and invention), which explicitly includes texts composed of combinational units,

[20] Ibid., p. 218, table 39.

84

stylizations (among which are "coded macro-ambiental features" and "literary genres"), vectors, programmed stimuli, and, above all, "invention as code-making."[21]

The formalistic correlative of these semiotic categories is to be found in the formula of the typical realistic description conceived by Hamon, in which each unit "can be more or less unconnected with the others, can be absent, or can change."[22]

Before applying the semiotic (and secondarily the formalistic) categories to the Verghian texts, it is necessary to note that for the clarity of my own discourse I shall follow Eco's graphic conventions, in which "single slashes indicate something intended as an expression or a sign-vehicle, while guillemets indicate something intended as content"; and since "objects, images or behavior intended as signs . . . must be expressed through verbal expressions," these are written "between double slashes and in italics. Therefore //*automobile*// is the object corresponding to the verbal expression /automobile/ and both refer to the content unit «automobile»."[23]

Hence we have: //*landscape*// →/landscape/→ «world view».

The first of Verga's texts to be analyzed according to the approach indicated above shows the character Gesualdo in action in the Sicilian landscape:

Still grumbling, he went off at the mule's pace under the boiling sun—a sun that split rocks now, and made the stubble pop as if it were on fire. In the ravine, between the two mountains, it felt like a furnace; and the town

---

21 Ibid., pp. 227 and 237–56.
22 Hamon, "Qu'est-ce qu'une description?" p. 475:

C + F + TH–I (N + PRq/PRf)

where C = character, F = function of the character (who can look at, speak of, or act upon an object—or a landscape), TH–I = introductory theme of the description, N = subthemes or nomenclature deriving from the theme through a flowing metonymy, and PR = predicative expansion (both qualitative and functional). Also note that the vector has its formalistic correspondent in the "vanishing point" on which the text is "focused" or "centered," "not only in descriptions, . . . but emotionally and ideologically as well." Hamon, "Un discours contraint," p. 436.
23 Eco, *A Theory*, p. xi.

on top of the hill, climbing above the precipices, scattered among enormous cliffs, undermined by caverns that left it as if suspended in air—blackish, rusty, looking abandoned, without a shadow, with all the windows opened wide in the torrid heat, like so many black holes, and the crosses of the bell towers swaying in the misty sky. Even the mule, covered with sweat, panted up the steep road. On the way Don Gesualdo met a poor old man, loaded with sheaves, exhausted, who began to grumble: "Oh, where are you going, sir, at this time? . . . You have so much money, and you give your soul to the devil!"[24]

This is a description, an iconic text organized by Verga through the transformation into a semantic model of the (pre-textual) perceptual stimuli given him by the objects //sun//, //rocks//, //stubble//, //ravine//, //cliffs//, //caverns//. These have been recognized by him, pointed out, and shown as samples, disregarding all those others that he considers not to be relevant. For example, there is no //shadow// for this is a landscape where there is no rain, no green, no coolness. (But they could be there, perhaps at a distance of a few kilometers or a few pages: as, for instance, in the veritable *locus amoenus* of Canziria, just at the end of the same chapter.)

The transformation/invention of the objective data occurs, then, through the various modes of Eco's table: vectors ("on top of the hill," "the steep road": the character's viewpoint, bottom-to-top direction, ascent); stylizations ("a sun that split rocks": a subcode of the spoken language); combinational units (the words /sun/, /rocks/, /stubble/, etc. combined with one another and with the adjectives that are related to them: /boiling/, /scattered/, /enormous/, and so on, according to a syntactic process of accumulation and parataxis); programmed stimuli ("it felt like a furnace," "as if suspended in the air," "looking abandoned," "the crosses of the bell towers

[24] Giovanni Verga, *Mastro-don Gesualdo*, tr. by Giovanni Cecchetti (Berkeley: University of California Press, 1979), p. 54; the second passage is on p. 59. In comparison with D. H. Lawrence's translation (London: Cape, 1925), Cecchetti uses a more seemingly "spoken" language. See also his important critical contributions in *Il Verga maggiore* (Florence: Nuova Italia, 1975).

swaying"). The description climaxes with the introduction of the /poor old man, loaded with sheaves, exhausted/ and of his final words, which are no longer a description but make the connotations of the description explicit, conveying its «meaning». There is an anti-epic irony in Guglielmi's interpretation of this meaning, an epiphany of the character's destiny in Bigazzi's. To each this is Verga's «world view».

If we apply to the text the formula used by Hamon to define the "circulation of knowledge" in realistic discourse,[25] there will be a significant variation.

Author: Verga (informed)—Sender
↓

Character 1: Gesualdo	Object-knowledge	Character 2: old man
→		←
Sender, pseudo-informed	landscape	Receiver, informed

↓

F3-acts on   Reader (not informed)—Receiver   F1-observes

In comparison with Hamon's original scheme, in Verga's text there is an inversion of roles and direction between C1 and C2. This corresponds to the difference between French naturalism (the hegemonic role of the professional, the engineer, and so on) and Italian *verismo*, in which the protagonist is one of the "vanquished" to start with. In the latter, true knowledge remains with those who do not believe in progress, those who with ancient wisdom observe the useless action of the character-hero upon the hostile setting.[26]

The second text by Verga repeats the same procedure and movement as the first:

[25] Hamon, "Un discours contraint," p. 429. In his original scheme, the direction of knowledge in the text is as follows: "Character C1→object-knowledge→Character C2."

[26] In this connection, one can make an eloquent comparison with the conclusions reached by recent sociological criticism concerning "the structural characteristics of the ruling class in Italy or at least of its most learned sector": "In the origins of Positivism and European naturalism it was possible to trace the presence of three great factors: science, industrialism, and the prevalence of urban over agricultural civilization. We believe we have demonstrated . . . how uncertain and contradictory these factors were in our national situation." Alberto Asor Rosa, "La cultura," in *Storia d'Italia*, vol. 4, *Dall'Unità a oggi* (Turin: Einaudi, 1975), p. 971.

And he went off under the scorching sun, pulling the tired mule behind him. It was suffocating in that Petraio gorge. The barren cliffs seemed red-hot. Not a patch of shade, not a blade of grass, hill after hill, piled upon one another, bare, parched, rocky, scattered with sparse and scrawny olive trees, with dusty prickly pear trees—the plain under Budarturo like a waste burned by the sun, the mountains dark with mist, in the distance. Some crows flew away croaking from a carcass that stank in the ditch. Sirocco flurries burnt his face and cut his breath short; a maddening thirst, the sun beating on his head just like the hammering of his men who were working on the Camemi road. But when he got there, he found them all lying on their stomachs in the ditch, here and there, their faces covered with flies, and their arms stretched out. Only an old man was breaking stones, seated on the ground under a dilapidated umbrella, his bare chest copper-colored and sprinkled with white hairs, his arms fleshless, his shins white with dust, just like his face, which seemed a mask—only his eyes burning in the midst of so much dust. . . .

As they saw him [Don Gesualdo] with that burning and parched face, white with dust only on his hair and in the sockets of his eyes—such eyes as those of the fever-stricken, his lips thin and pale, no one dared answer him. The hammering started again like a chorus in the vast silent valley, with the dust rising upon the sunburnt flesh of the men, upon their fluttering rags, together with a dry panting that accompanied every blow. The crows again flew overhead, croaking, in the ruthless sky. The old man then raised his dusty face to look at them, his eyes flaming, as if he knew what they wanted and were waiting for them.

The landscape described here is homologous to the first one, from the /mule/ and the /sun/ at the beginning to the /old man/ at the end, but here Verga seems to intensify his invention by putting the description—or, if you prefer, the iconicity of the text—on a secondary level. Let us see how.

First of all, he multiplies the programmed stimuli: "it was suffocating," "seemed red-hot," "like a waste burned by the sun," "a maddening thirst," "like the hammering," "his face, which seemed a mask," "eyes as those of the fever-stricken," "as if he knew and were waiting for them."

Secondly, he strengthens the text's connotation by means of the adjectives that accompany every noun, either by themselves or in multiple combinations: "the scorching sun"; "the tired mule"; "the barren cliffs"; "hill after hill, piled upon one another, bare, parched, rocky, scattered"; "sparse and scrawny olive trees"; "dusty prickly pear trees"; "waste burned"; "mountains dark with mist"; the men "lying on their stomachs . . . their arms stretched out"; "his bare chest copper-colored and sprinkled with white hairs, his arms flesh-less, his shins white with dust"; "burning and parched face, white with dust"; "his lips thin and pale"; "the vast silent valley"; "sunburnt flesh"; "fluttering rags"; "dry panting"; "the ruthless sky"; "his dusty face"; "his eyes flaming." Even the less attentive, the less "informed" reader cannot but perceive the connotation of aridity, fatigue, and desolation that is conveyed by this impressive, implacable series of adjectives.

Thirdly, by emphasizing accumulation and parataxis, Verga sets up two syntactical processes of combination that are present in the whole description but are particularly evident in the sentence that is without a single leading verb: "Not a patch of shade, not a blade of grass, hill after hill, piled upon one another, bare, parched, rocky, scattered with sparse and scrawny olive trees, with dusty prickly pear trees—the plain under Budarturo like a waste burned by the sun, the mountains dark with mist, in the distance." The deliberate repetition of key words such as "sun" (three times), "white," "dust" ("dusty"), and "eyes" is also part of the accumulation process.

In the fourth place, Verga increases the always arbitrary elements of invention: "some crows," "a carcass," "sirocco flurries" (none of which appeared in the first description), and especially the old man, who is no longer just an old man (albeit laden and exhausted), as in the first description, but a very specific stone-breaker. This old man is a visual, indeed a pictorial, invention that echoes the famous painting by Gustave Courbet, with its own connotation of hard work and fatigue. The Bakhtinian view of culture as a pluralistic interchange of different languages is indeed a genetic force in this example, which involves a "dialogue" between literature and painting, Italy and France, a conservative and a socialist ideology.[27] But let us return to the Verghian text, in which many remarkable details of the old stone-breaker are emphasized: his face, "which seemed a mask," his "burning" eyes, his "white hairs." In fact, he is a veritable double of Gesualdo, whose own face is also "burning and parched," who is "white with dust only on his hair," and whose eyes are "as those of the fever-stricken."

The final result of Verga's intensified invention is an increased textualization, or a lesser materiality, in comparison with the first description. This is evidenced especially in the change from the common noun /rocks/ in Verga 1 to the proper name /Petraio/ ("the stony place") and to the adjective /rocky/ in Verga 2, and above all in the symbolic intensification obtained by passing from the explicit final «message» of the /poor old man/ in Verga 1 to the sign /crows . . . in the ruthless sky/ toward which the /old man/ in Verga 2 lifts his face, «as if he knew what they wanted and were waiting for them». These «crows» take on the emblematic meaning of the whole epiphanic description. The desolation of this Sicilian landscape is indeed the desolation of the protagonist's destiny;

---

[27] There is a remarkable letter by Courbet about *The Stone-Breakers* that is worth quoting at length: "Would you like me to give you a description? On the one side is an old man, seventy, bent over his task, sledge-hammer in air, he is tanned by the sun, his head shaded by a straw hat; his trousers of poor material are all patched; in the cracked sabots torn stockings, once blue, show his bare heels. On the other side is a young fellow with dusty head and swarthy skin; his back and arms show through the holes in his filthy tattered shirt. . . . Alas, in labour such as this, one's life begins that way, it ends the same way. Here and there is scattered their gear: a basket, a stretcher, a hoe, a country boiler, etc. All this happens in the blazing sun, in the open countryside; at the edge of a highway ditch; the landscape fills the canvas." Jack Lindsay, *Gustave Courbet: His Life and Art* (London: Adams and Dart, 1973), p. 59. This letter is so revealing that any further comment on its cultural relevance for Verga's own description seems superfluous.

his failure as a bourgeois entrepreneur in a southern Italian province of the late nineteenth century is the very negation of "progress." Thus at the end Gesualdo the individual becomes "typical" in the Lukàcsian sense of the term.[28]

It seems to me that the whole preceding analysis clearly illustrates Eco's statement, according to which "the units composing an iconic text are established—if at all—by the context. Out of context these so-called 'signs' are not signs at all, because they are neither coded nor possess any resemblance to anything. Thus insofar as it establishes the coded value of a sign, the iconic text is an act of *code-making*." This code-making occurs first of all in the coherence and readability of the proposed text (and is therefore an equivalent of the "idiolect" of linguistic-oriented literary criticism). It also occurs, of course, with the collaboration of the receiver, who, using Verga's text, for instance, "as an imprint . . . makes his way *backward* inferring and extrapolating similitude rules, and finally reconstitutes the original percept" with the help of the artifacts offered by the sender. In describing how this takes place, we can definitely apply to literature what Eco says about painting:

> When this process is successful a new content-plane, lying between the percept (which is only remembered by the painter) and the physically testable expression is brought into being. This is not so much a unit as a discourse. What had been raw content-continuum perceptually organized by the painter [by Courbet, for example—or by

---

[28] Apropos of Gesualdo's "type," there are illuminating considerations in Alexandre Kojève: "The bourgeois worker presupposes—and conditions—an *Entsagung*, an Ab-negation of human existence; Man transcends himself, projects himself far from himself in projecting himself on the Idea of Private Property, of Capital, which—while being the work of the Proprietor—becomes independent of him and enslaves him completely, as the Master enslaves the Slave." *Introduction à la lecture de Hegel* (Paris: Gallimard, 1974), p. 191. Even more than a type, for Nicolas Perella the character Gesualdo is an archetype: he "seems the incarnation of the cruel sun visiting the earth with pestilence and death. . . . he takes on the features of a noontide demon"; but he is also "the victim" of his ambition, which "is reflected in the violent but arid noontide." *Midday in Italian Literature: Variations on an Archetypal Theme* (Princeton: Princeton University Press, 1979), p. 97.

Fig. 5. Giovanni Fattori (1825–1908), *The Stone-Breaker*, from Luigi Servolini, *177 incisioni di Fattori* (Milan: IGIS, 1965).

the writer Verga] in the first instance now gradually becomes a new cultural arrangement of the world. A sign function emerges from the exploratory labor of code-making, and so establishes itself that the painting [or the novel] generates habits, acquired expectations, and mannerisms.[29]

In order to understand (to visualize) the meaning of Eco's statement, we can take an etching by Giovanni Fattori, the greatest painter of late nineteenth-century Italy, entitled *The Stone-Breaker*, and relate it back, thematically as well as formally, to Courbet and his revolutionary, realistic code. In a strictly homologous way, we will also be able to say that in Italian literature the habits, expectations, and mannerisms

[29] Eco, *A Theory*, pp. 216 and 252–54. It should be remembered that for Eco a code actually is "a complex network of subcodes" (p. 125).

92

generated by the establishment of Verga's code will be reflected diachronically in and by readers, that is, in literary history and criticism.

This can be verified by analyzing those writers who lived after Verga and, like him, took Sicily and its nineteenth-century history as the object of their representation. Consequently, Luigi Capuana and Federico De Roberto are excluded from this analysis, since they are the other two valid spokesmen of that Italian *verismo* that is considered here as synchronic with Verga; and for different reasons other writers, such as Elio Vittorini and Vitaliano Brancati, are also excluded, because they did not deal with the same period of Sicilian history.

The first and foremost of the writers to be analyzed is Luigi Pirandello. Although he is a "great destroyer of naturalism," there is a particular moment of his work in which, as Giacomo Debenedetti says, "Sicily is the place where figures and facts can be shaped through a representation, a problematic bearing the naturalistic mark."[30]

Let us begin by considering the initial passage of the historical novel *I vecchi e i giovani*, which is so important for the ideological understanding of the whole Pirandellian oeuvre:

The rain, which had fallen in torrents during the night, had churned into a quagmire the long highroad that wound, in a succession of twists and turns, as though in search of some less laborious ascent, some less abrupt slope, over the broken surface of the vast, deserted plain. The damage done by the storm appeared all the more depressing, inasmuch as there were already signs, here and there, of the disregard, not to say the contempt, shown for the labours of those who had planned and constructed the road in order to give their fellow-men an easier passage over the harshness of the country by means of those bends and coils, erecting now a retaining wall, now a dyke. The retaining walls had fallen, the dykes had been trampled down, where craggy short cuts had come into being. It was drizzling still with downpours in

---

[30] Debenedetti, pp. 149 and 386.

the livid dawn, between the icy gusts that blew over from the west. And at every gust, over that strip of troubled countryside that was just beginning to emerge from the gloomy shadows of the stormy night, a long shudder seemed to run from the town, a huddled mass of yellow-ish houses, standing aloft and shrouded on its heights, and to pass over hill and dale, over the plain that bristled still with blackened stubble, to the boiling, crested sea beyond. Rain and wind seemed a ruthless act of cruelty on the part of the sky that overhung the desolation of those uttermost tracts of Sicily, upon which Girgenti, amid the piteous ruins of its primeval existence, rose a silent and awed survivor in the void of a time that would bring no changes, in the abandonment of a misery be-yond repair. The thickest hedges of prickly pear, or of withered brambles, or of agave, and the occasional crum-bling walls were interrupted here and there by a pair of tottering pillars supporting a crooked rusty gate, or by a rude and squalid shrine which, in the motionless soli-tude, watched over by the shaggy boughs of the dripping trees, instead of comfort inspired a certain sense of terror. . . . For some time Placido Sciaralla's aged white mare had been ploughing and splashing along this road, under the friendly encouragement of her weary rider, who sat, his hands stiff and purple with the cold, cowering be-neath the wind and rain, in the gay uniform of a Bourbon soldier: red breeches and a blue greatcoat.[31]

As a variant and completion of this long description, let us add two brief passages that appear just a bit later in the novel:

An inertia, whether for good or for evil, had taken root in the most profound distrust of destiny, in the conviction that nothing could possibly happen, that every effort must prove futile to shake off the utter desolation in which were engulfed not only the souls of men but everything else as well. And Sciaralla felt that he had a convincing

[31] Luigi Pirandello, *The Old and the Young*, tr. by C. K. Scott-Moncrieff (New York: Dutton, 1928), bk. 1, pp. 3–5. All references will be to this edition. I have corrected some of the (too many) liberties taken by the translator in order to make the text conform to the original.

proof of this in the dreary spectacle presented to him, that morning, by the surrounding country and by that endless road.

Indeed from that dreary tract of country, abominated by such peasants as were compelled by necessity to inhabit it, wasted, yellow, fever-ridden, there seemed to be exhaled in the squalor of the frigid dawn an agonizing oppression, by which even the trees were penetrated; those centenarian, writhing olives, those almonds stripped bare by the first winds of autumn. (bk. 1, pp. 13–14)

It is evident that, like Verga's texts, these descriptions constitute a specific labor for sign production, based above all on the recognition and ostension of objects or data such as //rain, highroad, slope// in the first sentence, or //dawn, gusts, town, hill, plain, stubble, sea// in the sentences that follow. In the textual replica these objects or data become respectively /rain, highroad, slope/ and so on until /stubble/ and /sea/. The text continues with other common, concrete nouns that crowd the passages just quoted: /prickly pear, brambles, agave, walls, pillars, gate, shrine, boughs, trees; mare, road, hands, wind, uniform; country, road; country (again), peasants, dawn, trees, olives, almonds, winds/.

Already, from a quick reading, one can establish similarities and contrasts between Verga and Pirandello: among the samples selected by the latter are the (autumn) rain instead of Verga's (summer) sun, and dawn instead of noon. But in both writers, the chosen elements have the same function of signaling an excess, a lack of measure, a pain, as will become apparent as soon as our attention is shifted to Pirandello's combinational units, above all the adjectives (but also some verbs) that are at the same time programmed stimuli: "laborious ascent," "abrupt slope"; "fallen" walls, dykes that have been "trampled down," "craggy short cuts"; the "livid dawn," "icy gusts." And then: "troubled," "gloomy," "stormy," "blackened," "boiling"; "ruthless," "uttermost," "piteous," "awed," "withered," "crumbling," "tottering," "squalid," "shaggy"; "aged," "weary," "stiff," "purple." Also notice the expressions that characterize an excess (in "torrents," "twists and turns," "with downpours") or a deprivation ("no changes," "beyond repair"). And consider the verbs as well that show excess or fatigue ("ploughing and splashing"). Furthermore, note the following in Pirandello 2 and 3: "futile," "engulfed"; "dreary"; "dreary," "abominated," "compelled," "wasted," "fever-ridden," "frigid," "agonizing," "writhing," "bare."

Indeed, the simple list of these combinational units is no less impressive than that made out from the Verghian texts. But Pirandello sharply distinguishes himself from Verga because of the elements of invention he introduces into his description. First of all, he focuses attention not on a hero but on the helper of one of the many protagonists of his novel, and completely eliminates the second character that in Verga had the function of making knowledge circulate, thus concentrating the human presence in the lone figure of Sciaralla, the "vanishing point" of his landscape, and concealing the author's *statut pedagogique* with an incomparably lesser effectiveness than Verga's. In fact, Pirandello uses numerous other explicit elements of invention in order to extract meaning from the landscape, to declare (even to cry out) the meaning of the signs of this landscape—signs that are clear to the reader who, aware of the code established by Verga, knows how to read them as imprints. Here is a revealing list of the *abstract* nouns inserted by Pirandello into the materiality of his landscape: /disregard, contempt, harshness, cruelty, desolation, void, abandonment, solitude, terror; inertia, distrust, desolation, spectacle; necessity, squalor, oppression/.

Such abstract nouns are of course not only an invention. They are also programmed stimuli and combinational units; they have a corresponding factor in the elaborate syntax, wrought with clauses and connections, that organizes every element of the description into a picture with an ample perspective. All the more than six hundred pages of the novel will be under the sign of this landscape-epiphany, this desolate and squalid vista that communicates the historical dismay of the author vis-à-vis the failure of the Risorgimento and its ideals.[32] The /ploughing and splashing/ along the road

[32] Cf. the well-known analysis by Carlo Salinari, *Miti e coscienza del deca-*

will become the «mud» of the Roman scandals, of public life in the united Italy; and Sciaralla, with his "gay uniform of a Bourbon soldier," this funny-looking "puppet" clashing with the dismal background of the livid landscape, will be the emblem of the defeat and disappearance of an entire world, just as Verga's Gesualdo had been a "typical" bourgeois in useless social ascent. Thus Pirandello has used Verga's code to convey a very similar message, one that is historically more complete (if for no other reason than the time that has elapsed), even if it is aesthetically less successful (perhaps because of his deliberately communicative intent).[33]

Before proceeding with our intertextual exploration, I would like briefly to analyze some passages of Pirandello's novel in which the emblematic atmosphere of the initial landscape is either taken up again or articulated according to precise historical occurrences and to the "cultural arrangement of the world" of which that landscape is an expression.

In this connection, one should remember that Verga, after following Gesualdo in his social ascent, then described his decline and fall in the second half of the novel. By this means, Verga showed how, through the events culminating in the "revolution" of 1848, the old aristocracy had formally absorbed the new bourgeoisie, which was by then hegemonic on the economic level, and had thus prevented it from establishing itself on the social and cultural level.[34] Gesualdo

dentismo italiano (Milan: Feltrinelli, 1962), pp. 249–84, and Vittorio Spinazzola, " 'I vecchi e i giovani' tra il caos e la rivolta," in Studi in memoria di Luigi Russo (Pisa: Nistri-Lischi, 1974), pp. 423–55, especially p. 429. For Robert Dombroski, the attention in Verga is focused on man's struggle, while in Pirandello this struggle is lost from the outset. "The Form of Chaos in Pirandello's I vecchi e i giovani," Yale Italian Studies, vol. 2, no. 2 (1978), pp. 85–113. It should also be noted that in Pirandello the landscape (not this landscape) has another epiphanic function—the revelation of Being—that is not considered here.
[33] It is interesting to note that realism has symbolic results in Verga and allegorical ones in Pirandello, perhaps in connection with the latter's communicative scheme. Renato Barilli, La linea Svevo-Pirandello (Milan: Mursia, 1972).
[34] Cf. Bigazzi, pp. 204–205, in particular: "At the core of Verga's rejection of contemporary bourgeois ideologies there is undoubtedly the recognized dominance of natural and economic laws, which annihilate the hope for new

begins to decay when he insists on desperately defending his own patrimony instead of "inserting himself with a quick-change into revolutions, as all those who had something to lose, *i.e.* the *notabili* of the town, had understood."[35] In Guglielmi's words, it can be asserted that "on one hand the movement of narrative forms—from Manzoni to Verga—critically acknowledges the failure of the Risorgimento program of renovation of society and of cultural unification of the country; on the other hand, the ideology of objectivity marks the limits of this *prise de conscience*," in so far as "positivism knows the fact but not the subversion of facts, mechanical legality but not historical dynamicism, the *datum* but not the process, the being of society but not its possibility."[36]

I think it is very significant that the Pirandello of *I vecchi e i giovani* adopts the Verghian code of *Mastro-don Gesualdo*, with a remarkable step backward in comparison with that revolutionary novel entitled *Il fu Mattia Pascal*, perhaps because he felt the need to know the data of history before being able to attack and subvert them.[37] It is precisely from such a perspective that one can frame the developments of the novel that are directly dependent upon the initial, emblematic landscape. Here is the broadening of /inertia/ and /agonizing oppression/ into a historical context that makes them more resonant than they were in the landscape background:

> The Akragas of the Greeks, the Agrigentum of the Romans had ended in the Kerkent of the Musulmans, and the brand of the Arabs had remained indelibly stamped

values: the failure of a whole Risorgimento generation has become a world view."

[35] Guglielmi, p. 109; cf. Verga, *Mastro-don Gesualdo*, part 4, chapters 2 and 3.

[36] Guglielmi, p. 127.

[37] In such an attitude, Pirandello has obviously also kept in mind the work of Federico De Roberto, in which the Risorgimento is "not only a betrayed revolution seen with the disillusioned eye of a southern writer, but also a historical process destined, with all its ideals, to be debased when faced with reality and its interests and passions." Carlo A. Madrignani, *Illusione e realtà nell'opera di Federico De Roberto* (Bari: De Donato, 1972), p. 116; cf. also Vittorio Spinazzola, *Federico De Roberto e il verismo* (Milan: Feltrinelli, 1964), p. 213.

on the minds and manners of the people. A taciturn inertia, a sensitive and jealous distrust. . . . Here, today, death sat enthroned. Commanded, from the top of the hill, by the old Norman cathedral dedicated to San Gerlando, the Bishop's palace and the Seminary, Girgenti was the city of priests and passing bells. From morning to night, the thirty churches exchanged, in long, slow peals, the note of mourning and the call to prayer, diffusing an agonizing oppression everywhere. (bk. 1, pp. 239–40)

And here, at the end of the novel, is the echo of the beginning: "The market place . . . , as soon as the smoke from their rifles melted in the livid glimmer of the dawn, seemed to the eyes of the soldiers . . ." (bk. 2, p. 368). Then one can read the statement by one of the characters that seems to translate into ideological terms the solar excess of Gesualdo's landscape-obstacle: "We all persist in being mere shadows, here in Sicily. . . . Inept or discouraged or servile. . . . The fault is a bit of the sun. The sun puts the very words to sleep on our lips!" (bk. 1, p. 292).

I do not wish to document all the passages in the novel where the historical events following Italy's unification are narrated or recalled; it is sufficient for my purpose to point out the documentary and at the same time impassioned punctiliousness with which Pirandello registers even minimal facts or mores (such as the song "La bella Gigogin," bk. 2, p. 6) that have to do with the background of history. I shall give only two examples: one is the "utter ruin" that "had come in Sicily to all the illusions, all the fervid faith, by which the torch of revolt had been kindled! Poor island, treated as conquered territory!" (bk. 1, p. 126); the other is the narration of the parliamentary elections, with the echo of the initial /rain/ transferred to the metaphorical /torrent/:

In the darkness of the night, beneath the faint glimmer of the street lamps, there passed in a tumult along the narrow street that torrent of people, who let themselves be swept on without the slightest enthusiasm, like a bellowing herd, by the will of two or three interested per-

99

sons. Flaminio Salvo's villa was illuminated from top to bottom, splendidly, so that it might be visible, as a sign of triumph from distant Colimbètra. . . . There came up to the villa a deputation from the crowd, who were received by Salvo with his habitual frigid smile, to which the slow stare of his eyes beneath their heavy lids gave a faintly ironical expression. And indeed those fifteen or sixteen excited townsfolk, newly emerging from the nameless multitude which down below in the darkness of the avenue sounded so imposing, assuming in an instant each his own name, his own appearance, standing there, timid, embarrassed, hesitating, bewildered, obsequious, their hands apparently sewn up in their sleeves, cut a sorry enough figure amid the splendours of the magnificent drawing-room. Flaminio Salvo expressed his gratitude to the townsfolk for this solemn affirmation of the popular feeling. . . . Whereupon one of the fifteen, swelling and reddening like a turkey cock, went to the balcony and, between the lamps held up by a pair of footmen, delivered an impassioned harangue to the crowd. (bk. 1, pp. 359–60)

The emblematic /darkness/-«darkness» that envelops the elections recurs later in the final pages of the novel, when Mauro Mortara, the surviving Garibaldinian hero, romantic and idealistic, pays a visit to the general's quarters, and there finds another, equally emblematic object:

In the darkness, from the corner of that room, the melancholy stuffed leopard, minus an eye, had been unable to make him see all the cobwebs that fastened it to the wall, all the dust that had fallen upon its skin, spotted now, in addition to its natural markings, with many patches of mould! (bk. 2, pp. 332–33)

I believe the reader has by now guessed where my exploration is leading: to Giuseppe Tomasi di Lampedusa's *Il Gattopardo*, which is entirely centered on the historical events of the Italian unification that occurred in Sicily, and on the relationship between the aristocracy and the bourgeoisie. *Il Gat-*

topardo takes on relevant aspects of Verga's and Pirandello's narrative code (much more so than that of De Roberto's *I Vicerè*),[38] through both a necessary updating and a felicitous anachronism.

The textual comparisons seem extremely eloquent, for the inertia of Gesualdo's workers and the Girgenti peasants returns in the impassioned peroration of Prince Salina against the emblematic background of the landscape:

In Sicily it doesn't matter whether things are done well or done badly; the sin which we Sicilians never forgive is simply that of "doing" at all. We are old, Chevalley, very old. For more than twenty-five centuries we've been bearing the weight of a superb and heterogeneous civilization, all from outside, none made by ourselves, none that we could call our own. We're as white as you are, Chevalley, and as the Queen of England; and yet for two thousand and five hundred years we've been a colony. I don't say that in complaint; it's our fault. But even so we're worn out and exhausted. . . . I have explained myself badly; I said Sicilians, I should have added Sicily, the atmosphere, the climate, the landscape of Sicily. Those are the forces which have formed our minds together with and perhaps more than alien pressure and varied invasions: this landscape which knows no mean between sensuous slackness and hellish drought; which is never petty, never ordinary, never relaxed, as a country made for rational beings to live in should be; this country of ours in which the inferno around Randazzo is a few miles from the loveliness of Taormina Bay; this climate which

[38] Giuseppe Paolo Samonà, in *Il Gattopardo, i Racconti, Lampedusa* (Florence: La Nuova Italia, 1974), p. 469, is decidedly opposed to the "so-called derivation of *Il Gattopardo* from *I Vicerè* (not to mention *Il Marchese di Roccaverdina* and *I vecchi e i giovani!*)." The semiotic approach I have adopted should prevent the ambiguity of such "derivations" by focusing on the intertextual relationships where they do exist and can be verified. Also Tom O'Neill, in "Lampedusa and De Roberto," *Italica*, vol. 47, no. 2 (Summer 1970), pp. 170–82, on p. 174 distinguishes between the two writers in the following terms: "It is a consciousness of the futility of action that takes *Il Gattopardo* beyond the realms of the historical novel [such as *I Vicerè*]."

inflicts us with six feverish months at a temperature of a
hundred and four; count them, Chevalley, count them:
May, June, July, August, September, October; six times
thirty days of sun sheer down on our heads; . . . and
then the rains, which are always tempestuous and set
dry river beds to frenzy, drown beasts and men on the
very spot where two weeks before both had been dying
of thirst. This violence of landscape, this cruelty of climate, this continual tension in everything, and these
monuments, even, of the past, . . . all those rulers who
landed by main force from all directions . . . : all these
things have formed our character, which is thus conditioned by events outside our control as well as by a terrifying insularity of mind.[39]

The prince's rhetorical eloquence is much more credible because Sicily's "violence of landscape" and "cruelty of climate"
are well known to us from Verga's and Pirandello's descriptions, which deal respectively with the summer sun and the
autumn rains. But the author wants to confirm the statements
of the prince through an impersonal process, from the viewpoint of Chevalley, the Piedmontese envoy, who is first the
receiver and now the sender of the same message:

In the livid light of five-thirty in the morning Donnafu-
gata was deserted and apparently despairing. . . . Chevalley hoisted himself up onto the post carriage, propped
on four wheels the color of vomit. The horse, all hunger
and sores, began its long journey. Day had just dawned;
the little light that managed to pass through the quilt of
clouds was held up once more by the immemorial filth
on the windows. Chevalley was alone; amid bumps and
shakes he moistened the tip of his index finger with saliva
and cleaned a pane for the width of an eye. He looked

[39] Giuseppe Tomasi di Lampedusa, *The Leopard*, tr. by A. Colquhoun (New
York: Signet, 1961), pp. 182 and 184–85. All subsequent references will be
to this edition. I have dealt with Lampedusa's landscape from a thematic
viewpoint in "The Prince and the Siren," *MLN*, vol. 78, no. 1 (January 1963),
pp. 31–50.

out: in front of him, under the ashen light, the landscape
lurched to and fro, irredeemable. (pp. 190–91)

If we pass from this //*landscape*//→/*landscape*/→«landscape-
judgment» to history, further confirmations of Lampedusa's
message will quickly follow. For example, consider this image
of a city (*i.e.* of culture, of history), which is Lampedusa's
analogue of Pirandello's Girgenti:

> Palermo could be seen very close, plunged in complete
> darkness, its low shattered houses weighted down by
> the huge edifices of convents and monasteries. There
> were dozens of these, all vast. . . . Here and there squat
> domes rose higher, in flaccid curves, like breasts emptied
> of milk; but it was the religious houses which gave the
> city its grimness and its character, its sedateness and also
> the sense of death which not even the vibrant Sicilian
> light could ever manage to disperse. (pp. 29–30)

Or Lampedusa's narration of the plebiscite:

> The day of the Plebiscite was windy and gray, and tired
> groups of youths had been seen going through the streets
> of the town with placards carrying "Yes" and the same
> on pieces of paper stuck in the ribbons of their hats.
> Among the papers and refuse swirled about by the wind
> were a few verses of *La Bella Gigugin* transformed into a
> kind of Arab wail, a fate to which any gay tune sung in
> Sicily is bound to succumb. They had also seen two or
> three "foreign faces" (that is, from Girgenti) installed in
> *Zzu* Menico's tavern, where they were declaiming about
> Leopardi's lines on the "magnificent and progressive des-
> tiny" of the new Sicily united to resurgent Italy. . . . Late
> that night the central balcony of the Town Hall was flung
> open and Don Calogero appeared with a tricolor sash
> over his middle, flanked by two ushers with lighted can-
> delabra which the wind blew out at once. To the invisible
> crowd in the shadows below he announced that the Pleb-
> iscite at Donnafugata had had the following results: Vot-
> ers listed, 515; Voted, 512; Yes, 512; No, zero. Applause
> and hurrahs rose from the dark background of the square;

on her little balcony Angelica, with her funereal maid, clapped lovely rapacious hands; speeches were made; adjectives loaded with superlatives and double consonants reverberated and echoed in the dark from one wall to another; amid the thunder of fireworks messages were sent off to the King (the new one) and to the General; a tricolor rocket or two climbed up from the village into the blackness toward the starless sky. By eight o'clock all was over, and nothing remained except the darkness as on any other night, as always. (pp. 112–13 and 115–16)

Here Lampedusa seems to take up some Pirandellian elements again, deliberately condensing and intensifying them. These include, in increasing importance: the mention of the popular song (noticed and cleverly emphasized by Luchino Visconti in the film version of the novel), which in Pirandello is just a *datum* of mores, is used here as a pretext for an improbable cultural fusion (Piedmontese-Arabic) and is accompanied by the ferocious sarcasm of the "magnificent and progressive destiny," which is as senseless and uselessly pompous as the adjectives "new" and "resurgent" that are used in reference to Sicily and Italy by the political rhetoric of the Risorgimento; the appearance on a balcony of a character ("one of the fifteen," Don Calogero) between two footmen (ushers) with lighted candelabra (lights), which "the wind blew out at once," as if to underline another crucial aspect: the «darkness» of the electoral results and related speeches, with the emblematic «darkness» here repeatedly insisted upon, «as always». Finally, in passing from Pirandello to Lampedusa an extremely significant transformation should be noted. In Lampedusa, we are dealing with a plebiscite (manipulated, alas, and therefore disastrous), with an event that is at least potentially capable of instituting a new historical period, and as such is certainly more important, more emblematic, than a simple parliamentary election like the one described by Pirandello.

Also, consider the *diminutio anti-aulica* (but not too much so) of the embalmed dog Bendicò that, just like the melancholic Garibaldinian leopard in *I vecchi e i giovani*, emblematically concludes the novel:

Anyone who looked carefully into the heap of moth-eaten fur would have noticed two erect ears, a snout of black wood, and two astonished eyes of yellow glass. . . . During the flight down from the window his form recomposed itself for an instant; in the air one could have seen dancing a quadruped with long whiskers, and its right foreleg seemed to be raised in imprecation. Then all found peace in a little heap of livid dust. (pp. 272 and 285)

Through intertextual analysis, one can clearly see how much the informative and aesthetic potential inherent in the Verghian code has generated "habits, acquired expectations, and mannerisms" that have then developed in a complex interaction with the subjective and stylistic elements of the authors who adopted them. In fact, one can say that Pirandello and Lampedusa have emphasized and made most evident the ideological elements of Verga's landscape code, which appears more and more explicitly as a motionless and unchangeable spatiality that defies man's temporality, development, and history.

This also means that, following the various levels of the text, my analysis, which started with description as a narrative function (landscape-epiphany) has gradually shifted to description as an ideological function (landscape-judgment). This other level has, in addition, an intellectual content that is ideologized by the poetics of impersonality to a second degree, inasmuch as it is a metatextual explanation based upon a partial world view (aristocratic-bourgeois, static, closed).

It is precisely this partiality that makes it semiotically relevant as an ideology. So far we have been interested in studying not so much its "mechanics of *motivation*" or its historical-economic *"genesis"* (an operation already performed by literary critics: remember Guglielmi's quotations) as its *"mechanism of organization,"* its *"structure"*[40]—the choice, for instance, of certain samples instead of others, the invention of certain elements instead of others.

As Eco says, and as our series of Sicilian landscapes clearly illustrates, "ideology is . . . a message which starts with a

---

[40] Umberto Eco, *Trattato di semiotica generale* (Milan: Bompiani, 1975), p. 360. These words do not appear in the English edition.

factual description, and then tries to justify it theoretically, gradually being accepted by society through a process of overcoding."[41] Certainly the Verghian poetics of impersonality can and must be considered as overcoding, especially when read and applied by such writers as Pirandello and Lampedusa.

Still, the critical hypothesis at the basis of this chapter remains to be verified *e contrario*, through a writer who rejects (but in doing so recognizes) the Verghian code, particularly the narrative and ideological functions of the Sicilian landscape descriptions as they have also been articulated through the complex filter of the other two authors examined so far. Naturally, even the writer who rejects this code will reveal his own world view; therefore it is necessary to keep in mind that "there is no theory of the ideologies that would be able to test and to improve them. There is a semiotic technique of analysis that allows one to destroy an ideology by opposing to it another ideology, the latter showing the falsity of the former (and vice versa)."[42]

In 1956, Leonardo Sciascia started his literary career with a book entitled *Le parrocchie di Regalpetra*, in whose fictional name ("royal stone") there remains an echo of the arid Sicilian landscape, ironically coupled with a hint at the pompous history of the island. As an *engagé* moralist, Sciascia uses this landscape and this history as a recurrent subject of his work, both as a narrator and an essayist. In particular, in the long story "Il quarantotto" he deals with the same events and the same setting that are treated by Verga, Pirandello, and Lampedusa in the passages we have analyzed so far, but he completely reverses their perspective at every level, from the stylistic to the ideological, because he knows historical facts can be subverted.

For Sciascia, this is done not merely to avoid investing his narrator with an objectivity or an impersonality that is no longer historically justified. By taking up the story in the first person, he allows his proletarian narrator to achieve a pro-

---

[41] Eco, *A Theory*, p. 290.
[42] Ibid., p. 312, n. 52.

gressive *prise de conscience* that is historical and political as well as personal. This *prise de conscience*, while agreeing with its famous predecessors in its objective evaluation of historical, political, and social events, and of the mechanisms that produced them, reverses their pragmatic and ideological direction. In other words, the narrator of "Il quarantotto" is not one of the vanquished like Gesualdo, nor is he disillusioned like the old and the young protagonists of Pirandello, nor is he a lucid elegiac figure like Lampedusa's prince. Instead he is an active and fighting character, notwithstanding his defeats and disappointments, and his parenthetical asides within the text seem to reinforce the subjectivity of his testimony:

> (I am writing these memoirs as I am sheltered, in solitude, in a country house near Campobello. Loyal friends have helped me to escape arrest; at Castro *carabinieri* and soldiers are looking for me; just as once the Bourbon soldiers and guards, so now *carabinieri* and soldiers of the kingdom of Italy arrest the men who fight for the future of other men, at Castro and in every town in Sicily. I feel remorse for having escaped arrest; but prison frightens me, I am tired and old. Writing seems a means of finding consolation and rest, a way of finding myself again finally in a destiny of truth, outside life's contradictions.)[43]

Through the eyes of this narrator we are told the facts of how the old landed aristocracy of Sicily was able to take advantage of the potentially revolutionary action of Garibaldi in order to retain power. In relation to these historical facts (and also in the context of Sciascia's whole oeuvre), the title of the story is significant. The epigraph (taken from Gaetano Peruzzo's Sicilian-Italian dictionary) explains it in its historical as well as its metaphorical implications: "QUARANTOTTU, n. disorder, confusion. 1. From the events of 1848 in Sicily. 2. *Fari lu quarantottu, finiri a quarantottu, apprufittari di lu quarantottu*, fig.

[43] Leonardo Sciascia, "Il quarantotto," in *Gli zii di Sicilia* (Turin: Einaudi, 1962), pp. 95–163, quotation on p. 110. All page references will be to this edition. On Sciascia and Lampedusa, see Walter Mauro, *Sciascia* (Florence: Le Monnier, 1974), pp. 66–91; and Giovanna Ghetti Abruzzi, *Leonardo Sciascia e la Sicilia* (Rome: Bulzoni, 1974), chapters 10 and 11.

stands for: to produce confusion, to take advantage of the confusion" (p. 95).

No wonder, then, that the only landscape into which the narrator delves at the beginning of the story (and returns to at the end) is quite different from those others that are already so familiar to us:

> My father used to take care of Baron Garziano's garden, a small piece of land fanning out around the palace; a land so rich that planting a pole would yield water, a black earth crowded with trees. There it seemed as if one were in the middle of night, inside that blackness of trees and earth, even if the sun was a scorching flame: there was coolness, as in caves, a sound of water that induced sleep and even fear, birds calling gaily to one another and sudden silences torn by the cry of the jay. The baron called it a garden because there were also magnolias and Indian trees with trunks that looked like masses of ropes, and branches that, like ropes, fell down to take root in the earth; and there was also, in the short semi-circle around the house, a rose hedge that during the month of May would light up with large roses that would soon be overblown. And the house, which the baron called the "palace," was large and ugly like a farmer's on the garden side, and equally ugly on the side facing the street, with two naked women in sandstone on the sides of the door, and big cats' heads under the balconies. (p. 97)

> In the garden the baron had the tables set; there were carafes of wine, pastries and cakes, and under the trees ice cream containers were lined up. Italian flags hung from the branches above. The baron said, "You, my lords, are guests in my house. . . ." Garibaldi, following him with his glance, said, "These Sicilians: what a great heart they have, what a passion they put in their things." (p. 160)

The most remarkable fact about this landscape is not so much that it is a //garden// of the nobility existing somewhere in Sicily in 1848 and 1860, a //garden//, by the way, that is seen with a very critical eye (only "a small piece of land," a "short semicircle," a land too "black" and "crowded with trees" whose trunks look "like masses of ropes," and "a rose hedge that during the month of May would light up with large roses that would soon be overblown"—not to mention the distancing notation: "the baron called it a garden," just as he called the house a "palace"). Hence it is a pompous and at the same time a meager //garden//, filtered through a very precise, Voltairean, demystifying design. Rather, the remarkable fact about this landscape is that it is precisely and deliberately a /garden/ rather than a /Petraio/, if one is to understand Sciascia's choice in the intertextual play of expectations created by the establishment of the Verghian code. Therefore this landscape must be read as a «garden», the *locus amoenus* in which serious historical events happened, but in which it should be possible for everyone, not just a privileged few, to live well.

The garden as hope, then. And in the story, a historical character is charged with the task of being the spokesman for this hope. He is Garibaldi's superintendent, "a young man with clear-cut features, a high forehead, his eyes continually veering from attention to boredom, from suavity to coldness." He is Ippolito Nievo, whose function is that of a historical guarantor, but above all that of the pre-Verghian literary model for the discourse that Sciascia is also performing through his emblematic «garden»:

"Because," Nievo said, "I believe in the Sicilians who speak little, in the Sicilians who do not get excited, in the Sicilians who worry inside and suffer: the poor people who greet us with a tired gesture, as if from a distance of centuries; and Colonel Carini, always so silent and apart, kneaded with melancholy and boredom but ready for action at any moment: a man who seems not to have any hopes, yet he is the heart itself of hope—the silent, fragile hope of the best Sicilians . . . a hope, I should say, that fears itself, that fears words and instead has death close and familiar. . . . These persons need to be known and loved in what they keep silent about, in the words they nurture in their hearts and do not speak." (p. 161)

This fragile hope, these silent words are perhaps the most eloquent and humane message transmitted so far to the reader through the written words of the Sicilian landscape. Discovered by an emblematic «Nievo» in an equally emblematic «garden», they cause a shift in a whole literary and ideological discourse that Sciascia has profoundly renewed, not to say made possible.

In fact, it is with an epigraph from Sciascia that Vincenzo Consolo begins his own novel *Il sorriso dell'ignoto marinaio*,[44] a book that cannot be examined here in detail as it deserves, but has as its foundation an encyclopaedic project (with an Enlightenment flavor) and a skilful and refined elaboration of literary languages and codes (à la Gadda). This project and this elaboration are not opposed but unified by a wholly modern awareness of ideology and metanarrativity.[45] Hence Consolo can freely utilize segments of Verga's, Pirandello's, Lampedusa's, and Sciascia's landscape codes (not to mention other authors and other codes), without being totally conditioned by any of them in particular.

The protagonist of the novel is Baron Enrico Pirajno di Mandralisca. Like Lampedusa's Prince Salina, he is a scientist (interested in malacology, the science of real as well as metaphorical snails) and an art connoisseur; and like Sciascia's Nievo, he understands the silence of the Sicilians:

What has history been so far, dear friend? A continuous writing by the privileged ones. . . . And even the writing by us so-called enlightened ones is an imposture, perhaps greater than that of those who are obtuse and confused by their privileges and caste passion. Let us add a question: beside the language, do we hold the key, the cipher

---

[44] Vincenzo Consolo, *Il sorriso dell'ignoto marinaio* (Turin: Einaudi, 1976). All page references will be to this edition.

[45] Another example of such a metanarrative conscience, ideologically different but perhaps somewhat pertinent to our subject, is found in Alberto Arbasino, *Specchio delle mie brame* (Turin: Einaudi, 1974). This is a "pseudo-libertine short novel," a *divertissement*, a true, narrative meta-kitsch in which Sicily is a mere pretext ("the usual Sicily can always do," p. 3), Verga becomes "the Tennessee Williams of the Deep South Italian-style" (p. 56), and the Leopard is transformed into an erotomaniac She-Leopard.

of being, feeling and resenting of all this people? We do hold as safe our own code, the code of our way of being and speaking, which we have imposed upon everyone else: the code of the right of property and possession, the political code of the acclaimed freedom and unity of Italy, the code of heroism, like that of Garibaldi the *condottiero* and all his followers, the code of poetry and science, the code of justice, or that of a sublime and remote utopia. (p. 97)

Mandralisca understands that behind the bloody revolts of the Sicilian peasants in 1860 (such as that at Alcàra Li Fusi, which is narrated in the novel with echoes from analogous events at Bronte that were related in Verga's story "Libertà")[46] there is "the true, material, eternal earth." Thus he "acts" coherently in the only way that seems logical and possible to him:

Ah the earth! It is because of it that the people of Alcàra rose, like the people of other towns—Biancavilla, Bronte— never because of snails. To act then, Interdonato? Not I, not I! The only worthy action I am about to do is that of

[46] Cf. Giovanni Verga, "Freedom," in *The She-Wolf and Other Stories*, tr. by Giovanni Cecchetti (Berkeley: University of California Press, 1973). A very persuasive example can be seen in the episode of the murder of Neddu, the public notary's son which ends with these words: "Another man shouted: 'Eh! After all, he would have been a notary too!' " (p. 209). Here is the analogous episode, evoked in one of the anonymous graffiti recorded by Mandralisca in Consolo's novel (p. 123): "I drag Turuzzo/ the notary's nephew outside/ I clutch him between my thighs/ with scissors I cut his throat/ he too would have been a notary." In the description of the revolt at Alcàra Li Fusi, Consolo has used many other writers beside Verga as his models (from Dante to Byron and the grandguignolesque Guerrazzi, p. 105). And even as far as Verga is concerned, Consolo must have taken into consideration Sciascia's own historical and ideological comments, which are outlined in "Verga e la libertà," in *La corda pazza* (Turin: Einaudi, 1970), pp. 79–94. It might be useful to point out that Verga's *Mastro-don Gesualdo* and "La libertà," taken together, clearly express the social struggles out of which the new landowning bourgeoisie in the south (the *galantuomini*) arose, according to Emilio Sereni, "at the expense of the nobility" but also and above all at the expense "of the large peasant masses." *Storia del paesaggio agrario italiano* (Bari: Laterza, 1961), pp. 346ff.

leaving my home and my estate for a school, to teach the sons of the people in this town of mine, Cefalù. So that, as I hope, their history, history itself, will be written by them, not by me, or by you, Interdonato, or a paid-for scribe, all by force of birth, by rank or by inclination ready to inscribe the pages with decorations, flourishes, aerial spirals, labyrinths. . . . Snails. (p. 100)

While visiting the Piranesian, snail-shell-like prison where some of the rioters were locked away, Mandralisca discovers their words, their graffiti, on the walls, and becomes their interpreter-advocate with Giovanni Interdonato, the lawyer from Messina who was first a conspirator and is now the public prosecutor who must decide "about the life of men who acted violently, yes, who can deny that? but were driven by much more serious violences perpetrated by others, centuries-old martyrdoms, abuses, oppressions, deceits" (p. 101). Hence the scientist moves from the collection of shells to the reading of the prison walls and becomes the intellectual who is aware that:

In ancient times they said *cochlìas legere*, in the sense of collecting shells along the shores as a pastime and a pleasant hobby. But now we *read this snail* as a dutiful task, with bitterness and at the same time with hope . . . : to know that history that comes from the depth, vortex-like; and to imagine as well the history that will be made in the future. (p. 120)

The result is a small *Spoon River Anthology* of oppressed and poor people, whose few bare words stand out all the more because they are inserted into the luxuriant language of the contemporary author and the artificial jargon of the judiciary records and official reports of the time in which they occurred. However, in the background there are always the two extreme poles of the code of the Sicilian landscape: those of Verga and Sciascia. Here is the rocky Sicily of Verga:

Peppe Sirna was at Baron Manca's "Sollazzo Verde" [a place called Green Delight], as if cut into it. Since dawn he had been working hard with his hoe, a blow after another, panting, hah hah, on that hard crust of the stony ground sloping down the hill, with just stale bread and water as his only meal at noon. Bent. His shirt, waistcoat and neckerchief all dripping with sweat, in that May sun which was still biting his shoulders. And he worked, with fury and passion, tied to the hope that those few yards of land perhaps soon, tomorrow, maybe. . . . And he did not know any longer he was a man, Giuseppe Sirna Papa, born at Alcàra, twenty-six years old, hired hand, son of Giuseppe, husband of Serafina. . . . And he did not know of the place, the hour and the season. There was only the screeching of his hoe on the soil and the rocks, and he stood enchanted after it, hah hah, like a blind donkey after the screeching of the pail at a well. (p. 85)

And here is the *locus amoenus*, which is not the equivalent of Verga's Canziria (a pause, a refreshment, a contemplation), but is Sciascia's polemical landscape of hope, because it is the place where the hired hands meet (among them Peppe Sirna) in order to organize the revolt:

The mountains were clear-cut in their dark blue masses against the clean, violet sky. One could still make out the reddish bastions of fortresses, the flowing veins of brooks, narrow at the top, then broadening down toward the rivers; at the foot and on the slopes of the mountains was the mobile, silvery gray foliage of the olive trees, and here and there, in the plain, the intense flame of poppies, the yellow of wheat, the shivering azure of flax. And one could make out the winding paths, passes, tracks; and the groups of peasants, with donkeys and goats, shepherds and hired hands returning from distant fields— Comune, Mangalavite, Scavioli, Bacco, Lémina, Murà. They were gathering festively, converging downward, toward the hidden hollow of Santa Marecùma. (p. 87)

In Consolo, the multiplication of names is a sure sign of an encyclopaedic and hence illuministic purpose lurking under the novel's lyrical, baroque appearances. Therefore, I shall conclude my long *excursus* on the Sicilian landscape code with

Mandralisca's reference to the hired hands, the poor wretches who do not share the values of the hegemonic class:

> Ah, a time will come when they, by themselves, will take over those values and speak of them with new words, words that are true for them and therefore for us too, true because names will be entirely filled by things. (p. 98)

These are well-wishing and hopeful words that also hold true for the critic who deals with mimesis and realism, and for the semiotician who studies the referents of cultural signs. In our vision of a sublime and remote utopia, a time will come when names will be entirely filled by things.

I BELIEVE THAT THE FIRST QUESTION TO BE
ASKED TODAY IS NOT "WHAT TO DO?" BUT
"WHAT TO THINK?" THEREFORE THE RE-
SPONSIBILITY OF THE INTELLECTUAL CLASS
IS THE FOREMOST AND THE GREATEST
OF ALL.

Nicola Chiaromonte

THE IDEA-CONTENT OF A WORK IS ITS
STRUCTURE. AN IDEA IN ART IS ALWAYS A
MODEL, FOR IT RECONSTRUCTS AN IMAGE
OF REALITY. CONSEQUENTLY, AN ARTISTIC
IDEA IS INCONCEIVABLE OUTSIDE
A STRUCTURE.

Yuri Lotman

Four. The Red or the Black

As HE THUS seemed to be gliding down, he thought:
"The horrible thing about our modern society is that it
lacks all right of asylum. If I get terror-stricken, if I am
pursued, whither am I to go for refuge? . . . I know where
my redemption would lie; in becoming a peasant and
tilling the soil,—a workman, even at the Adsum,—a sailor
on a vessel that would require six months to make its
voyage. But who'll take me? What trade am I good for?
Why, I'm a good-for-nothing! I'm an intellectual!"

He was close to the wall that the crowd was [lapping
on, flowing by]. As he was still very weak, one of the
mob, skirting along the wall in the opposite direction,
involuntarily thrust him off the sidewalk and cast him
into the human stream. Now he was a prey to fear. . . .
He raised his coat collar, despite the intense heat, so as
to hide his bourgeois aspect. But precisely because of this
he was recognized and they cried to him in scorn: "Cry

115

'Hurrah for Lenin!' " And he repeated: *"Hurrah for Lenin.*
Hurrah for Russia!" in a stifling voice, so as to save his
hide. . . . "Yes," he thought. "Bolshevism,—universal
prison barracks. But there'll be a place for every one in
that prison. And every one will be equal and anonymous."
Somebody thrust a red rag into his fist, and he seized
it. Another said to him: "Here, grab this; it's prettier,"
and stuck a black flag into his hand. In his left hand he
held the red flag and in his right the black. He staggered
along zig-zag, trying to reach the head of the procession
and work his way free. . . . When he had almost reached
his objective he heard another shout: "The cavalry!" And
this came from the human stream. It seemed as if the
crowd, pronouncing that word, seethed like foam. He
heard it with a vast delight. The cavalry was coming. It
would disperse the mob. He was free. . . .
The street ended in a large square, and the entire front
of this square was crammed with the cavalry. They looked
to him like the waves of the Lago Maggiore in the tempest,—these grey-green cavalrymen with the crested helmets.
As he gazed at the narrow empty space, which was
already filling in, still another thought came to him, as
dazzling as a discovery: "Eugenia was at the station this
morning. But it was my fate to follow the Unknown Traveller."
Then there was just enough time left for him to catch
a glimpse of the first cavalryman that struck him. He was
a very young man, blond, with a calm, kindly face. Certainly his eyes were the colour of the sky.

This is the concluding sequence of chapter five, part four, of
the novel *Rubè* by Giuseppe Antonio Borgese (published in
1921 but little known today),[1] and the scene it sets is the

[1] Giuseppe Antonio Borgese, *Rubè*, tr. by Isaac Goldberg (New York: Harcourt, Brace, 1923), pp. 383–86. All subsequent quotations will refer to this
edition. I have amended and/or completed the translation whenever necessary, indicating my changes within brackets.

Fig. 6. Umberto Boccioni (1882–1916), *The City Rises*,
1910, Galleria Civica d'Arte Moderna, Turin.

closest literary homologue that exists to the kind of painting
exemplified by Umberto Boccioni's *The City Rises*. Even without pursuing the homology, it is apparent that both the painting and the literary text deal with social as well as formal
problems that had a great impact on Italian culture in the
early twentieth century.

Let us look at the novel more closely. In the sequence under
examination, we find not only the climax of the story concerning the protagonist, Filippo Rubè, but also the strictly
literary and stylistic motifs of the work, as well as evidence
of the author's sociopolitical perspective. This sequence is
therefore a "hypersign" consisting of various textual levels,
of which in the following analysis I wish to concentrate above
all on "the form of the content," that is, "the structural unity
of the thematic, symbolic and ideological levels."[2]

First of all, I shall proceed by "inferences" from the proposed text,[3] which, going back to the context and the circum-

[2] Maria Corti, *An Introduction to Literary Semiotics*, tr. by Margherita Bogat
and Allen Mandelbaum (Bloomington: Indiana University Press, 1978), p.
106.

[3] Umberto Eco, *A Theory of Semiotics* (Bloomington: Indiana University Press,
1975), p. 17; cf. also the notion of extra-coding, p. 136.

stances, and then to the sender's codes and subcodes, should synchronically as well as diachronically explain the possible interpretive hypotheses of Borgese's idiolect.[4]

The Thematic Level

Assuming as an initial working hypothesis that Filippo Rubè is a deliberately emblematic antihero (intended as a cluster of signs constituting a theme, hence a code), the following characteristics will be immediately noted in the sequence under examination:

(1) "He thought" (repeated twice, with a third variant: "Still another thought came to him"): contemplation, logic.

(2) "He seemed to be gliding down," "they looked to him like the waves," and also "it seemed as if the crowd" (impersonal, but clearly referring to the protagonist's viewpoint): imagination, hypersensitivity.

(3) "A good-for-nothing," "an intellectual," "his bourgeois aspect": self-consciousness of social status and personal ineptitude (see also the clause "he was still very weak").

(4) "Fear," "to save his hide": a psychological condition of passivity. The only verbs denoting action on Rubè's part are "he repeated: 'Hurrah for Lenin' " (precisely "to save his hide"), "he staggered along zig-zag" (to underline the complete confusion or availability of the man with two opposing flags), and "trying to reach the head of the procession" (weak-willed direction). In all the other cases it can well be said that Rubè is acted upon: "one of the mob . . . thrust . . . and cast him," "somebody thrust a red rag into his fist," "another stuck a black flag into his hand," "the first cavalryman that struck him."

(5) "Our modern society" without "all rights of asylum" hints at an obscure sense if not of persecution at least of culpability.

(6) Bolshevism as a "universal prison barracks" in which "every one will be equal and anonymous" is the public and

[4] These and similar notions are systematically developed by Eco in *The Role of the Reader* (Bloomington: Indiana University Press, 1979).

historical projection of private preoccupations and obsessions, an abandonment to the irrational, with a related renunciation of individual identity and preeminence.

(7) "It was my fate to follow the Unknown Traveller" again expresses passivity (to *follow*), the mediation of the Other and, even more than fatalism, the acknowledgment and the acceptance of chance. The irrational is doubly embodied in the Traveller (a sememe leading not only to "travel" but also, through the capital initial, to "Authority") who is Unknown (a semantic marker that denies an actual, rational, knowledge).

From the very beginning of the novel, with a narrative movement that would be recalled by Vitaliano Brancati in *Il bell'Antonio* more than twenty years later, Borgese introduces Filippo Rubè as one of those "provincial youths who descend upon Rome with a lawyer's degree," but is endowed with "a logical mind capable of splitting a hair into four, an oratorical fire that burned his opponent's argument to the bone, and a certain faith that he had great things in him. This had been implanted in his heart by his father, who was the [town clerk] at Calinni, and who, well acquainted with the *Aeneid* in Latin and the life of Napoleon in French, considered everybody in the world—beginning with himself—an intruder with the exception of geniuses and heroes" (p. 3).

One immediately notices the derisory linking of the town clerk at Calinni, the *Aeneid*, and Napoleon. However, the fact remains that the ideal of greatness (*i.e.*, the shadow of the father) will be a determining factor in Rubè's life, marking the limit of an aspiration that is unreasonable with the forces available to him (at both the psychological and the economic level). This ideal also connotes the precise cultural point of reference against which the figure of the character as antihero is deliberately conceived and directed. Let us read the eloquent monologue on p. 322: "Bravoes, throw all these books into the fire; ten thousand, one hundred thousand volumes! Obey the Great Inquisitor, the Most Reverend Father Mariani! All of them, without exception! St. Helena's Memoirs, Stendhal, Nietzsche, D'Annunzio. All into the fire, dead or live superman!" Here the reader is explicitly warned; here the literary and cultural code (a Romantic and decadent one) necessary to interpret Rubè by antithesis is explicitly declared.

The death of the father and the beginning of World War I are the two events that set Rubè's novelistic story in motion— exactly as, two years later, in 1923, they will serve as both the beginning and the conclusion of the story of another antihero, Svevo's by now famous Zeno. All the characteristics noted in the sequence we have just examined recur in the plot of the novel and color its events. Thus it seems unnecessary to quote, or even to list, all the places where Rubè's contemplative attitude is at the center of the narration. Instead it will be sufficient merely to cite the most effective and meaningful examples. In these, contemplation is articulated into logic (which is analytic, introspective, dissecting) and imagination (tormenting, irrational, yet "logical"), both of which nurture each other and both of which by themselves constitute, through their powerful and obsessive prevalence, the substance of the "facts," which can be minimal when compared with the inner resonance of which they are the occasion and the pretext.

Rubè's logic is presented in a series of powerful, deadly images: "he ravelled and unravelled skeins of mad logic, denying all justification to himself, to others, to life" (p. 167); "and now again he began to spin his ratiocinations, fatally, as a spider spins its fibre. He was like a head that has just been chopped off upon the guillotine, but whose brain, through some miraculous intervention, continues to think, though severed from life and without a heart" (p. 226); "To extinguish this brooding conscience of mine needs death. Enough. Extinguish my conscience? It illuminates me like a veritable searchlight, enough to drive a fellow mad!" (p. 322).

In other cases, the narrator delegates the task of describing Rubè's logic to secondary but essential characters, such as Eugenia: "This maniacal self-introspection, this adoption of a convex lens to magnify the slightest things and reason them out (and, as Filippo explained, the lens concentrated the rays of the sun and burned what it was supposed to clarify) were among the chief causes of Filippo's ruination" (p. 264). For Father Mariani, Rubè is "the devotee of a religion that subjects the reality of the human being to the frenzy of reason, which confuses thought with action" (p. 317).

Imagination, like logic, is also a powerful force in Rubè: "his unbridled imagination shot through things like a flash of dazzling rays, corrupting his intelligence with a poisoned breath" (p. 50); after Celestina's death, he thinks about all its possible consequences, and among them is that of "cradling, perhaps within five months or little more, his own child in the same arms that had atrociously clasped a corpse beneath the water" (p. 297); he also recognizes his "horrendous disorder of imagination" in his reply to Father Mariani's arguments (p. 322, trans. mine).

Dissecting and introspective logic, imagination, and hypersensitivity all contribute to determine one of Rubè's fundamental conditions at the beginning of the novel: examining himself after an air raid, he fears he has been afraid (as Gérard Genot has perceptively noted):[5]

and gradually, gradually as he explored it, the emotion assumed inordinate proportions. At first he told himself that it was pity for his country at war, for the blood that was about to flow; and he was able to doze off. But toward the middle of the night he suddenly awoke in the fierce conviction that he had been afraid. Suffocated by shameful desperation, he feared that he would shriek this out; he got up; he dressed himself; hundred of times he measured the narrow length and breadth of the room, with the soul of a prisoner condemned to death. (p. 41)

It should be noted that such a feeling of shame at being fearful is more important than the fear itself (whether true or supposed), since it refers not so much to the character's psychology as to the cultural and social values by which he is molded, to that concept of honor the bourgeoisie inherited from the aristocracy. It is interesting that in dealing with aristocratic Russian culture of the eighteenth century, Lotman has emphasized how "the sphere of shame tends to become

[5] Gérard Genot, "La première guerre mondiale et le roman: l'Italie. *Rubè de Borgese,*" *Archives des Lettres Modernes,* vol. 2 (1968), n. 86, pp. 40–42.

the only governing factor of behavior, asserting itself precisely in those manifestations that imply that *to be afraid is a cause of shame*. To this concept are linked . . . the obligation of military courage during wars and the absolute value of boldness as such."[6] These words are thoroughly applicable to Rubè, and certainly not by chance.

As it appears in the sequence just quoted from the novel, hypersensitivity is strictly connected with contemplation. In this context, one should also remember the following passages: when Rubé analyzes his own body piece by piece, noting its physical as well as spiritual sensations (p. 327); when he imagines the beginning of the war ("Filippo, beholding the shot, had himself mentally added the click of the trigger," p. 11); when he, with microscopic attention, notices "that sort of shudder which rippled over upon Signora Rubè's nude skin" (p. 210); or when, listening to the bells tolling, he feels "as if he were bound in torture within one of those bells, devoured by a vortex of meaningless, pitiless sounds, with two rills of blood flowing from his tormented ears" (p. 353); or again, when "he had the sensation of the various layers rising from his brain like the peel of an onion being fried; his tendons were growing stiff as ropes dried in the sun after a rain" (p. 365).

Such hypersensitivity is the psychological prerequisite for the stylistic expressionism that is often noticeable in the novel.[7] It produces a continuous tension in Rubè, whose eyes are "somewhat hollow and hallucinated" the first time he passes in front of a mirror (p. 4), a movement that is typical of certain Pirandellian characters. Another time, in an even more Pirandellian fashion, "he was surprised, as he passed the mirror, to find himself mimicking the grimaces of the lunatic" (p. 137).

---

[6] Yuri Lotman, "Semiotica dei concetti di 'vergogna' e 'paura' " in Yuri Lotman and Boris Uspensky, *Tipologia della cultura*, Italian tr. (Milan: Bompiani, 1975), p. 274.

[7] Particularly meaningful examples are on pp. 31, 97, 168, 172, 189, 226, 247, 255, 352–53, and 383. There are grotesque distortions of images (monattos' carts, dentures, teeth), verbs with a high metaphoric potential (*fosforeggiare*), and violent colors (especially red).

This same hypersensitivity gives rise to the psychosomatic diseases by which Rubè is tormented (stomachaches, spasms in the throat, exhaustion, neurasthenia, dyspepsia, hypochondria, and so on). These ailments characterize the protagonist as an antihero and possess—or, better, achieve—a metaphoric but no less real dimension in that "hidden evil" that is his incapacity to live. They are also the single and recurring occasions of his own desire for a (real and serious) sickness as a flight from responsibility.[8] The great importance of this aspect of Rubè's character clearly appears on a contextual level in that it constitutes a motif tied to the similar and complementary ones of the train, war, sleep, prison, and death.[9] At an intertextual level, it is part of a great literary theme that continues even today—as seen, for instance, in Gadda's Gonzalo.[10] A particularly effective example, also because of the deliberately Marinettian and Dannunzian echoes, is the following, in which Rubè, while traveling on a train, "ever so gradually . . . felt himself become depersonalized, and he tasted the felicity of the journey, as dragging as opium fumes and similar to what he had imagined in moments of utter exhaustion, during which he would invoke some lethal disease such as typhus or meningitis that would exonerate him from the government of himself and turn him over to the [will] of others." But he knows that only his soul is sick, and that is precisely why he has chosen the life of the army:

The open air, fatigue, the renunciation of his free will, the freedom from pecuniary worriment and the cares of

[8] The motif of disease in its various articulations can be seen particularly on pp. 4, 5, 7, 14–16, 19, 21–22, 44, 64, 68–69, 72–73, 113–14, 142, 147–48, 165, 174, 187, 230, 267, 268–70, 298–99, 305–306, 322, 327, 347, 349, 352, 365. It is quite a presence, even from a purely quantitative viewpoint.

[9] In this connection, see Luciano De Maria, "Introduzione," in G. A. Borgese, Rubè (Milan: Oscar Mondadori, 1974), pp. x–xiii; and, above all, Mario Isnenghi, Il mito della grande guerra da Marinetti a Malaparte (Bari: Laterza, 1970).

[10] I have dealt with this theme in Literary Diseases (Austin: University of Texas Press, 1975). Referring to the inquisitional aspect of consciousness, it should be noted that Borgese transforms Filippo into "Don Felipe," just as Gadda (recalling Don Quixote as well) calls Gonzalo "Hidalgo" in Acquainted With Grief.

a career, would bring back his freshness and spontaneity. The war that was to prove *the healing of the world* would be his medicine, too. (p. 22, italics added)

Imprisonment in a certain manner was equivalent to what in other days he had hoped military service and war would be: an exemption by superior order from the obligation of making decisions in daily life. . . . Better still, it resembled the deep, torpid illness that the unfortunate invokes when he finds himself caught in an inextricable crisis,—the kindly typhus that gradually restores him to nature and society, which renders him as inert and inept as when he lay in his mother's womb. (pp. 297–98)[11]

After reading these passages, one understands how, by the end of the novel, Rubè can think of Bolshevism as a universal prison in which everyone will be equal and nameless.

This namelessness leads one to a consideration of the problem of the name, the sign of personal identity, which is strictly connected with Rubè's psychic regression.[12] It is a further aspect of his existential and social crisis, especially in the second half of the novel. Here there are nuances that inevitably recall Pirandello:

Again he was struck by this unexpected sound of his name, pronounced peasant fashion, with double r and double b. He had forgotten it, and thought that he was called only Rubè or Burè or Morello. "Four names," he said to himself. "And why not ten, a hundred, an infinite number, which would be the same as not having any? What sort of thing is this label branded in fire upon my flesh? This mark? Not to have a name! To disappear! Or else be called only Rubbè, as they called me when I was a child!" (p. 350)

---

[11] As De Maria has noted, the network of war-train-sleep-death, which is often connected with disease, also takes up a large space in the novel and gives its text a solid structure.

[12] Apropos of the problem of the name, one should also remember the episode of the anonymous soldier (pp. 135–38), because of both its immediate consequences on Rubè and its thematic echoes throughout the novel (e.g., p. 171).

If here Borgese's text anticipates *Uno, nessuno e centomila*, literally by four years, with the following example we should go back to *Il fu Mattia Pascal*:

"I'm really the unknown traveller. Unrecognizable. I've changed appearance. I've no card of identification upon me." "If I only were an unknown traveller! " he added. "Unknown to myself and to others. Nameless. Without memory." (p. 372)

The intertextual echo from *Il fu Mattia Pascal* (particularly chapter six) is even stronger and more obvious in another passage of *Rubè* when Filippo, "fanatically certain that luck was with him" (p. 236), gambles and wins a considerable sum of money, which allows him to flee his family, triggering a series of events that culminate first in the encounter with Celestina Lambert at Isola Bella, then in her death during a storm on Lake Maggiore, and finally in his own death during the cavalry charge at Bologna, after a hallucinatory series of travels throughout Italy: "all at once he saw himself rolling in the form of an ivory ball across the cloth of a billiard table. 'In fact Italy is as green as a billiard table. . . . Now this game that *I'm being shot about in*—is it the first stroke or the last?' " (p. 370, italics added). "Played" by chance, Rubè abandons himself to it completely:

He took out his watch and glanced at a hazard at the second dial. If the hand were between thirty and sixty, Eugenia would answer; if it were in the other half-circle, she would not. Or else he would open the book. If, at the page he opened, the tens were odd, she would answer; if the tens were even, she wouldn't. He even selected words from the context and counted the letters. Here, too, an uneven number was favorable, while an even was adverse. The fates thus consulted answered Yes, No, No, Yes, alternately, or in uneven series such as those of the roulette. (p. 376)

Later on Rubè, who has followed the "Unknown Traveller" at Bologna without seeing Eugenia, comments: "I never in my life believed in anything but Fortune, so that it's only just for Chance to decide. It decided, in the first place, on the reefs of San Maurizio. Now it decides on appeal in Bologna" (pp. 381–82). At the level of the character, such an abandonment to the irrational is more than justified psychologically: it corresponds perfectly to a deep attitude of Rubè's, strengthened by the historical and political circumstances under which he has lived, with disillusionment, during and after World War I. In this sense, the results of Genot's analysis should be read as a necessary prerequisite for Isnenghi's conclusions.

But there are also two other fundamental attitudes of Rubè's character, attitudes that derive from his self-awareness as a bourgeois intellectual: an obscure sense of guilt, of having to be judged always by others, and a clear and shattering perception of his own mediocrity, of being unfit, unable, inept.

The first attitude often follows his excessive and fantastic meditations: "he pronounced these atrocious insults with well-ordered oratorical complacency, as if they referred to some *accused party* or other" (p. 72, italics added); or "This is not delirium, [gentlemen. There are documented, palpable facts, gentlemen. The *findings* of the *proceedings* on this point are irrefutable]" (p. 322, trans. mine, italics added). Here the legal language is effectively coupled with the oratorical (Pirandellian) gesture of that "gentlemen, gentlemen," which technically speaking is an illocutionary act, involving the reader as a judge or a jury member. The legal language is also tied to the moral-religious one, as in the dialogue with Father Mariani. But perhaps the most meaningful passage is the following:

> Nothing compelled him to get off before that terminal. No military order, for example, no order of arrest. As a boy, he continued to recall, whenever he came upon any officers, he would stumble all over himself as if his feet were tired, though he certainly had been robbing no [peaches] from the stands. (p. 326)

Here one cannot help but recall Svevo's Zeno in the analogous episode in front of the newspaper stand. Other corollaries of this sense of guilt can be seen in Rubè's "unwittingly [giving] the right hand" to Garlandi, whom he has just met, and his stepping "half a pace backward as if Garlandi were his superior" (p. 26); or in his uneasiness in front of the "Unknown Traveller": "having adjusted himself as best he could, he felt the need of saying, 'Beg your pardon' " (p. 364), but "the eyes of that man opposite were inexorable, like those of certain pictures of saints or portraits of one's ancestors, which, from whatever part of the room they are looked upon, seem to fix their gaze upon the looker" (p. 367).

As for the second attitude (Rubè's perception of his ineptitude), it is immediately prefigured in the mention of his "absent-mindedness" (p. 29), the cause of the act *manqué* from which the shipwreck on the lake will derive (p. 284). But above all, it can well be said that Rubè's diversity, that is, his alienation at the intersubjective level, is realized in this very attitude. The examples are numerous: his peers in the army "were different. . . . They all appeared to him of Garlandi's type: adapted to life, as he defined them to himself" (p. 30); he considers himself "a cowardly wretch! His shadow, which followed him along the road, with the foppery and the [tightness] of his military uniform, seemed to him [an obscene] thing" (p. 42; I am reminded here of Eugenio Montale's "man who goes about sure of himself" and who "does not care about his shadow"); "He asked himself whether this imprecision of his memory might not be the cause of his inadaptability to happiness, of his constant detached and sated feeling" (p. 92); "it seemed that he had become a stranger in the company and in the battalion" (p. 102); the first time he faces an enemy soldier, "he needed but to raise his gun to kill him. But killing was not his affair, and in a moment he felt his forearm strangely weak and heavy" (pp. 118–19; one can think of Michele, in Alberto Moravia's *Gl'indifferenti*, who, when he decides to shoot Leo, forgets to load the gun); or again, like Svevo's Emilio in *Senilità*, "he was almost thirty-five years old and had learned nothing" (p. 191).

Rubè's diversity is made more anguishing by the continuous counterpoint of his desire to be the same as the others, "an average man" (p. 24): "And he came to the conclusion that it did not pay to be one of those few in whom the thought of death and immortality becomes exasperating or enfeebles the sense of life. To be like all the others: this is what he thought wisdom" (p. 74). But Rubè is denied this wisdom:

he is the man of contradictions, of unresolved tensions. In a letter to Eugenia, his self-awareness takes on definitive tones, pertinent to a whole generation, to an entire historical epoch:

> I belong to that most unhappy intellectual, provincial bourgeoisie, spoiled by the education of all or nothing, vitiated by the taste for definitive ascensions from which panoramas are contemplated. Our hands have no callouses; their tendons are weak; we can't grasp a spade or a shovel; all we can grasp is the void. (p. 99)

His condittion is reiterated in a lapidary manner, by articulating the syllables of the key word: "The fact is that I'm an intellectual. An in-tel-lect-u-al" (p. 322).

After this series of quotations, it seems to me that there cannot be any doubt about the central role of the sign function "antihero" in *Rubè*. On the one hand, the character traits of the protagonist constitute the content of the plot of the novel, which therefore has been rightly called "a book of a deep, powerful, unforgettable sadness."[13] On the other hand, they make up a thematic unit that is essential for the organization of the text, in that they constitute true codes through which the author can send his message and generate "habits, acquired expectations, and mannerisms" (like those engendered by the establishment of Verga's landscape code, which was analyzed in the preceding chapter). As codes, therefore, these character traits allow us to place *Rubè* along the following intertextual and diachronic axis: D'Annunzio—Pirandello—Tozzi—Borgese—Svevo—Montale—Moravia (or rather Sperelli—Mattia—Remigio—Rubè—Zeno—Moscarda—Arsenio—Michele). This axis, proposed in part by Salvatore Battaglia on the historical-literary level,[14] clarifies the figure of the antihero in all of its relevance as a cultural code.

---

[13] Mario Robertazzi, "Introduzione," in G. A. Borgese, *La città assoluta e altri scritti* (Milan: Mondadori, 1962), p. 20.

[14] Salvatore Battaglia, *Mitografia del personaggio* (Milan: Rizzoli, 1970), pp. 355–56 and 540–41; cf. also pp. 350–55 on Andrea Sperelli, and pp. 527–33 on Giorgio Aurispa, to understand the presence of D'Annunzio. The only author not mentioned by Battaglia is Montale.

The Symbolic Level

So far I have followed Borgese's own strategy and presented the reader with the traditional critical categories (such as "character" and "psychology") that appear at first sight in a naturalistic, psychological novel.

But throughout *Rubè*, and in particular in the sequence with which this chapter began, there is a level of writing that gives the text self-reflexivity (as a deliberate literary construction), and that has rightly been defined as "symbolic" and "expressionistic" by De Maria, who has proposed an intelligent preliminary analysis of the novel's motives and its network of correspondences, symmetries, and premonitions.[15]

In the sequence under examination here, this level is articulated above all in the metaphoric texture that thickens around the sememes "human stream" (repeated twice and reinforced by verbs, equally metaphoric, such as "lapping," "flowing," "seethed [like foam]," "filling in"). This metaphoric texture reaches its peak in the explicit comparison with which the cavalry charge is described ("They looked to him like the waves of the Lago Maggiore in the tempest," with the further nuance of the "crested" helmets), and finally slackens in the last vision of the cavalryman: "certainly his eyes were the colour of the sky."

This metaphoric texture can also be found throughout the novel, recurring along the same lines: there is a first semantic field of water, organized according to the dichotomy between *stream* (or *torrent*) and *swamp* (or *pond*, or *stagnation*), which connotes *life*; then there is a second semantic field, also relating to water, that is organized according to the dichotomy between *swimming* and *drowning* (or *shipwrecking*), which connotes *death*; and finally there is a semantic sub-field that relates to cavalry, beginning with the very name of the protagonist (Filippo, meaning "lover of horses") and connected with the water-shipwreck fields. It is remarkable that the images of all these semantic fields, considered as expressions of taste, independent of their signification, were also fairly common mo-

---

[15] De Maria, pp. xv, xvi, and xx.

Fig. 7. Walter Crane (1845–1915), *Neptune's Horses*, 1893, Neue Pinakothek, Munich.

tifs in the symbolic painting of the late nineteenth and early twentieth centuries, especially in the Art Nouveau style that was widespread in Europe. One of its most renowned representatives was Walter Crane, whose *Neptune's Horses* is perhaps the most fitting iconological correlative of our text.

But let us return to literature, and particularly to *Rubè* and note that these main semantic fields are a fundamental feature of Borgese's novel. They clearly illustrate Lotman's assertion that at the basis of the inner organization of the elements of a text there is, "as a rule, the principle of binary semantic opposition."[16]

Not only the events of the plot, but the very ideology of the text-world depend on this opposition. This is particularly evident in *Rubè*, for two reasons: first, the semantic fields are interconnected through a substantial series of correspondences that are used to prepare the premonitions or narrative epiphanies of the plot; and second, in their ambivalence (each of them contains the life/death dichotomy) they are the indispensable formal equivalent of the divided and ambiguous

[16] Yuri Lotman, *The Structure of the Artistic Text*, tr. by Ronald Vroon (Ann Arbor: University of Michigan Press, 1977), p. 237. This notion should be connected with the semiotics of cultural space, which is examined by Lotman himself in "Il metalinguaggio delle descrizioni tipologiche della cultura," in Lotman and Uspensky, *Tipologia della cultura*, pp. 145–82.

figure of the antihero, who is moving between juxtaposed worlds.

Let us briefly examine the three semantic fields that were noted above:

(1) The whole of Rubè's life is described in the metaphoric terms of running or stagnating water, from his adolescence to his experience of the war, from his time in the Dolomites to his removal to Paris. And at the crucial moment of the shipwreck, the metaphoric language is fundamental: "Another wave passed. In that instant a sinister thought occurred to him. 'Here, here,' he said to himself, as he felt the swell of the wave lifting him, 'here are the waters of my life moving at last, and how! I can't say any more that I'm stuck in a swamp' " (pp. 287–88). Here the signifieds seem indeed to be self-generated from the corresponding signifiers, metaphor comes before reality, the symbol causes the thing (the event). And if one passes from the private to the public plane, the situation is similar. Let us read the description of a socialist rally, made by Rubè as a weak-willed challenge in the house of his capitalist employer, De Sonnaz:

> No shouting. Just posters, inscriptions, pictures of Lenin and political prisoners, grotesque and pitiless caricatures. There was a religion in that stream of humanity. . . . As that procession flowed by, one thought of a stream as yet without banks, that may become wild and pull up the largest trunks, but that in the end will fertilize the earth. (p. 217)

Here Rubè uses the same metaphors he employed to define his own life, and his fascinated words become the textual prefiguration of the final sequence at Bologna when his destiny is fulfilled.[17]

(2) Before speaking of the semantic field of swimming-drowning-shipwrecking at the metaphoric level, it is necessary to underscore the fact that it also works throughout the

[17] Other examples of this semantic field are on pp. 49, 86, 91, 92, 128, 155, 178, 180, 232, and 233. It is taken up in connection with other characters (pp. 23, 24, 34, 62, 73, 74, 111, 117, 147–48, 161, 162, 201, 224, 244) and is also linked with brief landscape descriptions throughout the text.

novel at the literal level. On the one hand, Mary Corelli narrates the shipwreck of the *Ulysses* (p. 59) and remembers having thought: "Oh, how lucky I was to have learned how to swim that summer on Long Island!" (p. 62); the same sentence, shortened and ironically reversed, is taken up twice by Rubè (pp. 64 and 256), and during the shipwreck, "the waters rumbling in his ears repeated: 'You learned to swim on Long Island' " (p. 288). On the other hand, Celestina Lambert often speaks of her fear of drowning (e.g., pp. 151, 256, 287); Rubè echoes this by telling her that the stormy lake is "the colour of a drowned man" (p. 285), and repeats to himself that "the chief thing was . . . not to let her drown as the Sultans do in the Bosphorous with their unfaithful odalisks" (p. 288).

This frequent intertwining of "swimming" and "drowning," even if it is not metaphoric, makes up the network of correspondences and premonitions of the novel; it also reinforces the metaphoric field gravitating around the protagonist. At Novesa, waiting for the war, the sound of a church bell seems to Rubè "as useless as if invoking impossible aid amidst the certainty of shipwreck" (p. 32); later on, in the *pensione*, "at the sound of the second bell [for lunch] it seemed to him that he was in a wreck, descending spirally into the echoing darkness of slumber" (p. 44); at the De Sonnaz home, Rubè acts "as one who is trying not to drown" (p. 218); Eugenia thinks of stretching out a hand "to save him who was, perhaps, drowning and yet was ashamed to cry for help" (p. 268); before the boat trip, Rubè is already "drowning in the perfume that was shed" by Celestina (p. 283); during the encounter with Father Mariani, he still hopes for "a glimpse of purification. . . . If not, off I go, like a capsized boat, adrift" (p. 311); Rubè also speaks of Federico's "nauseating, unbearable wisdom, recited, as if committed to memory, with the benevolent condescension of the safe and sound, who, from their place upon the shore, give lessons in swimming to the shipwrecked" (p. 335). But the final metaphor is left to Eugenia, who, after the events at Bologna, "had her own opinions upon what had happened; but rather than an opinion, it was a phrase to which she could give no precise sense.

'Filippo,' she said to herself, 'was drowned in the crowd' "
(p. 391). This metaphor contains a judgment and a symbol:
Rubè is metaphorically drowned in the crowd, in the "human
stream" of the rally that is overwhelmed by the real waves
of the cavalry, exactly as Celestina was actually shipwrecked
in "the waves of the Lago Maggiore in the tempest." The two
destinies find a perfect correspondence in the juxtaposition
of the two levels of the text.

   (3) Witnessing a street battle between "Bolsheviki" and fascists in April 1919 in Milan, and "taking careful note of himself, he [Rubè] realized that his pulse was beating rapidly and
that his nostrils were quivering like those of a horse as he
sniffs the cool morning *on a river bank*" (p. 230). I have added
the italics to show the elevated (privileged) position that allows Rubè to watch the flowing of water (or of the "human
stream") below. However, this situation is completely reversed in the final sequence, which is foreshadowed by the
other sequence of the boat, "whose keel was entirely white
and whose gunwales were sorrel," and was therefore called
Balzana da quattro, "The Horse With the Four White Feet" (p.
255). After the shipwreck, this boat "with its white keel like
a mare in the wind, was adrift in the bouncing waves" (p.
288).[18] Now it is the cavalrymen, each with his own crested
helmet, who to Rubè look like "the waves of the Lago Maggiore in the tempest," caught as he is in the human stream
of the rally. Thus the private tragedy is lost and fused (completed) in the public one. However, before being trampled
upon, Rubè still has time to see the "calm, kindly" face of
the cavalryman, the connotations of which can perhaps be
understood only if one remembers the fascination with which
Rubè had witnessed the preceding violence between "Bolsheviki" and fascists in Milan, recognizing among the latter

---

[18] See Rubè's thoughts on p. 320 of the Italian edition (the English translation skips pp. 320–22 completely): "But, no, this is a table with four feet;
they are all sorrel, not white. No, it isn't a spiritist table." It is to be noted
that spiritism has a considerable importance in Borgese's second novel, *I vivi
e i morti*, and that séances are also described by Pirandello (*Il fu Mattia Pascal*)
and Svevo (*La coscienza di Zeno*).

one of his army peers, Massimo Ranieri: "under his helmet was his firm, arch-angelic countenance" (p. 232).

I have said that the metaphoric texture is an important part of the literary construction of *Rubè* in that it prepares and accompanies the technique of premonition that is the basis of the plot (thus underscoring its temporality), in addition to forming the network of correspondences that is the basis of the symbolist novel (thus underscoring its spatiality). Now it is necessary to clarify the fact that this metaphoric texture is not the only element that makes up such correspondence. For example, Borgese amply uses the device of repetition— of entire sequences, sentences, or details that might appear secondary at first glance.[19] I shall not undertake here a systematic analysis of this aspect of his art, but I do wish at least to touch upon the subject of repetition as symbolic overdetermination.

At this level, the figure of the consoling death—made up of a woman's hands (or fingers), exhortations to sleep, and the thought of a mother—is perhaps the most evident, and in any case one of the most complex, in the novel. It is centered in the character of Eugenia Berti, "with that neutral white complexion reminiscent of the communion wafer, as straight as a pre-Raphaelite virgin reconciling sleep with death" (p. 25), "a nun, a nurse, good for closing one's eyes in the last agony" (p. 225), whose beauty "exhaled a sort of sadness, [like a foreboding of death]" (p. 55), "a young Parce" (p. 143).[20] It is Eugenia who first places "her hand upon his forehead" when Rubè is in a crisis and tells him, "Sleep, sleep," so that "he was left in a quivering anguish, out of which from time to time rose the images of Calinni and of his mother, whom for so many days he had forgotten" (pp. 47–

[19] For instance, Celestina Lambert's garter with its small emeralds is mentioned on pp. 150, 282, 289, and 313. In this connection, there are excellent remarks in De Maria, *passim*.

[20] It is perhaps worth noting that the three women loved by Rubè are associated with different colors: the unattainable Mary Corelli is "dressed in [pink]" (p. 58), Celestina prefers red, and Eugenia is mostly dressed in white. The separation of the two colors of which pink is composed seems to be the expressionistic reflection of the male character's dissociation.

48). The same elements are taken up again and varied later
on, when Celestina, "placing both her hands upon his eyes,
closed them: 'So. You need sleep.' 'Don't say that,' he en-
treated. 'Somebody else told me that, too.' . . . Her hands
had become so incorporeal and soft that he was pervaded by
a childhood abandon. He felt that she was a mother" (p. 169).
Rubè thinks again of Eugenia, the consoling one, during his
exhausting train trips (p. 365). And finally, here is the moving
and solemn sequence that concludes the novel:

> Then, in the darkest depths of that consciousness, as at
> the furthermost bottom of a narrow well that reaches to
> the bowels of the earth, a tiny light had appeared; dim,
> incalculably dimmer than the bluish gleam that hangs
> from the top of the trains [compartments] at night with-
> out shedding any illumination. . . . It seemed that he was
> sleeping, at last; that he was dead. . . . At the foot of the
> bed, standing erect and tall, was Eugenia. . . . "Sleep.
> Sleep," she murmured to him, with her forehead upon
> his. And she cast a long glance of love into that glance
> which was already dying out. As he sank into death he
> heard the olden plaints of the violoncello. But it was no
> human voice that repeated the strains to him. And the
> long feminine fingers that lay upon his closed eyelashes
> had lost all weight. (pp. 393–94)

In the narrative sequences I have quoted, the crescendo from
a realistic and descriptive level to a symbolic one is achieved
through a clever modulation of three fundamental elements,
which recur throughout. The third of these elements, the
mother, is finally prevalent, even if it is doubly hidden first
of all in the figure itself of Eugenia (who is pregnant with
Rubè's son) and then in the reference to "the bowels of the
earth."[21] This is the chthonic image of the Great Mother to
whom Filippo has finally returned, and in whom all his con-

---

[21] Cf. the symmetrical, Jungian image at the beginning of the novel: "Nor
did he expect, at the top of that clear, native mountain, to recover his health,
which lay beyond reach at the bottom of his dark conscience, like a treasure
fallen into a well" (p. 64).

tradictions are smoothed and reconciled in a conscious abandonment to the forces of the irrational.[22]

The elements of the content of *Rubè* (thematic, narrative, symbolic) are strictly connected in an extremely coherent organization of the text. Thus, if an analysis of the ideological elements should give the same results, it will be possible to speak of an extraordinary structural unity of the different levels that compose the text as hypersign. Borgese's own intention of creating "an artistic construction," which he deliberately pursued, even to the point of theorizing "a poetics of unity,"[23] will be confirmed, then, in contemporary critical terms.

The Ideological Level

There is no doubt that in the narrative sequence under examination Borgese's discourse reaches its climax in the truly extraordinary figure of Rubè, who proceeds on a zig-zagging course, holding a red flag in his left hand "and in his right the black"—an unforgettable emblematic image, a real icon. It expresses, sums up, and emphasizes the whole ambivalence of the character, charging it with implications that demand to be analyzed.

The ambivalence (and hence availability) of Rubè, who is aware of being an "intellectual" and a "bourgeois," is underlined on the one hand by his fear of being caught in the midst of a "Bolshevik" rally (despite his attraction to socialism, in which "every one will have a place" and will be "equal and anonymous") and on the other hand by his fascination with the cavalry, which has arrived to disperse "the mob" and is received by him "with vast delight" (a fascination emblematically objectified in the "calm, kindly face" of the first cavalryman who strikes him). The psychological aspects of such an attitude are by now well known. Ideologically, they are

[22] Filippo's son will be called Demetrio, like his grandfather, to respect naturalistic verisimilitude, but above all, symbolically, as a masculine derivative of Demeter.

[23] See G. A. Borgese, *Tempo di edificare* and *Poetica dell'unità* (Milan: Treves, 1923 and 1934).

important because they explain Rubè's correlated public behavior, as well as the type of criticism the author is developing through it, making his character a true "paradigm of a certain Italian bourgeoisie," as Genot has rightly observed.[24] In this connection, the findings of the French critic and those arrived at by Isenghi make it possible for me to avoid carrying out a detailed analysis of the text. But, while summarizing these findings, I wish to complete them with some inferences that seem to me to be indispensable.

(1) *The economic motive as code*: I have no doubt that Borgese, who was a great admirer of Verga, wanted to carry on the lesson of realism by using one of its most characteristic codes, and therefore insisted throughout *Rubè* on the economic mechanisms, justifications, preoccupations, limitations, and conditions that are useful to define his character as a "petit bourgeois" and an "intellectual." Without them, the whole psychological construction of the novel would be gratuitous.[25] It is enough to think, at the very beginning of *Rubè*, of those "two hundred-lire notes" that his father sends Filippo at Rome, "perforating them with a bit of twine whose ends he fixed with putty seals of wax to the envelope of the registered letter" (p. 4); of the zeal used by Rubè to gain his employer's trust in order not to "endanger his daily bread" (p. 195); of his winning fifteen thousand lire at the gambling house, which makes materially possible his flight from home, his adventure at the Isola Bella, the train trips throughout Italy. I could, of course, go on and on.

(2) *The social classes as juxtaposed worlds*: It is appropriate to define the intellectual petite bourgeoisie, as Genot does, by examining its (failed) relationship with the *popolo* and socialism.[26] But at least of equal (if not more) importance is its

[24] Genot, p. 54.

[25] Cf. also Borgese's essay on "Giovanni Verga," in *Tempo di edificare*, pp. 1–22.

[26] Genot, pp. 45–53. In this connection, consider this revealing sentence from Borgese's *I vivi e i morti* (Milan-Rome: Mondadori, 1924), p. 97: "The *popolo* speak our same language, they live next door to us. Yet it is as if they breathe a different air. . . . We talk a lot about the *popolo*, but who knows anything about them?"

relationship with the grande bourgeoisie—the Sicilian landed gentry, the Parisian diplomatic and military class, the Milanese industrial magnates. For it is the grande bourgeoisie that dictates inexorable behavioral models in which the aspirations of the "inferior" class are manifested and concluded, a typical case of what René Girard has called *médiation*.

In *Rubè*, it can be said that the text is organized according to a juxtaposition of opposing worlds—the *grand* and the petit bourgeois. Using one of Lotman's spatial schemes,[27] the grand bourgeois world (the "high" world of the owners, of the capitalists) appears as an "external" space and, insofar as it is the bearer of models to be followed, a "good" one. In contrast, the petit bourgeois world (the "low" world of the employees, of the intellectual Rubè) appears as "inner" space. The world of the *popolo* is "external" space, and "bad," but it is only a virtual space, for everything important takes place between the former two.

The tragedy of the protagonist is that he is unable to belong to either of the two worlds, unable to cross the line that separates them. Again Lotman's analysis is pertinent here: "The classificatory border between opposing worlds assumes spatial features: Lethe, separating the living from the dead,

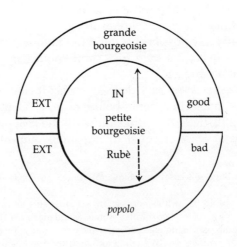

27 Lotman, "Il metalinguaggio delle descrizioni della cultura," p. 164.

the gates of hell with the inscription, 'Abandon all hope, ye who enter here,' the worn soles which mark the beggar as an outcast, denying him access to the world of the rich."[28] Let us see how this is borne out in *Rubè*:

> But despite the many praises of the judges and his acquaintances, he [Filippo] toiled away merely to triple that sum; and if he had a new suit his hat was a trifle soiled, and when his [tie] was spick and span his patent-leather shoes were sure to be somewhat cracked, so that evenings, when he sat conversing on the Taramanna's damasked sofa, it behooved him not to cross his legs comfortably lest the liberty lamp show up mercilessly every wrinkle and defect. (p. 4)

Here further comment is unnecessary. The literary text (with its nuances) and the critical text (with its categories) illuminate each other reciprocally. Other significant examples are the following: leaving for the war as an army officer, and "knowing that somebody would be there to see him off, he [Rubè] *felt obliged* to purchase a first-class ticket" (p. 18, italics added); in Paris, he "must" wait a few months before being able to buy "a fine black coat and striped trousers," which are necessary for the elegant parties in "the Auteuil apartments" (p. 144). Or let us read the descriptions, precise to the point of cruelty, of the two parties in Milan, one in "the small, provisional *ménage*" of Rubè, who is aware of having been hired by the Adsum company as a "guardian of the social order during the post-bellum period" (p. 194), and the other at the De Sonnazes', where "there was no one present [from the world of the masters]" (p. 214).

(3) *The narrative context and the historical circumstances*: The image of Rubè trampled upon while holding two flags is the perfect symbol of the intellectual petite bourgeoisie in the Italy of 1919, but it is not the end of the novel. It is only the climax, casual but possessing a "fatal logic," in terms of Rubè's story *a parte subiecti*. After it appears, there is a reprise by the omniscient narrator, who recounts the events following the cav-

---

[28] Lotman, *The Structure of the Artistic Text*, p. 237.

alry charge, and in particular the attention paid to Filippo, who has been seriously wounded:

> No sooner had the identification of the unknown traveller been officially established than there was plenty of discussion in the public gatherings and even some in the newspapers. The Bolshevik faction tried to inscribe Filippo Rubè upon its roll of martyrs, although it was somewhat embarrassed by the excessive amount of money found upon his person. The other faction insisted upon a version diametrically opposite, and spread it with resolute intransigence. Filippo Rubè, an immaculate citizen, a glorious veteran of the world war, had been fired with disgust at the sight of this filthy mob, and, seized with a sudden, irrepressible fury, had all by himself charged against the crowd. . . . Very few of either side referred to the "unfortunate incident upon the Lago Maggiore," and then only in passing, without attempting any absurd connection with the events of yesterday. (p. 390)

This sequence is important because the ironic—in fact, semiotic *ante litteram*—use of the two juxtaposed rhetorics detracts value from both.[29] The narrator, without revaluing his character and what he represents sociologically and ideologically, is distanced from the red as well as the black position. Both of them, after all, are presented as factions. Furthermore, soon afterward the narrator recounts an episode that is undoubtedly conclusive in ideological terms: a "delegation of Bolognese veterans" has gone to the hospital, and Eugenia, who has immediately run to assist her husband, speaks "little, moderately, and prudently; but enough to authorize, in general, the judgment of the veterans against the contrary thesis" (p. 391).

With it, the adherence to fascism of the petite bourgeoisie, which up to then had been available to the "opposite extremisms," is sealed in narrative terms. This is why Rubè is a

[29] Cf. Eco, *A Theory*, p. 312, n. 52: "There is a semiotic technique of analysis that allows one to destroy an ideology by opposing to it another ideology, the latter showing the falsity of the former (and vice versa)."

symbolic character, and why his story is paradigmatic and at least partially prophetic, as Borgese himself later noted.[30]

A confirmation can be found in contemporary historiography, particularly in Renzo Del Carria's *Proletari senza rivoluzione*, which illustrates the double availability of the intellectual petite bourgeoisie both toward revolution (on the side of the socialists against the parliamentary system) and toward reaction (on the side of the conservatives against the labor unions). Hence the Futurists sided with fascism because it had won those very fights of 1919 and 1920 that are the background of *Rubè*—but they could well have sided with the workers if the latter had prevailed.[31]

(4) *The cultural circumstances*: We have seen that the character of Rubè is conceived by the author as an antihero, and as such he is opposed to the superman with all of his codes of behavior, values, and so forth. In particular, this antihero is in deliberate opposition to the great Dannunzian model: "In *Rubè* Borgese exorcizes that mystique of the superman which had fascinated his generation."[32] But Borgese's criticism of D'Annunzio should not be considered an easy kick by an ass to a dying lion. In fact, just the contrary. Even the use of Verga's economic code is intended as a completion rather than as a substitution. Thus if one accepts the cultural scheme envisaged by Paolo Valesio, with its "reactionary" and "demosocialist" ideologemes,[33] it will be possible to formulate another ideologeme for Borgese, one we might call "liberal"

[30] Cf. G. A. Borgese, *Goliath* (New York: Viking, 1938), p. 294: "The symbol, perhaps an accidental one, was, however, significant as a prophecy of Italy"; and on p. 217: "In him [Mussolini] the petty bourgeoisie mirrored itself with its muddled restlessness and its guilty self-consciousness."

[31] Cf. Renzo Del Carria, *Proletari senza rivoluzione. Storia delle classi subalterne italiane dal 1860 al 1950* (Milan: Oriente, 1970), vol. 1, pp. 349–53. Teresa De Lauretis called my attention to these pages in a lecture on Marinetti that was subsequently published as "Futurism: A Post-Modern View" in *Quaderni di Italianistica*, vol. 2, no. 2 (Autumn 1981), pp. 143–59.

[32] De Maria, p. xvii.

[33] Paolo Valesio, "The Lion and the Ass: The Case for D'Annunzio's Novels," *Yale Italian Studies*, vol. 1, no. 1 (Winter 1977), pp. 67–82. The two ideologemes, formulated by Valesio from the models posed by Kenneth Burke and structural linguistics, are on pp. 74 and 75.

(but of a pre-fascist liberalism, of course). With all the necessary precautions, this ideologeme can be articulated as shown in the diagram.

Agent the intellectual	Role aspiration to greatness; failure	Focus analytical prose
Act weak-willed on the historical background	Purpose personal assertion, but also anonymity	Form literary language, symbolism
Scene Italy, Paris	Connotations poverty/luxury	Social Setting petite and grande bourgeoisie

Notice how Borgese replies to D'Annunzio partly on his own ground (Scene and Form), while making the Role, the Purpose, and the Connotations ambiguous (taking up one element but juxtaposing it with a contrary one that undermines it), and at the same time proposing a different discourse by modifying the Agent, the Act, the Focus, and the Social Setting, without identifying himself with the corresponding elements of the "demosocialist" ideologeme.

The "liberal" ideologeme I propose for Borgese is clearly an interpretive code for the hypersign *Rubè*, considered in its structural unity of different textual levels, of clusters of sign functions, and finally placed in the context of Italian culture.[34]

If we put this Borgese ideologeme in the middle, between the "demosocialist" and the "reactionary" ones, we have the critical confirmation of the extraordinary force, coherence, and originality of its central symbol: Filippo Rubè, the anti-hero, the intellectual, caught between the red and the black.

---

[34] Cf. Eco, *A Theory*, p. 310, n. 46: "The work of art is a text that is adapted by its concrete addressees so as to fulfill many different communicative purposes in diverse historical or psychological circumstances, without ever completely disregarding the underlying rule that has constituted it"—that is, the idiolect.

Five. The Laboratory and the Labyrinth

IT IS INTERESTING to note that while in medicine the science of symptoms is traditionally called "semeiotics," in literary criticism a similar word, "semiotics" (also used in medicine as a synonym of "semeiotics") is used to define the science of signs.[1]

My purpose in this chapter is to explore how literature deals with disease—more precisely, with mental disease—particularly at the semiotic level. Here symptoms become the signs of a language that the writer tries to decode and interpret in order to understand the Other, the sick person, and through the sick person disease itself, the irrational, what by a generally accepted definition seems incommunicable. In this way, the writer also seeks to understand himself and his writing.

Both literature and criticism have dealt with mental disease. With the economic boom of the fifties and the resulting social tensions and changes it produced, mental illness increased and, as a consequence, became the subject of many novels, diaries, and stories. However, this literary interest developed primarily at the realistic (documentary), metaphoric, and on-

---

[1] In this context, it seems important to recall Giorgio Prodi, *Le basi materiali della significazione* (Milan: Bompiani, 1977). A reflection of the enormous influence exerted today by biology, this work describes the language of cells from which human processes of communication and adaptation have gradually developed—including the distinction between symptoms and signs.

tological levels.[2] The prevailing emphasis was on neuroses, as in the cases described by Gadda (following the precedent of Svevo),[3] and on serious psychoses, as in the recent *Amore mio nemico* by Mario Isotti.[4] In all these cases, situations are described in which a certain normalcy of language, and hence of communication, is still present.[5]

But Isotti's novel also seems to suggest a growing interest in areas of psychopathology that have so far been little explored or are as yet altogether unknown.[6] Isotti is a neuropsychiatrist and a psychoanalyst who studied with Ludwig Binswanger (whose "existential analysis" is much closer to Jung than to Freud) and who is also familiar with explorations in advanced psychiatry, such as those of M. A. Séchehaye and R. D. Laing. (It should be remembered that it was from one of Séchehaye's cases that the poet Nelo Risi derived the memorable film, *Diario di una schizofrenica*.) One quote from Isotti's novel should suffice here:

> The third purpose of the book, the understanding of madness, was the most difficult: through an intimate and dialogical experience I wanted to transform a strange and chaotic mass into a story clear to everyone; I wanted to illuminate the positive elements of that world and the

[2] See the chapter "From Anatomy to Criticism" in my *Literary Diseases* (Austin: University of Texas Press, 1975).

[3] In this connection, see the proposals on Gadda's "obsessive neurosis" and Svevo's "hysterical neurosis" put forth and developed by Elio Gioanola in *L'uomo dei topazi: Saggio psicanalitico su C. E. Gadda* and *Un killer dolcissimo: Indagine psicanalitica sull'opera di Italo Svevo* (Genoa: Il Melangolo, 1977 and 1979), perhaps the most valid and stimulating discourses I have read on the subject.

[4] Mario Isotti, *Amore mio nemico* (Milan: Rizzoli, 1978).

[5] The case of Pirandello is different. He accepts madness as a *datum* and uses it polemically against society. Cf. "Moscarda's Mirror" in my *Literary Diseases*.

[6] Cf. Isotti for the references to Jung (p. 17), Séchehaye (p. 48), Laing (p. 34), and Binswanger (p. 276). The latter is quoted along with Heidegger, Merleau-Ponty, Buber, Jaspers, and Minkowski, but without the pretense of elaborating a philosophical system: "The causes of the crisis of traditional psychoanalysis as a means of help, the crisis of institutions and rehabilitation systems, or the frequent need to put mental patients on trial because of their being 'accusing mirrors,' only glimmer as logical consequences."

psychotic ones of ours, in order to bring two conditions of life closer to each other until they were joined; I wanted to give a human aspect to schizophrenia, to abolish distances, in order to do away with its monstrous, contaminated character of condemnation or curse.[7]

Isotti's novel offers impassioned testimony about a "great voyage" into the schizophrenic universe. It is filled with sober, technical statements about symptoms and psychotherapy, and I believe it could and should also be read as an argument in favor of opening up the traditional, institutional set-up of mental asylums, according to the proposals set forth by the late Dr. Franco Basaglia.[8]

There is another novel, published at the same time as Isotti's, that also deals with mental disease in a moving and revealing way: it is *Fratelli*, by Carmelo Samonà.[9] The importance of this novel is that it is the first by a writer who is neither a patient nor a doctor, the first in which disease is presented and analyzed *explicitly* as language, and the first in which the contemporary trend toward radical reform of mental institutions is reflected in the fictional situation of the characters, who do not live inside an asylum but in their own home.

Let us begin our analysis of this novel by briefly considering the hypersign *Fratelli* in its constitutive levels. We are dealing here with the story of two brothers, one sane and the other insane, who live together in a huge, semi-deserted apartment high above an unnamed city. The half-empty apartment provides them with ample space for their daily life, at times resembling a labyrinth in which it is difficult to find each other (or easy to hide), a space that affords the kind of isolation comparable with ideal laboratory conditions for the obser-

[7] Ibid., p. 273.

[8] See Franco Basaglia, *L'istituzione negata* and *La maggioranza deviante* (Turin: Einaudi, 1968 and 1971). On the latest developments of antipsychiatry, see Ernesto Venturini, ed., *Il giardino dei gelsi* and Anna Maria Bruzzone, *Ci chiamavano matti. Voci da un ospedale psichiatrico* (Turin: Einaudi, 1979); cf. also R. D. Laing, *Intervista sul folle e il saggio* (Bari: Laterza, 1979).

[9] Carmelo Samonà, *Fratelli* (Turin: Einaudi, 1978). All the quotations will refer to this edition.

vation of the basic manifestations of madness. Such an observation becomes much more difficult when the two brothers venture outside into the more complex space of the city, with its intertwining streets and alleys, its shops, public gardens, and crowds.

The sane brother, who is the narrator of the story, takes care of the insane one, helping him to eat, dress, and clean himself. In performing these humble duties, he doggedly tries to understand the fragmentary and absurd language of his brother, to decipher his behavior, decode his gestures. This gives his narrative a very special quality. Indeed, I believe there has never been another novel in which the human body has received so much attention, been scrutinized so minutely in its functions, been studied and rendered with so much insistence.[10] This insistence has the precise purpose of emphasizing the language of the body that is an alternative to words, forming a constant parallel to the narrator's search for a clear-cut, univocal meaning reducible to reason and normalcy. Thus the sane brother tries to establish contact with the Other, a contact that, while overtly physical (touching, embracing), is also more subtly spiritual (a "meaningful" glance, the exchange of some sort of dialogue). But in order to communicate, he is forced to adopt some of the behavior of the insane brother. And because of this, everything becomes play, theater, imagination—setting up an arena in which freedom of action is virtually unlimited by the boundaries of reason and logic. From this come the pretended "Great Voyages" the two brothers undertake together, as well as their role-playing and their gratuitous exchanges of food and clothes. From this too comes the gradual sensation, conveyed by the narrator, that *he* is no longer sure of his own Self, of his own meaning.

The narrator specifically refers to himself as a writer (in that he accumulates notes describing the illness of his brother), and his writing is posited against disease in a long, subtle meditation that involves not only the meaning but also the

[10] Particularly effective examples are on pp. 8, 11, 14, 15, 21, 22, 34, 49, 75, 89, 91, and 108.

values of Western civilization. These include the notions of personal identity and society, the cause-effect principle, and the laws of profit or of the maximum result obtained with the minimum of effort.[11]

The questioning of these meanings and values is particularly evident in two episodes: the gift of an apple by "the woman with the limping dog," a Giacometti-like figure met by the two brothers during an outing at the public gardens, and the suspicion by the narrator that the sick brother has stolen some of his notes, which results in a punishment that is followed by doubts about who committed what. Both episodes are connected by an element of violence that runs beneath the surface of the novel: public violence in the first episode (with the killing of the limping dog),[12] and private violence in the second. What prevails, however, is the effort at communication and understanding.

Beautifully written in a style that combines the pathos and compassion of a personal diary with the clarity and intelligence of a *conte philosophique*, *Fratelli* can be taken at face value as a very realistic (one suspects even autobiographical) story.[13]

[11] See, for example, pp. 25, 39, and 73.

[12] The scene of the killing (pp. 76–77) is concluded with a bitter meditation: "Perhaps we were the ones who cried, not those who stabbed. Yet we are also close to the murder, we fluctuate inside death, and in some small corner of the episode, perhaps, we raise our anguished and contradictory hands, defensive and aggressive at the same time, I don't know whether armed or not, but certainly intent upon suppressing and getting rid of. . . ." The metaphoric potential of this scene (which is prefigured by the episode in which the sane brother denies the madman, on pp. 60–63) cannot be underestimated: we are dealing with a scapegoat.

[13] Isotti's remarks come to mind (p. 278): "It is not easy to identify oneself with a madman because of an instinctive reaction of anguish; nor is it easy to identify with the therapeutic agent [the doctor] because nobody likes to walk among ruins, all the more if one does not know that in them there might be life. One would think: what if something like that should happen to one of us; what if it were our son, the one who remains buried under the ruins? Then everybody would move, would search the ruins, compelled by necessity and sorrow. In the present story I have lived such a sorrow outside a parental relationship, since the soul of a schizophrenic has the same power as a son's . . . , because every man, in every part of the world, represents us."

It can also be read at a metaphorical level: the brother's sickness is not really—or not only—madness, but everything that does not belong to the realm of reason and influences our lives, everything that is outside of our control. Finally, the novel can be read at the semiotic level as a self-reflexive or metanarrative inquiry into the nature of human language(s) and into the way in which people relate to one another through speech, silence, gestures, and especially the written word. Without the obscure force of sickness, the writer would not be able to write, or to understand himself or others or his writing.

The problems of communication involved in the text (the contact and the code between sender and addressee) inevitably lead to a process of interpretation of the context and the messages, according to Jakobson's well-known diagram,[14] which is a veritable cornerstone for semiotic practice.

```
                    context
                    message
    sender    . . . . . . . . . .    addressee
                    contact
                    code
```

In *Fratelli*, these six elements of the communicative act are all present, although I believe the contact (with its related phatic function) and the code (with its related metalinguistic function) are predominant, thereby confirming that a given message cannot, by itself, transmit a meaning.

In *Fratelli*, the process of interpretation is made a disquieting one by the fact that it starts with symptoms (the medical "semeiotics") and ends with signs (the literary "semiotics"). The correlation between medicine and literature could not be asserted more powerfully than in these two synonyms, which

[14] Roman Jakobson, "Closing Statement: Linguistics and Poetics," in Thomas Sebeok, ed., *Style in Language* (Cambridge, Mass.: MIT Press, 1960), p. 353. Cf. Umberto Eco, *A Theory of Semiotics* (Bloomington: Indiana University Press, 1975), 3.7.1 and 3.7.2; Yuri Lotman and Boris Uspensky, *Tipologia della cultura*, Italian tr. (Milan: Bompiani, 1975), pp. 111–33; and Yuri Lotman, *Testo e contesto* (Bari: Laterza, 1980), pp. 32ff., for an integration of Jakobson's model with a Bakhtinian, dialogic structure.

share the same classic Greek etymology.[15] To see how this occurs, let us examine the text of *Fratelli* in detail.

Samonà carefully emphasizes the nature of his narrator's quest: "I shall not give it a name," he says, referring to his brother's sickness, because for him sickness is "a sort of invisible object even more than a hostile force" (p. 8). However, he clarifies: "Although my brother's sickness concerns the area of thought above all, and the body only incidentally, its action always manifests itself materially" (p. 8). This statement suffices to "place" the sickness; the position of the narrator is given immediately following:

> I was the only one in my family who agreed to take care of my brother and to live with him in the large apartment, and since then I have never given up the idea of fighting this calamity with every possible means. I follow it closely, as if it had a shape; I spy on it; I carefully note down its symptoms and put them into relationships among themselves. I am so doggedly hunting, pursuing, finding it, that at times it might even seem that I am courting it. . . . Actually my behavior follows an entirely attentive and meticulous strategy. I have learned that one must pretend to accept disease as something that integrates and belongs to us, like an insane extension of our bodies: hence a sacred ceremony, capillary and incessant; a homely code rooted in our gestures. (pp. 8–9)

In this passage, the obsessive presence of sickness is reflected in the use of medical terms (from the very "disease" with its "symptoms" to the biological adjective "capillary"). The initial pretense that disease is accepted as an integral part of life is accompanied by a recognition of the mysterious and humble character of sickness (in that it involves both a "sacred ceremony" and a "homely code"). It is because of this recognition that one should emphasize the importance of the lexicon that is used in this passage. In addition to terms like

---

[15] Still following Jakobson, I think it is useful to emphasize that in such an interpretive process there is both a selective/associative element (the synchronic one, which in "normal" language produces metaphors) and a combinative/syntagmatic element (which expresses diachrony and metonymy).

"fighting," "calamity," "hunting," "pursuing," "strategy" (which are rightly denounced by Susan Sontag because of the sense of culpability they, or similar ones, induce in cancer-affected patients)[16] here one finds opposite terms like "courting," "ceremony," and "homely." This denotes an attitude toward disease that is both rigid and open. With fighting comes rejection, exclusion; but with courtship comes a desire to possess, to understand.

No matter how hard the narrator tries to imitate the sickness of his brother in order to identify with him, he knows that he is not obliged to *live* this sickness, that he can control it from the outside. Nevertheless, he states:

> While I try to snatch my brother from the condition in which he happens to be, I feel that he is performing on me an action somehow equal and opposite to mine: hunted by me, in his turn he follows me incessantly, visited by me he surprises me and obliges me to follow his movements. Our story consists wholly of these violations of territory, which are repeated until the names and the faces of the respective invaders become confused. (p. 10)

His use of the words "our story" (time) and "these violations of territory" (space) indicates that in facing disease the narrator becomes extremely aware of the coordinates within which both he and his brother move. These coordinates have been made explicit from the very beginning (even if they have not been connected directly with sickness) in the relationship between objects and memory, a relationship "deprived of affective resonances" (in that these objects no longer recall a familiar past that is forgotten, but are used only "to scan surfaces, to mark and separate itineraries"). Hence the relationship between objects and memory seems based upon "the illusion of an obstinate present" (pp. 4–5).

This "obstinate present," which corresponds to what is elsewhere called "achronic space" (p. 74), is perhaps the stylistic mark of the novel. It is clearly predominant over the

---

[16] Susan Sontag, *Illness as Metaphor* (New York: Farrar, Straus & Giroux, 1978).

THE LABORATORY AND THE LABYRINTH

other verbal tenses, which do exist and have their precise weight. On the one hand, the flow of time is subject to nuance and confusion, as on p. 78:

> Naturally, I do not know what duration I should assign to the existence of this relationship. I am inclined to feel it extending and multiplied into a space of years, but it is also possible, on the contrary, that it was only a season and a sequence of months.

On the other hand, time is also emphasized to the utmost, creating an effect of great pathos:

> A new problem faces me when I think of that indomitable body of my brother, which does not seem to be touched, as mine is, by the wear and tear of time. For how many more years, I ask myself, will I be able to follow him in his strange pilgrimages at home and in the city, to keep up with him? . . . I begin to feel old. (pp. 88–89)

In both quotations, the predominant verbal tense is the present, which is indeed a true *tempus*, as Harald Weinrich says, "the most frequent of 'commentative' tenses, indicating a certain communicative attitude."[17] In other words, even when the narrator shows himself most openly as a narrator, he clearly communicates to us that what interests him most is a commented world rather than a narrated world (indeed, his novel is more a *conte philosophique* than a diary).

There is another aspect of time that should be noted in *Fratelli*, also because of the importance attached to it by the narrator himself. He invents and prepares a "Time Table" that is intended to foresee and give order to his brother's actions and is based upon both the fundamental principle of the space/time relationship and the method of direct observation and accurate correlation of gestures and habits (pp. 39–40). But the unforeseeable and inventive variants of the brother's behavior destroy the pretense that the table could be a "regulator" of time, reducing it instead to "a commen-

---

[17] Harald Weinrich, *Tempus. Le funzioni dei tempi nel testo*, Italian trans. (Bologna: Il Mulino, 1978), p. 57.

tary, a glossary, an ornament" (p. 43). Thus the narrator turns to "pondering alternate times, oblique schedules, distorted yet perfect, in competition with those of calendars and clocks that normally appear [to him] to be dictated by wisdom" (p. 46).

The complete failure of the "Time Table," in addition to being so true at the level of common experience, can also be read as an ironic meditation on the pretense of a certain type of contemporary narratology (one that is commented upon by Cesare Segre)[18] at foreseeing and regulating all the possible combinations and developments of creative invention, of narrativity, of storytelling. The critic cannot foresee life (which after all is most original, as a great writer once said) any more than the narrator in Samonà's book, healthy and "wise," can predict the next move of the "mad" brother.

Together with time, space is the other coordinate that forms the frame within which the confrontation between the two brothers occurs. Following Lotman's spatial schemes, there is no doubt that such a confrontation takes place in two spaces:

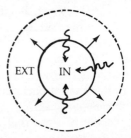

the internal one (of the narrator, of reason) with well-defined boundaries, and the external one (of the mad brother, of nonreason) with ill-defined and unknown boundaries.[19] For instance, when the narrator, tired and discomfited, retreats within

[18] Cf. Cesare Segre, *Structures and Time*, tr. by John Meddemmen (Chicago: University of Chicago Press, 1979), p. 55. It should be remembered that Samonà is also a knowledgeable literary critic.

[19] Lotman, "Il metalinguaggio delle descrizioni della cultura," in Lotman and Uspensky's *Tipologia della cultura*, p. 164; cf. also Yuri Lotman, *The Structure of the Artistic Text*, tr. by Ronald Vroon (Ann Arbor: University of Michigan Press, 1977), pp. 217ff.

the "limited geometry" of his room to seek order and harmony (by setting his books on the shelves, or reordering his personal objects), his gestures resemble "a slow gliding on a friendly territory from strange and limitless spaces" (p. 47). This sentence can be considered emblematic for the whole novel, whose spatial scheme could be diagrammed as shown. The arrows represent "violations" or "invasions" by one or the other brother into the adversary's "territory"; hence they represent the narrative movement and synthesize the nature of the narrator's human and intellectual quest. It is also to be noted that this graphic representation of the space of *Fratelli* is not concerned with the most immediate (and perhaps the most superficial) level of the text: the juxtaposition of the internal space of the apartment with the external space of the city. This is because such a juxtaposition simply is not an enlightening one.

With its solid and dotted lines, with its straight and sinuous arrows pointed in opposite directions, the graphic representation of the novel does, however, allude to the other juxtaposition that was mentioned at the beginning of this chapter. The apartment of the two brothers (and to a lesser extent the city) is a space-labyrinth as well as a space-laboratory; one leads to the meanderings of madness, the other to the calculations of reason.

In this connection, it is worth noting that the cover of the Italian edition of *Fratelli* bears a detail from an oil painting by Fabrizio Clerici entitled *ProMenade*. If a cover illustration was ever emblematic of the book inside, this is certainly the one. The illustration belongs to a diptych, itself a form of dichotomy, in which Clerici (a painter who has been linked with René Magritte and Giorgio De Chirico and their surrealistic, oneiric, and metaphysical poetics) shows the Euclidean geometry of an empty room with its clear, rational perspective à la Piero della Francesca being invaded or broken into by the fierce, red figure of a horse. The title reinforces the disquieting connotation of the painting: *ProMenade* includes both the figure of madness (the frenzied, Dionysian "Menade") and the figure of reason (the orderly, Apollonian "Promenade"). For our part, we know that the two brothers in the novel have

Fig. 8. Fabrizio Clerici (1913–), *ProMenade*, 1973, Galleria
Forni, Bologna, Catalogue of the Exhibition.

their own "promenades," their "Great Voyages," as they call
them.

An extremely significant example of how such a juxtaposition of reason and non-reason is achieved within the text
might be the following, which is worth quoting at length:

> Everything begins from the very manner we have of mov-
> ing and situating ourselves in the places where we live.
> When my brother moves, the spaces around him seem
> expanded and dull, the rooms are scanned by uncertain
> rhythms: any room can look like a desert for him, in
> which he risks getting lost or, conversely, it is too narrow
> a prison, in which he gropes like a lame bird. Brought
> on by a moment of ecstasy or a brief period of concen-
> tration, small aleatory universes emerge from his body:
> he moves into them for long periods, and I am given the
> privilege of entering them, from time to time, and of
> living there with him. Usually we call them the Great
> Voyages. . . . His most prevailing fantasies are about un-
> derground or flying homes. However, these are not flying
> machines or elaborate tombs but huts suspended in the

154

void, rooms summarily prepared among imaginary skies, tunnels and holes that were supposedly dug, tenaciously, by dint of fingernails, underneath us. As long as his voyage lasts, my brother could be said not to possess the notion of the horizontal and the plane on which we move, but only the notion of an *above* and a *below* that are conquered by tracing lines at certain points of the floor or in the air. . . .—Don't you see you are unable to fly?—I tell him . . .—Don't you realize that the floor is smooth and there are no holes? Now let's walk together. You look where you are putting your feet and begin to count, one by one, the true objects we see as we pass along. —True objects?—he answers with profound wonder, looking at me obliquely, as if I pointed at ghosts for him. (pp. 11–13)

There are, then, mental spaces, in which different languages are spoken, in which there develops a confrontation (a fight, a courtship, a ritual) between two ways of conveying messages, two sets of meanings. Thus a whole universe of communication is explored, a universe in which words are a minimal part, and gestures, silences, glances, and exchanges of various things are the predominant and most valuable elements.

This universe is divided into two parts. The first is the language of normalcy, rationality, order, cause and effect relationships, predictability, and limitedness; it is embodied in and written by the sane and wise narrator. The second is the language of abnormality, irrationality, chaos, chance, unpredictability, and limitlessness; it is embodied in and uttered (or acted out) by the sick and insane brother. The fascination of *Fratelli* is that the latter language has to be and is in fact described and conveyed through the former. The examples are numerous because the relationship between the two languages forms the very substance of the book. Let us examine some particularly meaningful passages, beginning with the following, in which words are shown as the most ambiguous channel of transmission because, even if they all belong to the code "Italian language" (or "English language"), they also and simultaneously belong to the code "madness" and the code "normalcy":

> We speak, but the form of our messages begins to become different: while mine are fast, neat, cohering to the line of my will and thought, his are almost always hindering or reluctant to follow faithfully the orders that his desire to communicate . . . must have transmitted to his vocal cords and lips. The strange thing is that he does not say anything inconclusive: every sentence is decisive and meaningful, every word is put forth by an incoercible inner determination. One would say they are lucid fragments of a discourse that has lost its cohesiveness because of a distant, terrifying explosion: during the centrifugal movement the links were shattered, the meanings upset and overturned, but shining bits of that ancient linguistic treasure still emerge on his lips. (pp. 21–22)

The fact is that the "exact key" by which to decipher "that universe of contradictions as if it were a legible system" (p. 22) is not in the hands of the narrator (and certainly not of the reader). Thus the situation described above leads to a continually repeated series of failures and new efforts at communicating. The narrator fails to establish "a unique meaning," and keeps trying and using other instruments to cause at least a contact: "oblique and cutting glances, small gestures of the hands, twists of the head" (p. 24).

One of the moments of most intense emotion—in fact, compassion—in the whole novel occurs when the mad brother utters a brief sentence, complete with meaning, and the narrator exults, but only for a very short time:

> In my brother's eyes I perceived a vacillation that softened the compactness of the gesture he had just made; in it, I also read a remote irony (perhaps similar to self-pity, while he was still motionless in front of me, obeying me) as well as a veiled abstractedness that was slowly filling his glance and seemed about to turn it toward other horizons. I shall never forget that premonition of absence that already touched him, nor that hint at a departure of that glance that was still fixed upon me. . . . At no other

moment did I think with such intimate conviction, looking at him going away: "You will never be like me." (pp. 25–26)

From this example it is obvious that words cannot be the code and channel for establishing contact and conveying messages and meanings between the two brothers. But could words at least be useful to describe adequately for us the code, the language of the Other? Could they be laboratory instruments to guide us in the labyrinth? In the following description— the rendering through written words (indeed, de-scription) of the sick brother sitting under a pine tree—symptoms of disease become the signs of a true, unknown, language:

> In his body, leaning tightly against the trunk and the ground, I observe imperceptible movements, like contacts, I should say, similar to mysterious pressures. Recently I have understood that he has an intense relationship with the old bark, the roots, the bits of moss covering the ground beneath him. The language he uses to explore them must be complicated. A sign of it is, for me, the very slow movement of his fingertips on the knots of the roots, different from the one he makes on the moss, more like a caress, and different as well from the way he presses against the trunk with his nape and back. You could say he is waiting for some signal. I have no choice but to enter the great wood by myself or to sit next to him and watch his behavior, without understanding it. (p. 86)

In another instance, it is no longer a question of decoding words, gestures, or bodily movements, but of deciphering things that are charged with meaning. The narrator finds certain small gifts ("presences") from his brother, such as bread crumbs or even little flakes of dried excrement:

> These collected presences make up a network of combinations that later on I try to decipher in solitude, as if they were an articulated discourse that cannot reach me except through that series of small, innumerable stages. I have the feeling that another language is coming forth, richer in innuendoes than the one that is sufficient to communicate elementary needs, such as "I am cold, I

THE LABORATORY AND THE LABYRINTH

want to dress," or "I am hungry, I want to eat"; it is a language turned upside down or astray, moving every time in the opposite direction from the desires and impulses I vainly believe I have foreseen. (p. 36)

Such a deciphering is obviously much harder than the relatively simple decoding of a well-known language. Therefore the importance of the linguistic dimension in the relationship between the two brothers cannot be underestimated. Because of it, the sane narrator can invent games in order to involve the insane brother in some sort of communication. Because of it, theatrical scenes can be enacted; the two brothers can play and exchange roles—and in so doing keep in touch. The notion of play, inherent in language, becomes crystallized in the "dramatic action" of theater. In fact, the sick brother can immerse himself rapidly and completely in a theatrical action, a theatrical role:

> this pulls him immediately out of his language. Not only is he capable of becoming interested in any given well-wrought plot, but he penetrates it happily, and his language profits from this disguise to the point that his lexicon and intonation are changed, and his body is compelled to have an economy of gesture that seemed unreachable before. (p. 14)

At this point, it is possible to perceive a metatextual dimension, in that the novel becomes a reflection on the storytelling process, on narrativity, while the activity of the theater becomes the quest for an Other and the loss of the Self— as it is, in fact, in Samuel Beckett's or Eugène Ionesco's theatrical pieces, which are based on the disintegration of words and personal identity:[20]

---

[20] Cf. Antonio Porta, "Se parla un 'sano di mente,' " *Il corriere della sera*, 19 March 1978, p. 12: "We are moving in the direction indicated by Samuel Beckett in Molloy, who doubles in Moron, with a very important variation: while Beckett's theme stops, so to speak, at the problem of the serialization of the Self, in *Fratelli* the Other, the madman, does not represent seriality but the negation of the person for the sake of an incomprehensible but existing order."

For a while we divided the roles between us accurately, respected the characters, the facts and the morals of the books. Then my brother began to be impatient: he always wanted new possibilities of stories, interrupted the play, asked me to go along with him, getting excited in his proposals of intrigues and dénouements, which became more and more unlikely. Fables, novels, melodramatic pieces were minutely broken up, reduced to a narrative mush that retained only imperceptible traces of the original texts. (p. 16)[21]

However, in the field of writing the boundary is clear. (Notice that I deliberately take up again a spatial metaphor, because I must add another dimension to the juxtaposition of different worlds that has already been examined, starting from Lotman.) The sick brother cannot accept books, including opera libretti, *I promessi sposi*, and children's stories (such as Carlo Collodi's *Pinocchio*), because the written texts,

> soon mastered and feared by him, weighed on him with an ambiguous authority that always hid a shadow of disillusionment. In his opinion, stories were no longer invented by me so that he could disassemble them; they were rigid plots, bottled up within signs, closed up within small and restrictive ingredients, distant from the sonorous flow of words, of gestures. Writing was the tomb of all the stories. (p. 19)

On the contrary, the narrator is characterized from the very beginning as *the one who writes*, the bearer of the story we are

[21] It might be banal to recall the ancient conception of the stage as the world (and vice versa), but it is a fact that between the two brothers everything is theater and at the same time everything is life: "the true dinner can be the third or the fourth act of a fictional pursuit," a walk can contain "fleeting interpolations of secondary or tertiary intrigues" (p. 90). Therefore it is no surprise that, "because of these quick shifts between the true and the fictional" (p. 91), the narrator often stresses his sense of the loss of the Self, which is experienced in a confusion of roles, fragmentary feelings, and swoonings. Particularly meaningful examples are found on pp. 38, 47, 56, 77, and 101–102.

reading: "I carefully note down the symptoms and put them in relationships among themselves" (p. 8); "I catalogue the words, the manners of speech, the silences" (p. 22); "to note gestures, to record and to define habits" (p. 40); "and I intend to note down these things accurately, talk about them, catalogue them" (p. 85); "the record of the facts, the papers on which I transcribe our story punctiliously, every day" (p. 92). Gradually, the one who writes is revealed as the one who writes because of the Other's sickness, as the one who is afraid and defends himself precisely by means of writing:

> In the situation I find myself in, I don't know a more effective means [than writing] to take some distance from the events that are pressing, from the person and the objects surrounding me, and hence to enable me to measure them and contemplate them from the outside. I cannot imagine a territory that is mostly mine, an area of which I can proclaim my exclusive possession most rightly, a space in which I can enter or leave without my brother knowing about it. . . . Writing builds possible universes around me, and proposals alternative to the reality I fear and in which I am constrained. It is not that my notes are not accurate; but I could not call them properly objective. They are rather divided in an equal way between the sequences of what actually happens and the line of the possible. (p. 93)

It is to be noted that such meditations—plausible or even necessary for the verisimilitude of the character—build yet another level of meaning, which is decidedly metanarrative and which becomes even more explicit immediately afterward. Under the seeming pretense of characterizing writing as the insuperable difference between the sane and the sick brothers, much else is hidden:

> The advantage of writing in comparison with oral discourse is that here my brother is not present and, as a consequence, cannot introduce variants. It is up to me alone to document or invent, test hypotheses or limit myself to sure data. When the sheet of paper is motion-

THE LABORATORY AND THE LABYRINTH

less and white on my desk, I can do everything. . . . And
I have some advantage over time. . . . While writing, I
can go back for days or weeks, or destroy an entire epoch
with a single stroke of my pen; or on the contrary I can
keep what I have already written and preserve it from
the menace of future disavowals. (pp. 93–94)

These words are extremely important because they describe
the complex and arbitrary nature of literature, revealed to the
narrator (as his own "internal space") by his constant contact
and experience with disease (the "external space"). Here the
contrast is not only between writing (on disease) and the
spoken discourse (of disease), but also between artificial order
and natural disorder, between health and madness, between
cosmos and chaos, between literature and life.

But perhaps what matters most is that this contrast is formulated in such a way as to be a recognition as well: writing
and madness, cosmos and chaos coexist, are interdependent,
exactly as normal psychology (reason) and psychopathology
(madness) are interdependent in the anthropological-cultural
interpretation of Jean-Michel Oughourlian and Guy Lefort,
who develop the thesis presented by René Girard in *Violence
and the Sacred*.[22]

In *Fratelli*, the figure who perhaps embodies the possibility
of dialogue and understanding between the wise man and
the madman, the possibility of a different and alternative

[22] René Girard, in *Violence and the Sacred* (Baltimore: Johns Hopkins University Press, 1978), maintains that civilization is born through the mechanism of the sacrifice of the scapegoat. By this means, the pre-existing violence
that is diffused in a universe based on mimetic symmetry and indifferentia-
tion is controlled and channeled into a structure that is based on asymmetry
and differentiation. Jean-Michel Oughourlian and Guy Lefort, in "Psychotic
Structure and Girard's Doubles," *Diacritcs*, vol. 8, no. 1 (Spring 1978), pp.
72–74, apply the Girardian conception to psychosis with extremely interesting
results. In their view, psychosis is a structure "of symmetry, of a double,"
"a return to the undifferentiated, pre-sacrificial mimetogony" (p. 73); "Girard's contribution to psychology and psychopathology seems to us to consist
in showing the absolute continuity between them on the level of their generative mechanism, and at the same time, in delineating this time T_0, or
degree D_0 of the structure that constitutes the most radical break between
them" (p. 74).

order, is "the woman with the limping dog," the one who simply "is there" (p. 66), the "hidden pawn" who causes "a triangular play" with the two brothers by "uncovering their tangles" (pp. 69–71). Unexpectedly and mysteriously appearing in the narration with the gift of an apple, the unknown woman complicates the narrator's quest:

> In fact, I found myself facing a linguistic dilemma. I supposed that woman was closer to my language [than to my brother's], since I thought of her, as of me, as intelligent and careful; yet I was unable to say "we shall do" or "we shall speak"; on the contrary, I could not trespass upon the enclosure of that expressive fortress of theirs, armed with plural desinences and third person endings, and surrounded by the "perhaps"'s and the "I suppose"'s of my reflections. (pp. 69–70)

Actually, the unknown woman possesses a language that is mysteriously superior to both the narrator's and the madman's:

> I have reasons to believe that the woman did not have, as I had, two different languages destined alternatively for my brother and for myself, but only one; only one, which however was rich in changing balances, restful and violent, airy and silent, intensely gestural, allusive, explicit, amiably ironic, self-contained, comprehensive, limpid, fragmentary, compact, involving, maternal: in sum, so mobile and omnivalent that it functioned as many languages, or at least displayed a power equivalent to that of our two languages together. (pp. 74–75)

With such an "omnivalent" and maternal language (similar, perhaps, to Andrea Zanzotto's *petèl*, the baby language with which mothers talk to their newborn children—and the poet to his readers), the woman influences the life of the two brothers and makes their communication possible "by uniting fragments of sentences like contiguous pieces of a broken vase," by "covering abysmal distances with the sudden modulations of a song," or else, "after having finished every stock of (usually inexhaustible) figurative or vocal signs, by finally having recourse to an embrace" (p. 75). In short, she becomes their "guide," their "helmsman" in their real and above all mental walks: "what is sure is that she was very useful to us, because she skilfully used to string together the distances between my brother and me, and opened the road toward the gardens" (p. 81). Then she vanishes, as mysteriously as she had originally appeared, leaving behind only fragments of memories and the gift of "objects that were absolutely gratuitous, unrequested, free from any complementary idea of reciprocation or exchange" (p. 79), small signals or models or warnings.

Then, as the novel comes closer to its conclusion, a "chain of disorders" begins to affect "the very thing that documents them" (p. 92). Strange disappearances of written sheets occur, as well as crucial dislocations in their order. Are they thefts by the madman or distractions of the sane brother, or both? In any case, by watching and hence punishing the sick man,[23] the narrator little by little diminishes his annotations and begins to fear "the end of writing" (p. 103). So too does his brother close himself up in "a progressive shedding of the encumbrance of words and in a clear-cut, definitive retreat into the inscrutable domain of silence" (p. 104). But such a "narrowing and coagulation of sounds" does not mean "a waning of his will to communicate":

> On the contrary, the more his language becomes thin and his words rarefied, sending me echoes and murmurs of their articulations instead of concepts and clear propositions, the more I have the impression that the thread binding us, the air separating our lips becomes filled with strange invitations, winks, seductions, and warnings. . . . It is not a rare occurrence when I too take any object whatever into my hands, bring it very close to my eyes, as he does, and study the movements of his lips in order to reproduce—when his words escape me—at least their clearest modulations, the bilabial and velar tremblings, the smacks of the implosives, the trills, the solfeggios,

---

[23] See the scene of the fight between the two brothers, perhaps obscurely desired by the narrator as a "reason" to be able to "use force" against the madman (pp. 98–100); cf. Michel Foucault, *Surveiller et punir: naissance de la prison* (Paris: Gallimard, 1975).

the sighs vibrating in exhaling or inhaling, the start of a song. (pp. 104–105)

Not all is lost, then. At the very moment when he confesses the failure of writing to account for disease, the narrator uses this very same writing to account for his unfinished quest, for his unending pursuit:

It is a fact that only while I take care of him in a material way do I find in him some echo of the old moods and am still able to snatch tenuous fragments of phrases resembling a prelude to a discourse with me. Since I help him, always, to dress, we find ourselves one in front of the other and touch our arms and shoulders lightly. Patiently I watch every single movement of his. In his combinative art (a word and a glance, a word and his tongue's smacking against his palate, a gesture contrary to the word accompanying it, or the cross of two opposite words), I read some clue of a meaning traveling toward me. There are moments when I seem to be nearing a gleam of truth, to grasp a transparence similar to a whole meaning. I concentrate, then, and stop every movement. I am as if on the verge of piercing a curtain at whose base, by dint of my fingernails, I am digging a passage. (p. 108)

This is the end of *Fratelli*, an end open to various possibilities, an end that does not preclude the discovery of a truth, the achievement of an understanding, the hope for a whole meaning that is also a recovery. The expressions "on the verge of" and "a passage" underline the temporal and spatial dimensions of a process (a progress?) that is still going on as the reader closes the book: the "curtain" veiling knowledge is not yet pierced. Confronted with disease, literature has explored its own nature while also exploring the object of its investigation; and, like medicine, literature continues its quest to understand the unresolved mystery of our life and our death, of which the irrational is such an integral part.[24]

---

[24] Guido Fink speaks of "the return of the repressed" apropos of *Fratelli*, a novel that "escapes the ruling language." "Lingua egemone e lingua marginale: il cinema italiano negli anni settanta," *Stanford Italian Review*, vol. 1, no. 1, Spring 1979, pp. 145–62, quotation on p. 155.

Fratelli is a splendid example of how the confrontation with disease brings about a heightened state of consciousness for the writer—and hence for the reader. First, he has become aware of the enormous importance of the body—the biological factor—as part of the totality of man (one remembers those "fingernails" in the very last sentence of the novel). It might seem paradoxical that it is a mental disease that brings about the awareness of the body, but the paradox disappears when one thinks of Michel Foucault's definition of madness as a "global structure."[25]

Secondly and perhaps most importantly, in meditating upon his own writing with a self-reflexive movement, Samonà has understood the "gleam of truth" that shines in the title of his book from the very beginning and that finally becomes clear: the languages of reason and unreason, notwithstanding their differences, derive from the same *matrix*, are fundamentally the same.

The sage and the madman are indeed brothers; they live together in the same space, in a writing that is both a laboratory and a labyrinth.

[25] Michel Foucault, *Maladie mentale et psychologie* (Paris: Presses Universitaires de France, 1960).

AND BEYOND VALLEYS THERE ARE OTHER
MOUNTAINS, AND SO ON *AD INFINITUM* UN-
TIL THE SPHERE IS CLOSED, WHICH IS THE
GEOMETRIC, TOPOGRAPHIC IMAGE
OF THE ONE-WHOLE.

Carlo Emilio Gadda

SUCH IS THE POWER OF LANGUAGE: BEING
WOVEN WITH SPACE, IT GIVES RISE TO
SPACE. . . . BUT LANGUAGE IS AGAIN DE-
VOTED TO SPACE: WHERE THEN COULD IT
FLOAT AND REST IF NOT ON THIS PLACE
WHICH IS THE PAGE, WITH ITS LINES AND
ITS SURFACE—IF NOT IN THIS *VOLUME*
WHICH IS THE BOOK?

Michel Foucault

Six. $4/3\pi r^3$

INTEREST in space, considered as a cognitive category, undoubtedly is a fundamental aspect of philosophic, scientific,
and cultural thought and can be formulated in very different
ways, of which the epigraphs for this chapter are only two
examples. These epigraphs are meaningful because they also
indicate the central position such an interest has in literature:
Gadda is a writer whose work has a strong philosophic content, and Foucault is a thinker and scientist who is interested
in literary criticism.[1]

The cognitive category "space" can be approached from
many directions, and considered in different moments and
different cultural contexts. For instance, it is inextricably linked
with objectivity, as in Newtonian physics and Kantian phi-

---

[1] Carlo Emilio Gadda, *Meditazione milanese* (Turin: Einaudi, 1974), p. 75;
and Michel Foucault, "Le langage de l'espace," *Critique*, vol. 20 (April 1964),
pp. 381–82.

$$4/3\pi r^3$$

losophy.[2] It can also be considered intrinsic to perception, of being and the Other, as in phenomenology, from Maurice Merleau-Ponty to Jean-Paul Sartre.[3] And it is, of course, associated with relativity and time, from non-Euclidean geometry to Albert Einstein's theoretical physics and beyond.[4] This interest is also present in anthropology, from the "human space" studied in Georges Matoré to Gilbert Durand's structures of the imaginary;[5] in psychoanalysis, where Jacques Lacan, for instance, explains the continuity between the unconscious and the conscious by means of the famous "Moebius's band";[6] and in the study of modern culture, where Marshall McLuhan emphasizes the emergence of spherical space not only in the discoveries and applications of electronics, but also in the work of artists like Paul Cézanne, and theorizes on the passage from the typographical man of the Gutenberg galaxy to the inhabitant of the global village.[7] Needless to say, an interest in space is also present in painting, where an artist like Lucio Fontana has staunchly explored "spatial concepts," some of which are the thorough, modern rendering of Turner's vortex.

An interest in space also enters subtly, even surreptitiously, into the structuralist and post-structuralist thought of contemporary France. For instance, in the writings of Lévi-Strauss

[2] Elio Vittorini, *Le due tensioni* (Milan: Il Saggiatore, 1967), especially pp. 13–33.

[3] In particular, see Maurice Merleau-Ponty, "L'oeil et l'esprit," *Les Temps Modernes*, vol. 17, nos. 184–85 (1961), pp. 7–227, and *Phénoménologie de la perception* (Paris: Gallimard, 1945); Jean-Paul Sartre, *L'imagination* (Paris: Presses Universitaires de France, 1936), and *L'imaginaire* (Paris: Gallimard, 1940).

[4] See Rolf Nevanlinna, *Space, Time, and Relativity* (Reading, Mass.: Addison-Wesley, 1968).

[5] Georges Matoré, *L'espace humain. L'expression de l'espace dans la vie, la pensée et l'art contemporains* (Paris: La Colombe, 1962); and Gilbert Durand, *Les structures anthropologiques de l'imaginaire* (Paris: Presses Universitaires de France, 1963).

[6] Jacques Lacan, *Ecrits* (Paris: Seuil, 1966).

[7] Marshall McLuhan, *The Gutenberg Galaxy* (Toronto: University of Toronto Press, 1962), and *The Medium is the Message* (New York: Random House, 1967). A stimulating discussion of McLuhan's "technological" aesthetics can be found in Renato Barilli, *Tra presenza e assenza* (Milan: Bompiani, 1974), especially pp. 45–85 and 150–54.

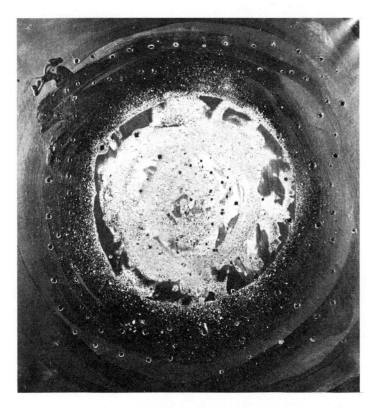

Fig. 9. Lucio Fontana (1899–1968), *Spatial Concept*,
1951, Private Collection, Milan.

a geological metaphor is used for the concrete manifestation
of the perfect transformation of time into space, while in the
work of Foucault an archaeological metaphor is employed to
suggest the transformation of the linear and temporal into
the discontinuous and spatial, thus underlining the clear hia-
tus between world and speech.[8] As for Derrida, he uses terms
such as "trace," "displacement," "dissemination" (which are
all spatial), and *"différance,"* a term in which the space of
writing becomes temporal (and the time spatial) in a neolog-

[8] Eugenio Donato, "Structuralism: The Aftermath," *Sub-stance*, vol. 7 (Fall
1973), pp. 9–26, quotation on pp. 14–15.

ism that combines difference in space with postponement in time.[9]

With these last examples, we have entered the most specifically literary field, that of language, which brings us to the question of the relationship between literature, criticism, and science.[10]

At the very outset it should be noted that the structure of scientific knowledge is such that in it a new paradigm takes the place of a preceding one, but without eliminating that predecessor completely. For instance, Euclidean geometry continues to be valid as a particular case of the new geometry of curved, non-Euclidean space. In this connection, Raimondi has noted that

in principle a paradigm is a measurement unit that is used to study the changes of a given system and its models of representation, and can be tested even in a literary system, provided of course that such a paradigm is derived from the kind of knowledge that can be reached through the language of literature and its formal elements. Then it will perhaps be possible to establish a new correlation between scientific and literary paradigms, taking into account the multiple and asynchronic time of their series of phenomena. . . . All this seems to me very close to the semiotics of culture that has been analytically outlined in the works of Lotman and Uspensky. . . . Lotman's hypothesis that every phenomenon, once it has

[9] In particular, see Jacques Derrida, *Of Grammatology*, tr. by Gayatrik Spivak (Baltimore: Johns Hopkins University Press, 1978); *Writing and Difference*, tr. by Alan Bass (Chicago: University of Chicago Press, 1980); and *La dissémination* (Paris: Seuil, 1972). Different and complementary discussions involving McLuhan on one side, and Foucault and Deleuze on the other, are found in Barilli, *Tra presenza e assenza*, pp. 143–71 and 172–94, and in Umberto Eco, *La struttura assente* (Milan: Bompiani, 1968), pp. 278–84 and 343–54.

[10] Cf. Ezio Raimondi, "La strada verso Xanadu," *Scienza e letteratura* (Turin: Einaudi, 1978), pp. 3–54. Raimondi also deals with the visualization and hence spatialization of knowledge in his essay "Verso il realismo," in *Il romanzo senza idillio* (Turin: Einaudi, 1974), pp. 3–56. Cf. Mario Petrucciani, *Scienza e letteratura del secondo Novecento* (Milan: Mursia, 1978), and the essays by Roland Barthes ("Science vs. Literature") and Raymond Queneau ("Science and Literature") in the *Times Literary Supplement*, 28 September 1978. These are important, opposite points of reference for Italo Calvino.

entered culture, becomes a sign, and that, like science, art is a modeling activity, with specific rules concerning its construction, is the literary and semiotic correlative of *The Structure of Scientific Revolutions*.[11]

These remarks are important because they establish a necessary correlation between art and science as modeling activities (through Thomas Kuhn's notion of "paradigm") and because they provide the equally necessary link for understanding the unitary functioning of culture in semiotic terms. In fact, Lotman and Uspensky call our attention to a phenomenon that is very important for our research: in the scientific-technological field, cybernetics has developed in a non-Euclidean space and has evident similarities with semiotics. For both of them, "the difficulties of contact" among men in today's world "are not situated in spatial categories" but in "the problems of communication"—exactly as is the case in art and literature.[12]

However, even more than the phenomenological analysis of a text (à la Gaston Bachelard or, to be more precise, Georges Poulet),[13] formal analysis peculiarly emphasizes the problem of the juxtaposition of artistic "space" with empirical or scientific space. I am referring, of course, to the famous essay

[11] Raimondi, *Scienza e letteratura*, pp. 51–52. Cf. Nevanlinna, ch. 9; Thomas Kuhn, *The Structure of Scientific Revolutions* (Chicago: University of Chicago Press, 1970); and Gaston Bachelard, *La formation de l'esprit scientifique* (Paris: Vrin, 1947).

[12] Yuri Lotman and Boris Uspensky, "Introduzione," in *Ricerche semiotiche*, Italian tr. (Turin: Einaudi, 1973), pp. xvi and xviii.

[13] Gaston Bachelard's *La Poétique de l'espace* (Paris: Presses Universitaire de France, 1957) and Georges Poulet's *Les Métamorphoses du cercle* (Paris: Plon, 1961) and *L'espace proustien* (Paris: Gallimard, 1963) remain fundamental and unique. Equally memorable is Mauriche Blanchot's *L'espace littéraire* (Paris: Gallimard, 1955), which discusses the conditions that make literary experience possible, especially in the face of death. An interesting example of ontological criticism, which fuses formalist and ethical concerns, is Charles Sherry's "The Fit of Gogol's 'Overcoat': An Ontological View of Narrative Form," *Genre*, vol. 7, no. 1 (March 1974), pp. 1–29, particularly p. 3: "Just as in the Einsteinian universe the curvature of space becomes measurable through the density of the matter it contains, because that density bends it, so the spatiality of the world of the narrative is contoured by the density of the being revealed in it."

by Joseph Frank entitled "Spatial Form in Modern Literature," an essay that is fundamental to the conclusive demonstration of how the novel (traditionally considered as the temporal form of art par excellence) actually organizes time spatially, according to a simultaneity of perceptions that takes the place of narrative sequence and is the indispensable condition for the self-reflexivity of the work.[14] Above all, I am referring to Lotman's *The Structure of the Artistic Text*, in which a whole chapter is devoted to "The Composition of the Verbal Work of Art" and in particular to "The Problem of Artistic Space."[15]

Lotman explicitly recalls a statement in Nicolai Lobachevsky's non-Euclidean geometry according to which it is possible to trace through a single point more than one parallel to a given straight line that is inscribed within a circle. He then links this statement directly with "the problem of the frame in art": "In modeling an infinite object (reality) by means of a finite text, a work of art substitutes its own space not for a part (or rather not only for a part), but also for the whole of that reality, the aggregate of all its parts. Each individual text simultaneously models both a particular and a universal object" (p. 211).[16] In other words, in every text one can dis-

[14] Joseph Frank, "Spatial Form in Modern Literature," in *The Widening Gyre* (Bloomington: Indiana University Press, 1968), pp. 3–62. To those who raised objections, citing "the physical impossibility" of spatial form, "since reading is a time-act," Frank replied: "I could not agree more. But this has not stopped modern writers from working out techniques to achieve the impossible—as much as possible" (p. 60n). Cf. also his later work: "Spatial Form: An Answer to Critics," *Critical Inquiry*, vol. 14, no. 2 (Winter 1977), pp. 231–52, and "Spatial Form: Some Further Reflections," *Critical Inquiry*, vol. 5, no. 2 (Winter 1978), pp. 275–90, as well as the summation of his whole trend of thought in W.J.T. Mitchell, "Spatial Form in Literature," *Critical Inquiry*, vol. 6, no. 3 (Spring 1980), pp. 539–67.

[15] Yuri Lotman, *The Structure of the Artistic Text*, tr. by Ronald Vroon (Ann Arbor: University of Michigan Press, 1977), pp. 209ff. and 217–31.

[16] In addition, the notion of "register" is connected with the problem of "frame" in art: Cesare Segre, *Structures and Time*, tr. by John Meddemmen (Chicago: University of Chicago Press, 1979), especially pp. 23–24. A sociological approach is found in Erving Goffman, *Frame Analysis: An Essay in the Organization of Experience* (New York: Harper and Row, 1974). Cf. also Joy Potter, *Five Frames for the Decameron: Communication and Social Systems in the Cornice* (Princeton: Princeton University Press, 1982).

tinguish a "mythological" aspect (the modeling of a whole universe) as well as a "story," a "fabulistic" aspect (the representation of some episode of reality). It will be remembered that for Lotman "the iconic principle and a graphic quality are wholly peculiar to verbal models" (whereby, for instance, the very concept of universality has a markedly "spatial character" for the majority of people). As a consequence, "the structure of the space of a text becomes a model of the structure of the space of the universe, and the internal syntagmatics of the elements within a text becomes the language of spatial modeling" (p. 217). We have seen this demonstrated earlier in the analysis of Foscolo's sonnet "Alla sera," which is an expression of the new relationship between conscience and universe in Romanticism.[17]

An important consequence of such premises is that "the spatial structure of a text . . . always represents not only a variant of the general system, but also conflicts in some way with the system by de-automatizing its language"; another consequence is that "the concept of event is dependent on the structure of space assumed by the text, or its classificatory aspect," which governs the development (or absence) of the plot (p. 238). As we have already seen, particularly in connection with the diegetic function of the Sicilian landscape:

> At the foundation of text construction lies a semantic structure and actions which always represent an attempt to surmount it. Therefore two types of functions are always given: Classificatory functions (passive) and the functions of the agent (active). A map is a good example

[17] In *The Structure of the Artistic Text*, Lotman gives some examples: "Even on the level of supra-textual, purely ideational modeling, the language of spatial relations turns out to be one of the basic means for comprehending reality. The concepts 'high-low,' 'right-left,' 'near-far' . . . prove to be the material for constructing cultural models with a completely non-spatial content and come to mean 'valuable-non valuable,' 'good-bad.' . . . All these things are couched [framed] in models of the world invested with distinctly spatial features" (p. 218). On this problem, see also his "Il metalinguaggio delle descrizioni tipologiche della cultura" in Yuri Lotman and Boris Uspensky, *Tipologia della cultura*, Italian tr. (Milan: Bompiani, 1975), pp. 145–81; and Matoré, pp. 29–45 and 54–57.

of a classificatory (plotless) text. Other such examples are calendars, descriptions of signs or omens, texts designating normalized, regular actions—a train schedule, a code of laws. . . . But if we draw a line across the map to indicate, say, the possible sea or air routes, the text then assumes a plot: an action will have been introduced which surmounts the structure (in this case geographical). (p. 239)

Lotman concludes that "the special character of the artistic plot, repeating on another level the specific character of metaphor, consists in the simultaneous presence of several meanings of each plot element, none of which annuls another, even when they are totally contradictory" (p. 245). Therefore the text "forms a single structure in which all semantic systems function simultaneously in a complex 'interplay,' " while on the contrary "scientific truth exists in [only] one semantic field" (p. 249). Lotman's remarks on the cinematographic concept of "depth" in relation to the literary text, and on the use of montage (or cutting), "the juxtaposition of heterogeneous elements as a compositional principle" (pp. 261–79), are also worth mentioning.

Lotman's theory, in which formal analysis clearly achieves semiotic results, is the only one that gives systematic emphasis to space as a constitutive element of the text. It can therefore be used as a point of reference for a comparison of literary space with scientific space. When considering the latter, the following important factors should be noted: the emergence of non-Euclidean geometry with curved spaces and n dimensions; the preservation of Euclidean geometry as a particular case of the former; the establishment of the spatiotemporal systems of relativity in physics; and the preeminence of spherical space at the level of technological experience—in the field that encompasses electronics, the mass media, and cybernetics.

Each one of these factors has its own corresponding literary reflection (by "reflection" I mean not "mimesis" or "cause/effect," but "translation," after Lotman, p. 210). For instance, it is evident that landscape or interior descriptions are still

$$4/3\pi r^3$$

based on Euclidean geometry, as the chapter on "Sicilian Epiphanies" has already demonstrated. But even at this level the relationship between literature and science (or technology) is no less interesting.[18]

On the other hand, literature as a whole has actually anticipated in its own terms discoveries that were later made by science in the field of relativity, as Ricardo Gullòn has proudly and rightly stated:

> Whereas in mathematics the theory of relativity relating time and space added a fourth dimension to reality, literature has always acknowledged the temporal dimension of space. Indeed, the contradiction between Kantian philosophy and non-Euclidean geometries is resolved in literary creation without difficulty and, I would venture to say, spontaneously.[19]

In the present chapter I shall limit myself to exploring the relationship between literature and science as it concerns the last point—spherical space. When I write or pronounce the *words* constituting the signs and numbers of the mathematical formula for the volume of the sphere, it is evident that I am carrying out a reductive operation, a "translation"—from the metalanguage of science into a natural language such as English or Italian—that claims its literariness at different levels. Let us begin by examining them:

(1) In Italian the formula for the volume of the sphere is a rhymed response to a question in the youthful *aide-mémoire*: "Il volume della sfera qual'è?/ Quattro terzi, pi greco, erre

[18] For example, Umberto Eco remarked: "When the first trains begin to pollute the country, aren't our nineteenth-century grandparents trying to go back to medieval forests, to solitary castles covered with ivy? Thus, the notion of an ecological utopia and the development of new forms of energy go together; Tytirus' syndrome is always a consequence of Prometheus': the proof of it is the final bad faith of Giosuè Carducci, who succeeds in praising the train as a symbol of progress while he rolls by Bolgheri in a first-class compartment, but at the same time dreams of the pious ox and the chamois jumping on those crested and shining peaks under which the rock drills of the great international tunnels are already at work." "Muoia Sansone con tutti gli operai," *L'Espresso*, 26 January 1975, p. 71.

[19] Ricardo Gullòn, "On Space in the Novel," *Critical Inquiry*, vol. 2, no. 1 (Autumn 1975), pp. 11–28, quotation on p. 12.

$$4/3\pi r^3$$

tre" (roughly, in English, "What is the volume of the sphere?/
Four thirds, pi, r cubed, my dear"). Rather than a mathematical formula, then, it is indeed a "programmatically mne-
monic verse" of the type that begins, "Thirty days hath September." As such, it is part of that "secondary orality"
considered by Walter Ong in connection with the survival of
primitive orality in our still "typographical" civilization.
Therefore, with some necessary adjustments, it is linked with
McLuhan's all-encompassing electronic and audiovisual technology.[20]

(2) It also becomes the metaphor of the globality of the
empirical (if not really scientific or technological) experience
of time-space that every writer must have in order to create
artistic expression. The following remark by Gullòn on space
in general can be applied to the volume of the sphere: "Space
as a reality and as a force includes what is and what can be,
what we see (hardly anything), and what we intuit or imagine
(potentially)."[21]

(3) It can be a more adequate metaphor than circularity for
the critical description of a literary text—a description that
includes thematics, lexicon, and self-reflexivity, in addition
to consciousness and point of view. For example, consider
the following statement by Sharon Spencer: "A work with a
closed structure based upon a single perspective will require
only one circle to indicate the relation between perspective
and subject, but a book with an open structure will require
as many circles as there are perspectives, each wheeling about
the same center."[22] Clearly, if the circles (with the same ra-
dius) are conceived not as situated on the same plane, but as
intersecting with one another on different planes while maintaining a common center, the result will be a sphere.

(4) Finally, the choice of the volume of the sphere as a
literary emblem, while testifying to the permanence of Eu-

[20] Walter Ong, *Rhetoric, Romance, and Technology* (Ithaca: Cornell University
Press, 1971), pp. 284ff. The clarification is on p. 296: "our most sophisticated
knowledge storing and retrieving tool is the computer, essentially a visual
device, with a print-out."

[21] Gullòn, p. 18.

[22] Sharon Spencer, *Space, Time and Structure in the Modern Novel* (New York:
New York University Press, 1971), p. 187.

$$4/3\pi r^3$$

clidean geometry in the context of the new non-Euclidean and post-Einsteinian paradigms, also testifies by analogy to the permanence of the printed word in a cultural context that, through audiovisual media, would seem to negate the typographical civilization. But in this connection it should suffice to remember that under the external pressure of modern technology writers have tried to overcome the structure of the book-object, as well as linear writing, through a variety of means. These include, for example: the use of different typographical and alphabetical characters; the use of signs, symbols, numbers, and ideograms; the choice of layouts that "open up" and "disorganize" the traditional printed page (from the Futurists' *parole in libertà* up to the contemporary and complex examples of Michel Butor and Maurice Roche);[23] the visualization of the "contents" of the text in its typographical form (calligrams, concrete poetry, or even the recent poetry-epitaph by Giorgio Bassani); or the use of a ludic element that organizes the spatiality of the text in the sense of discontinuity (Edoardo Sanguineti's *Il gioco dell'oca*, Julio Cortàzar's *Rayuela*).

In order to verify the preceding theoretical statements, I have chosen some texts by Italo Calvino that are particularly suited to such an examination. I shall conduct this examination by using Lotman's categories of literary space and the scientific data that have been discussed above.

In Calvino's *Le cosmicomiche* and *Ti con zero*,[24] space is undoubtedly preeminent, so much so that Guido Fink has taken these two works as a point of reference and comparison for

[23] See Gérard Genette, "La littérature et l'espace," *Figures II* (Paris: Seuil, 1969), pp. 44–47; Michel Butor, "Le livre comme object," *Essais sur le roman* (Paris: Gallimard, 1972); and on Roche, the special section in *Sub-stance*, no. 17 (1977), pp. 3–66, and in particular Dina Sherzer, "Circus: An Exercise in Semiotics," pp. 37–45. It is worth noting that the (typo)graphical elements of literature are also employed aesthetically in the artistic field by such contemporary artists as Luca Patella or Emilio Isgrò, who play on the disjunction between signifier and signified.

[24] Italo Calvino, *Cosmicomics* and *t zero*, tr. by William Weaver (New York: Harcourt, Brace and World, 1968, and Collier Books, 1970). Quotations will refer to these editions (*Cosmicomics*, page numbers followed by C, and *t zero*, page numbers followed by T).

$4/3\pi r^3$

Stanley Kubrick's *2001: A Space Odyssey* (a title in which the word *space* should be highlighted): "time . . . does not exist any longer, or is prolonged to such an extent that it coincides with nothingness: in this movie 'things' happen one next to another and not one after another."[25]

The globality of empiric-scientific experience has a first and rather obvious correspondence in Calvino's work at the thematic level. From its very title, *Le cosmicomiche* includes the whole universe—from the atom to the galaxies and from the protozoan to the computer—in its open neologism. In a similar fashion, *Ti con zero* takes up the (geometrical) formula of spatio-temporal coordination as its emblematic title. Together the two texts are thematically complementary; in fact, it can be stated that they are one "cosmicomic" corpus, a true "macrotext."[26]

Initially, the frame of this macrotext is a scientific postulate that defines the beginning of writing. In it, science is mythologized (the text models the whole universe; the narrator Qfwfq stands or could stand for any person, for any human consciousness). At the same time, science is also "fabulized"—that is, made into a story (the text represents some episode of scientific reality, from the attraction of the moon on the tides to the evolution of the gastropods; the narrator Qfwfq, even reduced to a minimum in its individual role of "protagonist," is different from the other "characters" he evokes).[27] In other words, we pass from the millennia of the

[25] Guido Fink, "2001: Il cinema e lo spazio," *Paragone*, vol. 232 (June 1969), pp. 56–65, quotation on p. 60.

[26] Francesca Bernardini Napoletano, *I segni nuovi di Italo Calvino* (Rome: Bulzoni, 1977), pp. 61–62. Cf. also her "Letteratura e scienza. Linguaggio poetico e linguaggio scientifico ne *Le cosmicomiche* e in *Ti con zero* di Italo Calvino," in *Letteratura e scienza nella storia della cultura italiana. Atti del IX Congresso AISLLI* (Palermo: Manfredi, 1978), pp. 852–59.

[27] On this subject there are sharp and entertaining remarks in Teresa De Lauretis, "Narrative Discourse in Calvino: Praxis or Poiesis?" *PMLA*, vol. 90, no. 3 (May 1975), p. 417: "Particularly original to Calvino are the purely graphic signifiers like the names of the characters of *Cosmicomics*, which are totally impossible to articulate as sounds, but visually suggest the qualities of their referents: the symmetrical, orderly molecular structure of Qfwfq, the unimaginative and gossipy narrow-mindedness of Mr. $Pber^tPber^d$, archetypal Fellinesque sexuality in Mrs. $Ph(i)Nk_o$, introverted visionary complexity in the sister $G'd(w)^n$, or the terrestrial long-leggedness of Lll."

evolutionary process (which is natural, scientific) to the single event that is necessary for the narration, intrinsically essential to the plot.

As for the other element of the frame—that is, the ending—it is rightly open, in progress, because world history continues, because science is made up of new discoveries, new paradigms that continuously widen knowledge, and because the text can continue or renew itself indefinitely according to the creative invention inherent in its language, in its idiolect. *Le cosmicomiche* ends with the words "without shores, without boundaries" and is taken up again and literally continued by "more of Qfwfq" in *Ti con zero*, which in turn is concluded with the search for a possibility of escape—a search that continues, a possibility that is opened, an escape that perhaps will be achieved (in future pages?). In this sense, the sphericity of the text is perfect—and infinite.

Calvino's cosmicomic corpus also presents a linguistic "sphericity," if I can use a term that undoubtedly widens to a different level the "iconic aspects" of language of which Jakobson has spoken. This linguistic sphericity consists of two main elements.

The first is chaotic enumeration, from the "Moon-milk" at the beginning of "The Distance of the Moon" to the splendid "kind of eye-dust" at the end of "The Spiral" (p. 153C) and to the "cap" of signs, a true "duplicate of the Earth's crust" with which "Priscilla" ends (p. 98T).

The second (and most important) element is the artistic use of numerous specialized and scientific languages, together with others taken from common speech, which form an amalgam that in its genre (and with all due differences) is just as good as Gadda's celebrated verbal pastiches. In this area, Teresa De Lauretis has already carried out a skillful preliminary analysis, pointing out six different main lexicons in a passage taken from "The Form of Space": colloquial language ("The universe, therefore, had to be considered not *a crude swelling placed there like a turnip*"); geometric or geological classification ("*a smooth-walled solid, a compenetration of polyhedrons, a cluster of crystals*"); architectural terminology ("the space in which we moved was *all battlemented and perforated with spires*

*and pinnacles . . .; with cupolas and balustrades and peristyles, with
rose windows, with double- and triple-arched fenestrations"*); bo-
tanical references ("space breaks up *around every cherry* tree
and *every leaf of every bough* that moves in the wind, and at
every indentation at the edge of every leaf"); terms from pho-
tography ("all *printed in negative*"); and, finally, anatomical
language ("the *pimple* growing on a *caliph's nose* or the soap
bubble resting on a *laundress's bosom* changes the general form
of space in all its dimensions").[28]

The passage analyzed by De Lauretis is a beautiful example
of what Lotman calls montage, "the juxtaposition of heterogeneous elements as a compositional principle." Of course,
other languages could also be traced, described, and cata-
logued within it: for example, those of mathematics, cybernetics, biology, and genetics; and beyond the sciences, those
of history, journalism, sports, finance, and so on. But the
example given above should suffice.

The use Calvino makes of such a rich vocabulary is not only
"ironic" (in the sense both of creative self-awareness and of
deliberate "distortion"), but also poetic and totalizing. Thus
the language of science (chemistry, physics, and biology) becomes the language of poetry in a description that could be
defined as "nostalgic":

> On those nights the water was very calm, so silvery it
> looked like mercury, and the fish in it, violet-colored,
> unable to resist the Moon's attraction, rose to the surface,
> all of them, and so did the octopuses and the saffron
> medusas. There was always a flight of tiny creatures—
> little crabs, squid, and even some weeds, light and filmy,
> and coral plants—that broke from the sea and ended up
> on the Moon, hanging down from that lime-white ceiling,
> or else they stayed in midair, a phosphorescent swarm

[28] De Lauretis, pp. 419–20, her italics. See also the following: "In Calvino,
metalinguistic and metanarrative references have the main function of ex-
posing, or even exploding, the code so that a new one may be created";
Calvino makes a continuous effort to build "new models of possible uni-
verses, of invisible cities, of systems closed but constantly and dialectically
reopened" (p. 423).

we had to drive off, waving banana leaves at them. (p. 4C)

It is worth repeating with Lotman that this passage is "a single structure in which all semantic systems function simultaneously in a complex 'interplay' " that vertiginously increases the number of signifying marks of every element, and particularly of every element of the scientific languages, which become "de-automatized."

The totalizing exigency (the globality or sphericity of the language) is also present at another level, not in the use and manipulation of different lexicons, but in the explicit intellectual contemplation of "the work written in all languages" (which is at the same time a good example of chaotic enumeration):

I see all this and I feel no amazement because making the shell implied also making the honey in the wax comb and the coal and the telescopes and the reign of Cleopatra and the films about Cleopatra and the pyramids and the design of the zodiac of the Chaldean astrologers and the wars and empires Herodotus speaks of and the words written by Herodotus and the works written in all languages including those of Spinoza in Dutch and the fourteen-line summary of Spinoza's life and works in the installment of the encyclopedia in the truck passed by the ice-cream wagon, and so I feel as if, in making the shell, I had also made the rest. (p. 148C)

The same totalizing, linguistic exigency is repeated in the following concise but very effective statement:

Each second is a universe, the second I live is the second I live in, la seconde que je vis c'est la seconde où je demeure, I must get used to conceiving *my speech simultaneously in all possible languages* if I want to live my universe-instant extensively. (p. 116T, italics added)

This statement, which is of an explicitly metalinguistic type, can also be used to introduce the third level of the literary correspondence in Calvino of the globality of scientific experience: the self-reflexivity of the text, which closes in upon itself from every direction, mirrors itself, encompasses itself, and becomes a metanarrative, a discourse on literature. (Incidentally, I should metacritically emphasize the fact that here I am using not so much the sphere as its *volume* in a metaphoric sense.)

There is no doubt that *Le cosmicomiche* and *Ti con zero* are metanarrative texts. Basic to this analysis is the fact that they are both structured mainly on the presence of two narrators. The Narrator-Author appropriates for himself the language of science (in italics) in brief denotative-referential messages that are situated at the beginning of every narrative episode. Immediately afterward, still in italics, the Narrator-Author introduces the poetical or textual narrator, linking this second narrator with his own initial scientific statement through referential expressions like the following: *old Qfwfq cried, confirmed, said, narrated, recalled, explained, asked, corrected, remarked, went on.* Such an explicit presentation of Qfwfq is absent (perhaps simply for variation) only from "The Form of Space" and "The Light Years" in *Le cosmicomiche*, and from the third part of *Ti con zero*.[29] Every narrative episode is then printed in roman type and taken up in the first person by the "narrator" Qfwfq. For example:

At one time, according to Sir George H. Darwin, the Moon was very close to the Earth. Then the tides gradually pushed her far away: the tides that the Moon herself causes in the Earth's waters, where the Earth slowly loses energy.

[29] To be more precise: the scientific statements introducing the second part of *t zero*, "Priscilla," are quoted directly from the originals and are printed in small roman type in the Italian edition and in regular roman type in the English edition (instead of being enunciated by the Narrator in italics), and do not appear at all in the third part. The narrator of "t zero" is identified with the letter Q, while those of the "The Chase" and "The Night Driver" are clearly a logical and combinative derivation from "Games Without End": "And so after every Qfwfq there was a Pfwfp, and after every Pfwfp a Qfwfq, and every Pfwfp was chasing a Qfwfq, who was pursuing him and vice versa" (p. 68C). The narrator of the last story in *Ti con zero*, "The Count of Monte Cristo," is even a character from another book, as if to confirm the metanarrativity of the text.

$$4/3\pi r^3$$

How well I know!—*old Qfwfq cried,*—the rest of you can't remember, but I can. We had her on top of us all the time, that enormous Moon: when she was full—nights as bright as day, but with a butter-colored light—it looked as if she were going to crush us. (p. 3C)

This spatial organization of the text, with two narrators and two different typographical styles, is used very effectively to institute the metanarrative discourse. Through it, Calvino calls the reader's attention to the process of writing, which transforms an oral tale into a written text—the first-person memories of the "old" narrator. Such a spatial organization also lets us view, as through a filigree, both the semantic structure of the text itself and the "action" that according to Lotman is always "an attempt to surmount" such a structure. In this way, we are allowed to see the two corresponding types of functions. The first are the classificatory or passive ones—that is, the scientific paradigms, constituting a precise code or a classificatory plotless text, which can be arranged in a series of diverse combinations (hence these paradigms are also, in Calvino, the obvious antecedents of the Tarot cards and the types of cities). The second functions are those of the agent, the active ones—the tales by Qfwfq, the texts with a plot that we literally see being born from the paradigms. In addition, one cannot exclude the fact that in Qfwfq, who is so impertinent and punctilious in his ubiquity and atemporality, Calvino also wanted to give us an ironic view of the traditional naturalistic narrator, who knows everything about each one of his characters.

The self-reflexivity (metanarrativity) of the texts is continuous. "A Sign in Space" is the transcribing in fantastic terms of writing, with the Saussurean arbitrariness of sign, Derrida's "erasure" and "trace," and Ludwig Wittgenstein's notion of play applied to graphic expression. "The Light Years" can (or perhaps must) be read as a metaphor of the relationship between the writer and writing and the reader and reading, in all its possible articulations and complications. "The Spiral" is a metaphor of the process of artistic creation, with the mollusk symbolizing writing, which cannot see itself but cre-

$4/3\pi r^3$

ates sight in the reader by giving him the raw material, the images, which are infinite and continuously generated from the *langue/parole* relationship (furthermore, in the middle italics of this work, synchrony and diachrony coincide, and the oral and the written discourse become one). Finally, "t zero" is the narrative and literal application of a Derridian image—the sheaf of lines of meaning (or force)—that sums up the whole system of *différance* and therefore, again, of writing.

One could continue to point out such metanarrative references in these texts and even go beyond them to *Il castello dei destini incrociati* and *Le città invisibili*.[30] It is sufficient, however, to recall what Flavia Ravazzoli has noted in connection with the use of italics in the latter book, as a full confirmation of the preceding remarks on the cosmicomic corpus: the text in italics "is then a mega-story whose subject is the act of narrating and not the cities that are narrated" in the text in roman type;[31] and "the difficult textual relation between Marco and Kublai, first level *actants*, foreshadows the analogous, metatextual difficulty at a second level between Calvino and his addressee, which is the difficulty of every literary communication."[32] We could also consider Calvino's recent book, which is a novel about the self-reflexivity and metanarrativity of the novel. It begins with the words, "You are about to begin reading Italo Calvino's new novel *If on a Winter's Night a Traveler*,"[33] and ends in a circle (or sphere) with these words, told by the "Reader" in a "large matrimonial bed" where his

[30] Italo Calvino, *The Castle of Crossed Destinies* and *Invisible Cities*, tr. by William Weaver (New York: Harcourt, Brace, Jovanovich, 1977 and 1974). With reference to these, see, among others, Maria Corti, "Le Jeu comme génération du texte: Des tarots au récit," *Semiotica*, vol. 7 (1973), pp. 33–48; Gianni Celati, "Il racconto di superficie," *il verri*, vol. 1 (March 1973); Alain Jullian, "T₀ et l'écriture labyrinthique," *Prévue*, vol. 3 (May 1975), pp. 43–51; and Barilli, *Tra presenza e assenza*, pp. 252–61.

[31] Flavia Ravazzoli, "Alla ricerca del lettore perduto in *Le città invisibili* di Italo Calvino," *Strumenti critici*, vol. 35 (February 1978), pp. 97–117, quotation on p. 104.

[32] Ibid., p. 114.

[33] Italo Calvino, *If on a Winter's Night a Traveler*, tr. by William Weaver (New York: Harcourt, Brace, Jovanovich, 1981), p. 3, from the original Italian *Se una notte d'inverno un viaggiatore* (Turin: Einaudi, 1979).

story with the "She-Reader" is finally and happily concluded after passing through ten beginnings of ten different novels: "Just a moment, I've almost finished *If on a Winter's Night a Traveler* by Italo Calvino."[34]

But rather than straying afield, let us return to the cosmi-comic stories and choose some particularly meaningful examples of self-reflexivity, examples that should fix the preceding statements in precise textual correspondences. Consider, for instance, the use of the sub-code "comic strips" in "The Origin of the Birds":

> Each figure will have its little balloon with the words it says, or with the noise it makes, but there's no need for you to read everything written there letter for letter, you only need a general idea, according to what I'm going to tell you. To begin with, you can read a lot of exclamation marks and question marks spurting from our heads, and these mean we were looking at the bird full of amazement. . . . I like telling things in cartoon form, but I would have to alternate the action frames with idea frames, and explain for example this stubborness of U(h)'s in not wanting to admit the existence of the bird. So imagine one of those little frames all filled with writing, which are used to bring you up to date on what went before: *After the failure of the Pterosauria, for millions and millions of years all trace of animals with wings had been lost.* ("Except for Insects," a footnote can clarify.) (pp. 21–22T)

It is not so much, or not only, the use of the sub-code in itself that is interesting at this point (notwithstanding its extraordinary elegance and refined *divertissement*), as its use for un-

[34] Ibid., p. 260. Another meaningful example appears on p. 108: "I am producing too many stories at once because what I want is for you to feel, around the story, a saturation of other stories that I could and maybe will tell or who knows may already have told on some other occasion, a space full of stories that perhaps is simply my lifetime, where you can move in all directions, as in space, always finding stories that cannot be told until other stories are told first." Cf. Cesare Segre, "Se una notte d'inverno uno scrittore sognasse un aleph di dieci colori," *Strumenti critici*, vols. 39–40 (October 1979), pp. 177–214: Calvino's book is not "the novel of a Reader" but "of the Writer" (p. 195).

184

derlining and accompanying writing in general, and Calvino's
text in particular, with those "idea frames" *in italics* that look
like the ironical, metanarrative wink of the author to the scientific paradigms and spatial organization of his text.

Also, many spatial references are co-extensive with the notion of writing, as at the end of "A Sign in Space":

> In the universe now there was no longer a container and
> a thing contained, but only a general thickness of signs
> superimposed and coagulated, occupying the whole vol-
> ume of space; it was constantly being dotted, minutely,
> a network of lines and scratches and reliefs and engrav-
> ings; the universe was scrawled over on all sides, along
> all its dimensions. There was no longer any way to es-
> tablish a point of reference: the Galaxy went on turning
> but I could no longer count the revolutions, any point
> could be the point of departure, any sign heaped up with
> the others could be mine, but discovering it would have
> served no purpose, because it was clear that, independ-
> ent of signs, space didn't exist and perhaps had never
> existed. (p. 39C)

We should also examine the monologue of "The Form of
Space," which seems to fuse the pretypographical and Gu-
tenbergian man with the Einsteinian curved universe, literally
playing with the literariness of the text:

> What you might consider straight, one-dimensional lines
> were similar, in effect, to lines of handwriting made on
> a white page by a pen that shifts words and fragments
> of sentences from one line to another, with insertions
> and cross-references, in the haste to finish an exposition
> which has gone through successive, approximate drafts,
> always unsatisfactory; and so we pursued each other,
> Lieutenant Fenimore and I, hiding behind the loops of
> the *l*'s, especially the *l*'s of the word "parallel," in order
> to shoot and take cover from the bullets and pretend to
> be dead and wait, say, till Fenimore went past in order
> to trip him up and drag him by his feet, slamming his
> chin against the bottom of the *v*'s and the *u*'s and the *m*'s

and the n's which, written all evenly in an italic hand, became a bumpy succession of holes in the pavement (for example, in the expression "unmeasurable universe"), leaving him stretched out in a place all trampled with erasings and x-ings, then standing up there again, stained with clotted ink, to run toward Ursula H'x, who was trying to act sly, slipping behind the tails of the f which trail off until they become wisps, but I could seize her by the hair and bend her against a d or a t just as I write them now, in haste, bent, so you can recline against them. . . . Whereas naturally the same lines, rather than remain series of letters and words, can easily be drawn out in their black thread and unwound in continuous, parallel, straight lines which mean nothing beyond themselves in their constant flow, never meeting, just as we never meet in our constant fall: I, Ursula H'x, Lieutenant Fenimore, and all the others. (p. 123C)

From the point of view of self-reflexivity, this text is so evident and such a virtuoso performance that no comment is really necessary. Suffice it to say that in this passage writing, which is made up of "straight lines which mean nothing beyond themselves," literally coincides with the universe, which is governed (as we are reminded at the beginning of the piece) by *"the equations of the gravitational field which relate the curve of space to the distribution of matter"* (p. 115C). Here the inventive felicity of the narrator has as its subject (together the source, force, and goal) not so much Barthes' or Girard's *désir*, exploding through the use of the sub-code "Western genre" and the technique of the interior monologue, but rather the letters, the graphic signs, the words themselves that are born under the pen. By this means one can say that writing is self-generated, creating itself by itself in a perfect, spherical entropy.

The literariness of the text, the globality of the universe of cells and cybernetics, and their indissoluble relationship are also reaffirmed at the end of the vertiginous journey (from mitosis to meiosis to Death) of "Priscilla":

Everything at a certain point tends to cling around me, even this page where my story is seeking a finale that

$$4/3\pi r^3$$

doesn't conclude it, a net of words where a written I and a written Priscilla meet and multiply into other words and other thoughts, where they may set into motion the chain reaction through which things done or used by men, that is, the elements of their language, can also acquire speech, where machines can speak, exchange the words by which they are constructed, the messages that cause them to move. The circuit of vital information that runs from the nucleic acids to writing is prolonged in the punched tapes of the automata, children of other automata: generations of machines, perhaps better than we, will go on living and speaking lives and words that were also ours; and translated into electronic instructions, the word "I" and the word "Priscilla" will meet again. (p. 99T)

A final quotation, with its image-metaphor, will conclude our initial critical assumption and seal it in the rigorous invention of a metanarrative character (metanarrative insofar as it belongs to a novel by Alexandre Dumas while narrating Calvino's text entitled "The Count of Monte Cristo"):

The search for the center of If-Monte Cristo does not lead to results that are more sure than those of the march toward its unreachable circumference: in whatever point I find myself the hypersphere stretches out around me in every direction; the center is all around where I am. (p. 155T)

Hence the sphericity—in fact, the hypersphericity—of the text is valid; the initial formula has found its demonstration. By mythologizing and fabulizing the paradigms of science, Calvino has taken up geological eras and millennia in the spatial form of his art, in the force of a geometrical writing that is continually renewed in an inexhaustible combinative process.[35]

Like other great writers of the twentieth century, Calvino is a worthy representative of that modern art rightly called "spatial" by Joseph Frank, who followed Wilhelm Worrin-

[35] Italo Calvino, "Notes Towards a Definition of the Narrative Form as a Combinative Process," *Twentieth Century Studies*, vol. 3 (1970), pp. 93–101.

187

ger's distinction between the naturalism of periods of harmony between man and cosmos, and the antinaturalism of periods of disharmony and uncertainty:

> Just as the dimension of depth has vanished from the sphere of visual creation, so the dimension of historical depth has vanished from the content of the major works of modern literature. Past and present are apprehended spatially, locked in a timeless unity that, while it may accentuate surface differences, eliminates any feeling of sequence by the very act of juxtaposition. . . . What has occurred, at least so far as literature is concerned, may be described as the transformation of the historical imagination into myth.[36]

To support his statement, Frank quotes Mircea Eliade, who in *Cosmos and History* spoke of "the fear of history" of both primitive as well as modern man. But I prefer to go back to the conclusions reached by Gilbert Durand because they seem more consonant with Calvino's intelligent "eroticism" and ideological optimism.

In a treatise in which he examines and systematizes the anthropological structures of the imaginary, Durand has noted that, like ritual, all aesthetic activities (and especially imagination) possess a "euphemistic function," are forms of "the struggle against putrefaction, an exorcism against death and temporal decomposition"; they are used for "insuring perennity and hope, in time, both for individuals and society." The a priori form of the euphemistic power of thought is space, which is "the place of representations, since it is the symbol that achieves the controlled distancing."[37] In the "fantastic space" studied by Durand, "topology, projective relations, similitude are nothing but three perceptible and genetic aspects of the image's *ocularity*, *depth*, and *ubiquity*,"[38] the

[36] Frank, pp. 59–60.
[37] Durand, part 3, ch. 2, *passim*.
[38] Ibid. More precisely: as for depth, "every 'thought of' space implies control of distance within itself. This distance, when abstracted from time, spontaneously and globally recorded, becomes a 'dimension' in which the

$$4/3\pi r^3$$

three qualities from which the "ambivalence," the "euphemism," and the "Hope" of the fantastic function derive.[39]

Such anthropological categories correspond to the formalistic-semiotic ones that have been used so far: the spatial qualities of (Calvino's) artistic text are visual (= ocularity) and totalizing (= depth and ubiquity); its semantic polyvalence is its poeticity (= ambivalence); its information potential (= euphemistic function, Hope) is confirmed and concluded in and by self-reflexivity and mythopoesis.

Thus it is possible to refer Calvino's "spherical" writing to the need for a "renewed mythopoesis" that was pointed out years ago by Gillo Dorfles, who had quoted Durand, and not by chance.[40] This renewed mythopoesis runs precisely parallel to the philosophical and scientific developments of contemporary thought, in which the notions of structure, code (communication), and model (function) have replaced, or at least devalued, the notion of Subject, while the "text" (be it literary, genetic, or tribal) has become the catalyzer of the different strategies through which the "structural revolution" has occurred.[41]

---

succession of distancing fades away in favor of the simultaneity of dimensions"; as for ubiquity, "the power of repetition, of redoubling, the synchrony of myth, if it is extraneous to a physical space, certainly is the fundamental quality of Euclidean space, in which homogeneity insures the instantaneous displacing of figures—ubiquity through similitude." It is almost useless to emphasize how much these definitions can be applied to Calvino's texts, and particularly to Qfwfq, a true personification of the fantastic function.

[39] Ibid.

[40] In *Gruppo 63. Il romanzo sperimentale* (Milan: Feltrinelli, 1966), p. 150.

[41] See Jean–Marie Benoist, *La Révolution structurale* (Paris: Grasset, 1975), and Robert Scholes, *Structuralism in Literature* (New Haven: Yale University Press, 1974), pp. 190–91: "In the sciences, the structuralist imagination has emphasized the universal and systematic at the expense of the individual and idiosyncratic. And it would be a very *un*systematic world indeed if the arts remained oblivious to these new emphases. . . . The resurgence of interest in mythology, among both writers and critics, is an aspect of the general structuralist movement in fiction." It is useless to say that the "structuralist revolution" prepared the ground for post-structuralist developments, such as semiotics. Wolfgang Iser has emphasized the importance of such notions as structure, function, and communication in contemporary thought and criticism: "The Current Situation of Literary Theory: Key Concepts and the Imaginary," *New Literary History*, vol. 9, no. 1 (Autumn 1979), pp. 1–20.

In order to "overcome" time (death), the literary text, by using the only means at its disposal, obliterates it, "erases its letters." That is, it becomes spatial and ends up by telling itself, creating itself while encompassing the universe within itself by naming it. Thus the literary text becomes the spherical space, the volume that is no longer (of) geometry but (of) the word.

Index

Petrucciani, Mario, 169n
Pinto, Sandra, 48, 56n, 72n
Pirandello, Luigi, 14, 20, 93–104,
106, 107, 110, 122, 124–26, 128,
133n, 144n
Piranesi, Giambattista, 112
plot. See story and plot
Pollock, Jackson, 20
Porta, Antonio, 158n
Portinari, Folco, 56n, 70n, 74
Potter, Joy, 171n
Poulet, Georges, 170
Praz, Mario, 22, 26n, 64
Prodi, Giorgio, 143n
Propp, Vladimir, 5, 64, 65, 78, 83

Queneau, Raymond, 169n

Radcliffe, Ann, 28n
Radcliff-Umstead, Douglas, 31n
Ragusa, Olga, 22n
Raimondi, Ezio, 3, 9, 38n, 55n, 68n,
69, 70, 71n, 169–70
Ravazzoli, Flavia, 183
referentiality, 4, 11–14, 26–27, 81–
82, 114
Reis, Marion, 8n, 69n
Rembrandt, van Rijn, 20, 23
representation, 14, 25, 78–114, 173–
74
Reybaud, Louis, 64
Reynolds, Graham, 28n
Riffaterre, Michel, 13n, 81
Risi, Nelo, 144
Robertazzi, Mario, 128n
Roche, Maurice, 176
Romagnoli, Sergio, 53n, 55n, 56n,
60n, 64n
Romano, Massimo, 70n
Romanticism, 14, 18–47, 172; "ex-
treme," 21; "minor," 48–77;
"moderate," 21, 48, 54–55; and
Enlightenment, 23; and moder-
nity, 46–47; and neoclassicism,
22–24; and organicism, 23, 31, 32
Rossi, Aldo, 69n
Rougemont, Denis de, 67
Rousseau, Jean Jacques, 24

Ruffini, Giovanni, 55
Russo, Luigi, 35

Sade, Marquis de, 64n
Salinari, Carlo, 96n
Samonà, Carmelo, 14, 145–65
Samonà, Giuseppe Paolo, 101n
Sanguineti, Edoardo, 176
Santarosa, Santorre, 55
Sapegno, Natalino, 24n, 53n
Sartre, Jean-Paul, 167
Saussure, Ferdinand de, 5, 6n, 182
Schefer, Jean-Louis, 23
Scholes, Robert, 189n
Sciascia, Leonardo, 14, 106–10, 111,
112, 113
Scott, Laurence, 64n
Scott, Walter, 51–55
Scott-Moncrieff, C. K., 94n
Searle, J. R., 82
Sebeok, Thomas, 148n
Séchehaye, M. A., 144
Segre, Cesare, 5, 7, 23, 25, 40n, 61,
65–66, 69, 152, 171n, 184n
selection of theme, 14, 51, 56–59
self-reflexivity, 12–13, 14, 110, 129,
148, 160–61, 171, 179n, 181–89
semiotics, 3–17, 82–85, 143, 148–49,
169–73; cultural, 10–11; literary,
11–13; practical, 13–14; and de-
construction, 12–13, 81n; and
Marxism, 11–12; and painting,
24–26, 91–93
sender. See communication
Sereni, Emilio, 111n
Settembrini, Luigi, 56n
Shaftesbury, Anthony, 23
Shakespeare, William, 75n
Shelley, Percy Bysshe, 21
Sherry, Charles, 170n
Sherzer, Dina, 176n
Shklovsky, Victor, 7, 8, 61n, 65
sign-production, 14, 83–85, 95
Sini, Carlo, 5
Smith, Robert Jerome, 76n
Sollers, Philippe, 6
Sontag, Susan, 150
space, 15, 18–19, 29, 33–36, 37, 39,

197

198

The Image of the City in Modern Literature.
By Burton Pike

The Imaginary Library: An Essay on Literature and Society.
By Alvin B. Kernan

Pope's "Iliad": Homer in the Age of Passion
By Steven Shankman

199

Library of Congress Cataloging in Publication Data

Biasin, Gian Paolo.
Italian literary icons.

(Princeton essays in literature)
Rev. translation of: Icone italiane.
Includes index.
1. Italian literature—19th century—History and criticism—Addresses, essays, lectures. 2. Italian literature—20th century—History and criticism—Addresses, essays, lectures. 3. Criticism—Addresses, essays, lectures. 4. Semiotics and literature—Addresses, essays, lectures. I. Title. II. Series.

PQ4086.B53 1985   850'.9   84-42876
ISBN 0-691-06632-9